ALPHA ONE SIXTEEN

A Combat Infantryman's Year in Vietnam

Peter Clark

CASEMATE

Philadelphia & Oxford

Published in the United States of America and Great Britain in 2018 by
CASEMATE PUBLISHERS
1950 Lawrence Road, Havertown, PA 19083, USA
and
The Old Music Hall, 106–108 Cowley Road, Oxford OX4 1JE, UK

Hardcover Edition: ISBN 978-1-61200-599-7
Digital Edition: ISBN 978-1-61200-600-0

A CIP record for this book is available from the British Library

Printed and bound in the United States of America

For a complete list of Casemate titles, please contact:

CASEMATE PUBLISHERS (US)
Telephone (610) 853-9131
Fax (610) 853-9146
Email: casemate@casematepublishers.com
www.casematepublishers.com

CASEMATE PUBLISHERS (UK)
Telephone (01865) 241249
Email: casemate-uk@casematepublishers.co.uk
www.casematepublishers.co.uk

For my daughters, Jessica, Natalie, and Naomi, and my grandson, James

Contents

CHAPTER I

Getting in

Near the end of a hot and overcast August day, I was seated on a folding metal chair in an undistinguished windowless room deep within a grey barn of a building on Van Buren Street in Chicago. Forty or so other young men in various iterations of the male clothing choices of 1965 were seated around me, some silent, some chattering nervously. At our feet were the little suitcases or gym bags that contained a change of clothes and toilet stuff, which we had been directed to bring from home when reporting to the induction station. All of us held big brown paper envelopes with our names, last name first, printed on the front in black magic marker. These contained the paper and cardboard residue of the last few hours of processing through the Army Induction Center, during which I had stood in long lines of guys, sometimes clothed, sometimes naked, as bored and impatient soldiers chivvied us from room to room. We had been tested, subjected to group physical examinations—"Turn round! Ben' over! Spread th' cheeks a yur butt apart wit yur hans!"—and had 30 seconds of attention from somebody with a stethoscope. The results of these activities had been collected, perforated, and inserted into the twin prongs of a cardboard folder with mysterious printed boxes and notations, stuffed into the brown paper envelopes, and thrust into our hands by young men in uniforms. These guys, all of whom presumably had been anxious civilians like us a short time ago, were like beings from another planet: they had gone through what we were about to undertake and come out the other side. Their indifference to us as individuals contrasted with the nervous regard I at least gave them.

At some point all the chairs in the room were occupied, and an older man in a light tan uniform, with a bunch of chevrons on his short sleeves and bright brass insignia on his open collar, appeared to our front, followed by another fellow in a similar outfit but with metal bars on his epaulettes instead of stripes on his sleeves.

The first guy said, "Listen up, you are about to be given the oath of enlistment."

The officer stepped up and told us to stand. "Raise your right hand, and repeat after me."

We all did as we were told, and mumbled our way through the oath: "I, Peter Clark, do solemnly swear that I will support and defend the Constitution of the United States against all enemies, foreign and domestic; that I will bear true faith and allegiance to the same; and that I will obey the orders of the President of the United States and the orders of the officers appointed over me, according to regulations and the Uniform Code of Military Justice." And that was that.

We picked up our suitcases and were herded out of the back of the building, where we boarded a bus that took us to Chicago's Union Station. From there our group was moved through the station and into a dusty Illinois Central passenger car. Night had fallen before we departed, and the sun was up when we arrived, dirty and tired, in Louisville. By then our ranks had been augmented by a cohort of inductees who had boarded in Indianapolis. Perhaps a hundred of us climbed on a couple of buses for the trip to Fort Knox.

In 1965 Fort Knox was famed as the location of the United States Treasury gold depository, and had figured prominently in the 1964 James Bond film *Goldfinger*. For our purposes, the gold could have been on Mars, as the fort was also a massive army base, home to the Armor School and a rapidly expanding collection of basic training units as the Vietnam War geared up. Our buses dropped us in the middle of one of these units, numberless World War II-era, red-brick, two-story buildings, in the middle of a field of dirt divided into lanes and rectangles by lines of rocks painted white. We processed through these buildings for a couple of days, during which we were measured for and provided with fatigue pants and blouses, khaki summer dress uniforms and heavy green winter dress uniforms, boots and shoes, coats, hats, socks, and underwear. These were crammed into a canvas duffel bag that weighed around 50 pounds when full. Our civvies went into the little overnight bags, where they were destined to molder for the next eight weeks, and our bodies went into the rough olive drab fatigues. White tapes printed with our last names were sewn over the right breast pocket flap, and a similar tape, black with yellow letters, was sewn over the left pocket, and read U. S. Army. Every couple of minutes I caught myself looking down at that U. S. Army tag, and feeling a flush of pride: I was finally a soldier. We also received our dog-tags: two lozenges of aluminum stamped with our service number, name, religion, and blood type. When asked by the dog-tag-stamper about my religion, I answered "none," which drew a snarl and a nasty observation. But I was also proud of not caving in to 1960s cultural pressure by claiming a generic protestant affiliation, which my sporadic exposure to Unitarianism would have permitted. I was certainly going to try to be the atheist in the foxhole.

During this transitional interval I had, along with the other recruits, gaped at the formations of troops marching or double-timing along the asphalt, 50 or so young men dressed all the same and marching or running in what appeared to be perfect step, either to the melodious cadence of campaign-hatted drill sergeants, or singing their own accompaniment to the thud of all those boots hitting the ground in unison. The platoons, for that is what the groups were, were dressed in anything from white tees over khaki fatigue pants to full combat gear, with steel helmets, M-14 rifles, and bayonets hanging from scabbards attached to web belts. Compared to the unstructured gaggle of random recruits in which we slouched about, these formations exuded competence and purpose. I found it hard to believe that none of these soldiers was more than eight weeks ahead of us in his journey from civilian to soldier. The gulf appeared immense and almost unbridgeable.

During a couple of days of being herded around in our new uniforms and boots, inoculated, indoctrinated, and examined, we were introduced to the simplest and most basic elements of army etiquette, such as how to distinguish officers from sergeants, and how to salute the former and obey the latter. This training allowed us to be sort-of-marched down some army roads to our new home, a training company occupying five large two-story brick barracks and a smaller structure labeled "A Co. Orderly Room." There we were sorted by the prefix to our service numbers: RA stood for Regular Army, and designated those of us who had enlisted; US was for those drafted under Selective Service; ER for Enlisted Reserve; and NG for National Guard, the latter two categories embarking on a six-month tour of active duty before returning to civilian life as weekend warriors. Draftees served a two-year tour of active duty, and Regular Army guys were mostly in for three years, the minimum enlistment, and some longer, such as the folks who had enlisted for a helicopter pilot program which would, about a year later, find them with a warrant officer's rank and another three years to serve. There was one barracks for RAs, including me, two for draftees, and one each for ERs and NGs. Each barracks held a platoon of about 50 kids.

Quickly I learned that the prefixes were markers for more than just the mode of entry into the service. While the US folks were a fairly representative sample of young American men, college attendance as well as marriage qualified as draft deferments, so the guys in those barracks tended to be single and with little education past high school. Political connections were useful in obtaining slots in the Guard or the Army Reserve, and those connections, then as now, went along with money and social standing. Both the ERs and the NGs were thus more likely to be older, with more of them married and quite a few of them college grads as well. Overwhelmingly they were Caucasian. If there were any black or Hispanic kids in the ER or NG barracks, I don't remember them.

My Regular Army barracks-mates were another breed of cat entirely. Most of us were from the poorer neighborhoods and industrial suburbs of Chicago, lots of kids of Polish or other Eastern European ancestry, along with Irish, Italians and a few blacks. Maybe half a dozen out of the 50 in my platoon were college kids like me, who had joined up for a variety of reasons, which no doubt had seemed like good ideas at the time. Many of the other guys had joined up to improve their lives, or maybe to avoid jail. At least a couple joined for the dental care. One kid had all of his teeth pulled in the first week of training and got fitted with false teeth. He had never had dental care before and must have been in huge discomfort, as he was beamingly happy after the extractions.

My own motivation for enlisting was more complicated. I had always loved army stuff, and growing up in the 1950s I was surrounded by men who had served during World War II, my father for a start, and most of my male teachers and the fathers of my friends as well. I was bored and largely unmotivated in college, and after several unhappy romances there was no compelling reason for me to continue, academic or otherwise. Even though I didn't really think fighting a land war in Asia was a smart idea, the notion of serving my country in wartime was something I had long accepted as my duty. While Vietnam wasn't likely to be a good war, it was the one I had. And if I was going to serve, I wanted it to be in combat, not stuck behind a desk in the rear. I had never faced real danger or adversity, and in my ignorance I imagined I would enjoy the immersion in what for me was the stuff of legend.

I relished the actuality of wearing a uniform, qualifying on the M-14 rifle, crawling under barbed wire while live bullets whistled overhead, and all the other incidents of basic training. Harder for me, an only child, was the adjustment to barracks life with 50 or so other young men, most of whom were more or less tough kids, who came from families in the bottom ten percent of income and education. Few of these kids were represented in my suburban high school, which sent about 94 percent of its graduates to four-year colleges. At the beginning of basic I hadn't a clue about how to fit in with my new comrades, but by the end I was starting to figure out that character, both good and bad, was pretty evenly distributed without regard to race or privilege.

I wasn't very good at basic training, although I got in decent physical shape and had at least been introduced into the enlisted man's culture. Advanced Infantry Training was another matter. The eight-week course was stuffed with weapons training, in classrooms, on the range, and in the field. Here for the first time I became good at some useful things. Map-reading and orientation were particularly fun for me, and I was proud to be chosen as a tutor for this subject. Here I learned that some folks just couldn't move from the map to the territory, no matter how hard they tried and how much effort was spent by their teacher. I was also selected to tutor fieldstripping the Colt M1911A1 automatic pistol, but was humbled by my inexplicable failure to complete the reassembly on the graded test. Tactical exercises were engrossing, sort of like playing soldiers with really good toys, and lots of willing playmates. All in all, AIT was the best eight weeks of my life, so far.

My hope at that point was to go to Officer Candidate School, preferably the Infantry School at Fort Benning, but that was not to be. I was selected instead for Ordnance OCS, probably because I had gushed about weapons when I was called before a selection board of officers during the OCS screening process. Initially I refused the assignment, officer training being one of few things the army allows an enlisted man the opportunity to refuse. I settled down to wait for my orders to Vietnam, but my commanding officer convinced me that I could go to Ordnance OCS and transfer to infantry once I got there. Of course this turned out to be untrue, but I spent nine weeks training to become a second lieutenant nonetheless.

The first part of OCS was conducted at the Armor School in Fort Knox, where I had my basic training, and elements of the curriculum were great fun, including learning the rudiments of driving all sizes of trucks, armored personnel carriers, and tanks. Likewise the classroom instruction was fascinating and I had the best academic record in my company. Where I failed miserably was at the interpersonal level. Most if not all of my peers were career army noncoms who saw a commission as a chance for job advancement. Older, less physically fit, and decidedly opposed to the kind of adventures I imagined I sought, I am certain my classmates considered me a royal pain the ass and were delighted to rate me accordingly when we had the opportunity at the end of the first half of the course, before the company moved to Aberdeen Proving Grounds and the more technical aspects of ordnance. This process, known as "paneling out," was an effective way of reducing the number of square pegs the army had to pound into round holes, and while I was devastated for a bit, as it was my first failure at army life, I dimly understood the justice of it, and consoled myself with thoughts of the mysterious jungles and rice paddies in which I could again imagine myself, facing the test of ground combat.

CHAPTER 2

Can You Type?

So after almost a year in the army, I finally had my orders for the 1st Infantry Division, Republic of Vietnam. Getting those orders for Vietnam was like getting into the college of my choice, and I was supremely happy. In late July 1966 a lot of troops going to Vietnam as replacements were processed out of the Presidio, near San Francisco. Every day hundreds of mostly young men flew out on commercial passenger jets operated by various contractors. Processing took a couple of days, mainly filling out forms and getting the 201, the army's personnel file, up to date with encouraging things like next-of-kin forms. Mostly I sat along with many other bored and apprehensive young men in classrooms. I do recall an exquisite rendering of Popeye the Sailorman guiding an enormous erect penis into some babe from *Terry and the Pirates* on one of the desks, and another graffito with a name, recent date, and the words "Bound for Vietnam If I live I'll erase this in one year," which struck me as kind of stupid. But I wished I could draw as well as the Popeye artist.

Near the end of the processing time I was sitting in an enclosed courtyard waiting for a bus to take me and a bunch of other troops, none of whom I had seen before or since, watching dust devils move leaves and trash around. I was wearing khaki summer Class As, my private first class stripe carefully sewn on, and lugging a duffel bag filled with fatigues, combat boots, and other army junk, including a couple of civilian knives which were permitted. Drinking Coke, smoking Marlboros, and going to Vietnam. Right then there was no place I would rather be. After a long wait we were bused to an airport, where some more processing took place, our duffels were collected, and we were herded up a movable stair into a civilian aircraft.

The flight seemed interminable; every seat filled with a GI of one sort or another, officers in front, noncoms in the middle, the rest of us thereafter. Stewardesses served us meals, and I ate them and smoked, and made small talk with my seat mates. The aircraft was probably a 707, maybe a DC-8, and I had a window seat near the rear of the cabin. We stopped in Guam to refuel, and were warned not to take pictures out the windows. My dad had given me a Minox 8mm camera, and I happily circumvented the no-picture rule, taking shots of various military aircraft and installations. I still have some grainy pictures of F-16s laden with fuel tanks and other pod-like structures that I imagined were bombs, the sight of which fed my enthusiasm for real war adventures.

My first sight of Vietnam was from several miles in the air as we came in to Tan Son Nhut airport near Saigon. The plane came down in a tight spiral rather than the long descents typical of more peaceful landings. I got a bit of a show as it was getting dark and there were a few flashes and some red tracers visible against the general blackness, but the landing was uneventful. Processing was minimal as we were checked off somebody's list and loaded into buses, for a quick trip to the 90th Replacement Battalion in a place called Long Binh. At that time the road between Tan Son Nhut and Long Binh was open for unarmored vehicles. The bus was a big disappointment, as its only warlike characteristics were heavy screens on the windows to protect against grenades. For now we might as well have been driving along in a stateside post, except for the exotic views out the windows. Pony traps and brightly painted miniature buses jockeyed for road space with American trucks and jeeps, with petite Vietnamese policemen standing on concrete tubs trying to stay out the way. Arrival at the Long Binh perimeter presented me with a gratifying panorama of barbed wire and sandbags, raising my hopes of doing something warlike, but we were merely hustled into tents, fed, and left to our own devices. During the night some nearby batteries were firing, probably scheduled harassment & interdiction, but of course I didn't know that, so it was pretty exciting and a little scary, even after somebody told me that they were outgoing rounds.

The evening's impression of entering a besieged fortress was offset the following morning by the many Vietnamese in colorful outfits performing chores about the base. Here and there bored GIs with M-14s lounged about in bunkers, but overall there was an air of business as usual as we were processed once again and assigned to a barracks. At least I was out of my Class As and into regular fatigues. The air temperature was probably around 100° F. but I was confident I would soon be getting lightweight jungle fatigues and boots, and maybe even a weapon. As usual there were fatigue duties and one of mine was to shepherd a detail of Vietnamese civilians. I can't recall what the task was, but I was issued an M-14 with no ammunition, and followed the Vietnamese around as they did what they were supposed to do, or not, under the direction of a Vietnamese straw boss. This was my first opportunity to win the hearts and minds of our allies, and I tried to engage in friendly discourse. Of course I was immediately the object of derision; the more engaging of the workers trained me that the words "*Chao Co dep lam*" and "*Chao Ong dep lam*" were same-same as "hello" in American. I used my new language skills at every opportunity over the next few days, though I was often bemused at the response, usually snickers. Later I found this was a much more intimate form of greeting than would be considered proper by the Vietnamese.

Next day I was in a long line of GIs getting processed again; the goal here was assignment to an actual unit. Personnel soldiers sat on one side of the row of tables, some with typewriters, checking, correcting, and completing the forms for each of the replacements filing down the row. Each of us clutched our 201 file, surrendering it to the clerk on the other side of the table, each of whom performed some task or other before returning the file and waving us on. Most of the tables were under canvas, but the one at the end was shaded by a fly, open to the pleasant breezes of the early morning. The sergeant under the fly was heavy, balding, and clearly had been in the army a while. Like all soldiers, I was characterized by Military Occupational Specialty, or MOS. My MOS, earned in Advanced Infantry Training, was 11B20, Light Weapons Infantryman. Proud as I was of this designation, most career soldiers looked down on the infantry as embodiments of the strong backs and weak minds who had neither useful skills nor the capacity to acquire any. The average amount of time at this station was about five seconds as the sergeant did a final check of the 201 before sending it and its owner to a nearby wall tent where the transportation clerks handled the last stage of the process. In my case, the five seconds became ten, then twenty. Checking the jacket of my 201 file, he had probably noted my scores on the Armed Forces Qualifying Test, the Clerical Aptitude sub-test, and my two years of college. From behind the long folding table, he finally looked up from my 201 file.

"Can you type?"

I instantly knew he was offering me a chance to stay in a nice tent and shuffle papers for a year. I could be safe, dry, and comfortable. But no way was I going to be cheated out of the reason I was in Vietnam, to serve my country in ground combat! This was one of those times when the brain can do a lot of processing in a very short time, but what my brain came up with, was to look him in the eyes, and say "No." He raised his eyebrows, shook his head, and handed me my 201. I was going to have a lot of opportunities to replay this particular 20 seconds in the year to come, and, each time, to regret with more intensity that I had not fallen to my knees and begged him to give me a table and a typewriter so I could show my stuff.

In the next tent, at yet another table, a Specialist Fourth Class, or SP4, pronounced Spec 4, glanced at the top sheet of my 201 and gave me a handwritten order for air transportation to Company A, 1st Battalion, 16th Infantry Regiment, usually written A Co., 1/16 Infantry, at a place called Lai Khe. He also offered to sell me brand-new jungle boots for $30 US.

"Why would I want to pay you for boots?" I asked. "I'll be issued boots free when I get to my outfit."

The SP4 gave me a junior version of the bald sergeant's look, shook his head, and handed me my papers. Hoisting my duffel, I trudged over to another tent, wondering at the extent to which venal Rear Echelon Mother Fuckers would try to take advantage of an innocent GI.

After a bunch of us had gathered in the tent, we climbed into the back of a two-and-one-half-ton truck, known universally as a deuce-and-a-half, the basic form of ground transport if a jeep was too small. We rode a short distance to an airstrip paved with pierced steel planks, aka PSP, and were herded up the rear ramp of an army Caribou, in which I had my first experience flying in a military aircraft, notable for its lack of amenities. Little did I know then that the Caribou was a model of grace, agility, and comfort compared to the C-123 and C-130. The Caribou wasn't as primitive as these aircraft, but the exposed wires and hydraulics, lack of interior paneling, and uncomfortable nylon-and-steel-tube sling seats certainly contrasted with the commercial aircraft in which I'd flown. The Caribou and the other transport aircraft were notable for their ability to take off from, and land on, very short, unimproved, runways. This was accomplished by locking the brakes and revving the two un-mufflered engines, or four on the C-130, driving the propellers to an excruciating volume of sound, while the airframe shuddered and whined, and various loose components banged and clattered. After straining against the brakes, the ship was turned loose and bounded forward, almost immediately nosing up and losing speed as it clawed for altitude. Typically at this point various parts of the aircraft would fall off or at least sound like they had broken. At Long Binh the runway was longer than a football field and didn't end in triple canopy jungle, but at the time I discovered a newfound fear of flying which, nurtured and abetted many times in the next few months, provided an interesting counterpoint to other fears which I had yet to experience.

CHAPTER 3

Welcome to Lai Khe

The flight to Lai Khe was noisy and bumpy, but brief, and the landing was predictably exciting. Unlike the C-123 and C-130, the Caribou had seats and windows, so I was able to appreciate the low-altitude flying, the very short landing, and the overwhelming green-ness of the Vietnamese countryside. Exiting from the tail ramp of the Caribou, I was struck by the heat and the primitive collection of low structures which straggled out from the narrow PSP strip, which bordered a red dirt road, Vietnam Highway 13. Scattered about a large cleared area and the apparently randomly placed scruffy buildings were helicopters and a few jeeps and trucks. One of the Caribou crewmen pointed me and a couple of other replacements to a shed-like building. Waiting in the shade was another bored sergeant who told us to get in the back of a truck, then proceeded to drop us off at various company orderly rooms after a five-minute drive down the dirt road. By now the heat was intense, and seemed to boil up from the road surface.

I was the only replacement for Alpha Company that day. A short distance off the red dirt main road, on a sandy track in the middle of tall, regularly spaced trees which I later learned were part of a Michelin rubber plantation, I found a small, crowded collection of unpainted, weathered structures including a tin-roofed wooden shack identified by a stenciled sign as the Alpha Company orderly room. Next to it were a couple of sandbagged bunkers, one of which sprouted lofty antennas, and some cleared spaces and stacked lumber and other building materials. The noncom in the truck told me to report to the orderly room, so I shouldered my duffel and entered the gloom, glad to be out of the sun. I found another bored noncom who took my orders, told me that the company was out in the field, on what I found out later was Operation El Paso, and led me down a gentle slope through the plantation of rubber trees. Interspersed among the trees were large wall tents with wooden platforms for floors, mostly with a dozen or so cots and footlockers lined up on each side. Other amenities included crude wooden latrines with a few toilet seats over 55-gallon drums, a sandbagged ammo bunker with a wooden door, and more sandbagged windowless bunkers about ten feet wide and 30 feet long, dug into the earth and covered with three or four layers of sandbags, the entrances protected by blast walls of the same material. We stopped outside a tent and I was told to find an empty bunk, leave my duffel, and report back to the orderly room.

The supply room was another shed with a tin roof near the orderly room, and yet another noncom was summoned out of its depths by the first one, who told me to report back after I had my gear. I was given a naked steel pot, web gear, a poncho, and a gas mask. The noncom unlocked a steel arms locker and gave me an M-14, a couple of magazines and a box or two of 7.62 rounds.

"Hey, can I get some jungle boots and fatigues?" I asked.

"Don't have your size," said the sergeant. "Maybe next week, check back in."

Next week, good enough, I thought, reassured that the army would make sure I had the gear I needed.

Chow was served in a large wall tent with folding tables and benches, and was served straight off the chow line into stainless steel trays, just like back in the States. Despite the company being in the field the handful of us in the rear area got the same hot meals, which were also sent out to the troops in the bush, via chopper, in Mermite insulated containers.

After chow a sergeant led a few of us down a slope covered with regular lines of rubber trees, each topped with a canopy of glossy green leaves reaching 40 or so feet high, still with spiral runnels carved into the bark and white ceramic bowls stuck in wire holders catching the milky sap, though no one seemed to be collecting the product. The rubber trees stopped along another sandy track, which we reached by stepping over a stone marker set flush to the ground, inscribed with the name and rank, in French, of a Vietnamese veteran of some other war. The track ran along the rubber trees in a gentle curve. On the outer side of the track were large sandbag bunkers, roofed with tin and sandbags, each about a meter tall and four or so wide, with low entryways in the back and narrow embrasures facing away from the rubber. The ground sloped down towards a green valley, lush with rice paddies and fields, bordering the small river, really a creek, which paralleled the track we were on. Rows of barbed-wire strands stretched between steel posts, and further rows of accordion coils of wire, concertina wire, followed the bunker line on my left around the rubber to the south and west, and on my right to the north and east. Two or three hundred meters across the valley, low hills covered with vegetation stretched as far as could be seen. I was told to man one of the bunkers until a company from another battalion, just in from the field, arrived to take over the perimeter for the night.

I scanned the far treeline anxiously, trying to imagine what I would do if black pajama-clad figures started to emerge from the jungle. The sun was setting to my left when the first GIs walked down the sandy path from beneath the rubber trees behind me. All thoughts of the lurking menace across the valley fled; the sight of the slender young men who filed down the path in all shades of faded green uniforms, enriched by the red underlay of laterite dust, their skin golden in the long sunlight, their eyes flicking quickly over me as each turned to his left, then scanning the distant trees, struck me like a blow. They were utterly silent, and moved with an economical grace, despite the burdens with which they were draped: web gear, grenades, canteens, bandoliers of ammunition, all in shades of faded green, all with a brick-red undertone. Their eyes seemed huge, and each one, as he turned the corner, fixed me with a quick glance, and then changed the focus of his gaze to the woodline. Most carried sleek black M-16 assault rifles, some had M-60 machine guns balanced on their right shoulders, with one leg of the bipods extended and held in their right hands. Some had stumpy M-79 grenade launchers and .45 pistols. Their weapons alone were free of the red dust, and had an oily black sheen. Officers were recognizable only by the radio-telephone operators who followed them, antennas jutting above the bulky PRC-25 radios on their backs. They were beautiful, dangerous, and damned, every one.

Never had I felt so trivial and insignificant, not so much like a child watching the veterans' parade on the Fourth of July, but like a mortal watching the gods coming down from Asgaard on their way to some incomprehensible meeting. One after another, about a hundred times a soldier's eyes touched mine, then moved away. The last of them disappeared up the perimeter path, leaving me in my awkward, thick fatigues and clutching my clumsy wooden-stocked rifle. The sun set, the darkness came. I followed the sergeant back up the path through the rubber, found my tent, and eventually, I suppose, I fell asleep.

The visiting company stayed for a few days, and I fell into a routine of light duty around the company area, hanging out at the fringes of the groups of veterans when I wasn't working. I don't remember what battalion that company was from, but I envied beyond words their natural grace and obvious competence, and yearned to be like them. They stayed in our company tents, and by the second night had gotten pretty relaxed. Small groups from time to time disappeared down the dirt road towards Lai Khe, while others hung out in the tents, drinking, smoking, and listening to music on portable tape players.

On the second or third night, while I was in my bunk trying to sleep, I heard a single shot from nearby. Looking up through the screen walls of the tent, I saw a cluster of GIs in the darkness around an adjoining tent, and a flurry of shouts and activity which quickly moved up towards the company hooches. When all became quiet, I relaxed enough to go to sleep; this was just one more inexplicable occurrence in a strange new world. Next morning I heard that a guy in the neighboring tent had been maintaining that a .45 automatic pistol couldn't fire if you were grasping the muzzle so the slide couldn't retract, and that if anybody pulled a .45 on you all you had to do was grab the muzzle and hit him upside the head. This assertion was met with the derision it deserved, but the GI, who had probably had a couple of pops, insisted it was so, and convinced a buddy to hold a cocked .45 with a chambered round while he grabbed the muzzle and told the guy to pull the trigger and prove that he was correct. Of course the weapon fired, and the round went through the hand of the guy holding the muzzle, which would have been fine if it had ended there, but went on through the chest of a beloved medic, who had been with the company until a recent move to battalion, and was visiting his old buddies. The doc was killed, and I never discovered how the responsible parties got sorted out, as the visitors left and Alpha came back home that afternoon. (And while it's true that a .45 won't fire if you push the slide back a bit, doing it correctly requires a deft touch and more than a little practice. Please don't try this at home.)

A day or so after the company came back in, the new guys were summoned up to the orderly room hooch. There were four or five of us, PFCs and SP4s, with maybe an average age of 19, standing in line while a sergeant gave us a summary of our next few days, which would mostly consist of training given by the battalion headquarters. He called us to attention, and the Old Man came out of the hooch. Peter Knight looked to be in his late twenties, dark haired, short and stocky, with a linebacker's build and a southern gentleman's drawl. He was a soldier out of another era, soft-spoken, gentle, and tough. A former varsity footballer, he was built like a tank and seemed just as indestructible. He seemed to care about his men and his mission, and I think in that order. I remember that somebody had told me he was a West Pointer, but that was about all I thought I knew. I later found out he hadn't been to the Academy, but had attended University of Florida, and had gotten his commission from OCS. He had us stand easy, and spoke for maybe ten minutes. He pitched his voice just to us, much quieter than I at least expected, with no bombast or cheerleading at all. Most of what he said I have forgotten, but the gist of it was that we were welcomed to his family, the best company in the infantry; we were to do our duty, pay attention to the experienced troops, and he would do his best to take care of us during the year ahead. What I do remember clearly was the gentleness and intelligence that he projected, manly in the best sense: strong, competent, and caring. During those ten minutes a burden of which I had not been aware was lifted, and I felt a certainty that this calm and muscular officer could bring me through the coming year with safety and honor.

Training at the battalion HQ was mostly directed at familiarization with the weapons we were to carry. At that time most U. S. Army units were equipped with the M-14 rifle, designed to be carried by armored infantry in the fields of Europe and the tundra of the Soviet Union. While I had qualified on the M-16 rifle just before I was sent to Vietnam, not all of my co-replacements had any experience with that weapon. We also spent some time on the M18A1 Claymore mine, a wicked three-pound piece of plastic about the size of an opened paperback book, filled with hundreds of ball bearings and about a pound of plastic explosive, and the M-72 Light Antitank Weapon, or LAW, another plastic concoction which weighed about five pounds, and launched a three-inch rocket in the general direction it was pointed. Both of these weapons would have been useful in the Korean War, probably, and we dutifully tried to understand their operation, and even got to shoot some of them off. We had several classes on booby traps, mines, and other pitfalls for the unwary, which made much less impression on me than the weapons. Soon enough we were done, and the real job began.

I checked back in the supply hooch after the last training day, but there were still no fatigues or jungle boots in my size. "Maybe next week," I was told by an SP4 who was apparently the supply sergeant's understudy.

When I had arrived in Vietnam I was at the peak of my physical condition, up to that point. I could do a hundred push-ups, run a mile in six minutes in combat boots, and max the army PT test. But once I had strapped on my allotted gear and started to go out with the platoon, and later the company, on what were called local operations but were actually training exercises, I realized the shallowness of my conditioning.

First, the stuff we carried. If you haven't read the book, here is the list, from top to bottom: steel pot, helmet liner, web gear consisting of suspenders, on the front of which were clipped a field dressing and a smoke or teargas grenade; the suspenders were holding up a pistol belt, to which was clipped a butt pack, with either an entrenching tool or a machete attached, and a rolled poncho tied beneath. The pistol belt also supported two canteen covers with canteens and a canteen cup, two ammo pouches which each held 80 rounds of 5.56 ammo in four 20-round steel box magazines, though we usually only kept 18 or 19 rounds in the magazines to reduce the chances of a jam. The rounds were usually divided between tracer, ball, and armor-piercing, when available. Four fragmentation grenades clipped to the sides of the ammo pouches completed our offensive armament. Draped over the shoulders were more 5.56 ammo magazines in cloth bandoliers, and a Claymore mine, with wire and detonator, in its cloth bag. In the butt pack were at least a couple of cardboard boxes each containing 20 rounds of 5.56, one or two trip flares and cords, plus personal stuff like spare cigarettes, matches, toothbrush and paste, deodorant, soap, writing pad and pens, paperback book for breaks, spare socks, an olive drab towel, called a sweat towel and often worn around the neck, and a T-shirt for warmth while sleeping. A gas mask in a canvas cover hung on its own waist belt and leg strap. Fastened wherever there was an empty spot would be a small brought-from-home hunting knife in a sheath, and how many ever days of C-rations, depending on the length of the mission, stuffed into black or olive drab GI socks and tied to D-rings, straps, or carabineers. Plus stuff I have forgotten, and anything a sergeant might decide would enhance the mission and was nominally portable. This included belts of 7.62 ammo for the M-60 machine guns, and perhaps a LAW or an 81mm mortar round. If you were very lucky, you had on canvas and leather jungle boots with knobby rubber soles, otherwise leather GI combat boots with slick soles and no drain holes. And in my case an M-16 rifle. Other folks had an M-79 grenade launcher or a machine gun. Those who carried the latter weapons had a somewhat different load, including a .45 Colt automatic pistol, but humping anything less than 60 pounds would have been considered slacking.

Did I mention it is hot in Vietnam? Highs were in the nineties, lows in the seventies, and during the monsoon season, May through October, which was just beginning when I arrived in-country, it rained every day and when it wasn't raining the humidity was such that it might as well have been. I would start to sweat at about sunrise and by 6 a.m. every inch of my fatigues was soaked and remained so throughout the day.

So moving through dense jungle, muddy rice paddy, or even along sandy roads during those first few weeks left me gasping and sick with fatigue. I was always extremely thirsty, and usually out of water. Dozens of insect bites swelled and festered; rashes of unknown origin appeared in all the usual and several hitherto unaffected body places; and everywhere a strap or a belt or a suspended object touched the skin, abrasions, blisters, and bruises appeared and made each step, or even just standing still, at best deeply uncomfortable.

Worst of all was the godlike indifference of the veterans, who were carrying larger loads, for longer periods, while conducting the business of an infantry squad without obvious effort, and occasional enjoyment, while I was expending every bit of energy and will simply to keep up. There is, as any veteran will tell you, a place to stand in the back of a deuce-and-a-half; or a place to sit on an M-113 Armored Personnel Carrier, or APC, usually just called a track; or a Huey, which will provide the person occupying that place a comfortable and pleasant ride, with opportunity to chat with buddies and observe the passing scene. Likewise there are places on the same vehicles in which the hapless occupant, to avoid sharp corners, red-hot manifolds, or forcible ejection from the conveyance, must expend great and sometimes painful effort for the duration of the trip. Those latter places were the ones I invariably found during that first month.

Although the general attitude of the vets towards me as a replacement was one of aloof amusement, there were some exceptions. A rifle squad consists of ten or so men, a couple of whom carry the M-79 grenade launcher, and the rest M-16 rifles. Three or four squads make a rifle platoon, commanded by a lieutenant and a platoon sergeant. Three rifle platoons, plus a weapons platoon armed with M-60 machine guns and 81mm mortars, complete the infantry company, commanded by a captain and a first sergeant. Each rifle squad, along with its roster of riflemen and M-79 grenade-launcher-men, had a three-man machine-gun team, consisting of a gunner, an assistant gunner, and an ammo bearer, assigned from the weapons platoon. Unlike our 5.56-caliber M-16s, the M-60 machine gun fired the 7.62-caliber NATO round (pronounced seven-six-deuce), and did a pretty good job of it. The ammo came in shiny brass and copper belts of 100 rounds, held together by black steel clips which flew out of the gun, along with the spent cartridge case, when the gun was fired. Altogether the three men on the team carried about a thousand rounds of 7.62, which for a gun which fired at a rate of 500 or so rounds a minute, wasn't much at all. The gunners were technically part of the weapons platoon, but in practice were usually assigned to one of the rifle platoons, and worked with the same rifle squad. My squad's regular gun team consisted of Jim Emerson, Mike Kish, and a guy named Roland Wilson. Emerson was a little older than me, a draftee from the state of Washington, well over six feet tall and thin, but strong. He had large features and dirty blond hair, and with his GI glasses and beaky nose he could look kind of goofy, but he carried the heavy M-60 with grace and skill. Kish was another draftee, from Michigan, and about my height and age. Wilson was a muscular black man with a sly sense of humor. While they didn't exactly take me in hand, the three of them were more than usually kind when circumstances joined us together. Several of the quiet days on the Lai Khe company line were spent hanging out with them, trying to absorb the wisdom of the veterans.

Sandbags came in two flavors in 1966, natural jute and synthetic nylon. Both were equally fashionable as architectural elements on the Lai Khe perimeter. The perimeter for which Alpha was responsible ran in a gentle north-to-south curve for about a kilometer along the western flank of the base camp. A narrow stream, the Suoi Ba Lang, made the bottom of a V down the center of a 500-meter-wide belt of rice paddy. On the far side of the stream the paddy sloped up towards a dense treeline punctuated by a few clearings. On our side of the stream the ground sloped back up towards a belt of barbed-wire entanglements, including coils of concertina wire and single strands stretched between steel stakes in a tangle-foot pattern. The wire was festooned with suspended beer cans, each containing a couple of cartridge cases to act as doorbells in case of nocturnal visitors. The wire ran roughly parallel to the stream, followed by the bunker line, and then the sandy track ran between all that and the rubber trees from the defunct Michelin operation. When that perimeter had been constructed, about a year before my arrival, the sandbag bunkers had been placed along the sandy road at 50-meter intervals just behind the wire. Each bunker was about three meters wide and two deep, dug a meter or so into the ground. A double row of sandbags was laid around the edge of the excavation, then another double row laid at right angles to the first. This was continued until the walls surrounding the dugout allowed a man to stand upright and observe or fire through slits in the sandbag walls framed by wooden artillery boxes with the top and bottom removed. Steel fence posts laid across the final ashlar of sandbags were then covered with a double or triple layer of bags, over some plastic sheeting or corrugated tin to keep the monsoon at bay. The finished structure was surprisingly stable, and provided shade and shelter as well as protection against most of the incoming ordnance we were likely to get, short of a direct hit by an RPG or a heavy mortar round.

But sandbags, whether woven of jute or nylon, deteriorated and needed replacement from time to time. During my first few weeks I spent a fair amount of time filling and moving sandbags. It is almost impossible for one man to fill a sandbag unaided. But two to four GIs can quickly produce a respectable pile of sandbags, with one person holding the empty bag open and tying it off when full, and the remainder digging and filling. The work is not arduous and there is plenty of time to fool around.

My introduction to the craft was spent in the company of Emerson's gun team, along with some other Second Platoon guys, including a skinny, sandy-haired city kid about my age; I'll call him Switek. I had gone to college in Portland, Oregon for a couple of years before I enlisted, and in the course of filling and tying, I discovered Emerson was from South Bend, Washington, on the Pacific coast about midway between Portland and Seattle. We bonded a bit over banana slugs and rain. Switek, meanwhile, was squinting at me with his pale, close-set eyes as I shoveled sand. I'd taken off my fatigue shirt; I was endowed with minimal chest hair but had a really hairy belly.

Switek spoke up: "Hey, Clark, squeeze your belly—no, from the sides."

Bemused, and wondering if this was some sort of rookie hazing, I did as I was told.

"Oh man, that looks just like a pussy!" he chortled.

I looked down, and had to agree there was some similarity, as my navel was reduced to a vertical slit surrounded by hair. There were some appreciative snickers from the group.

Wilson weighed in: "Switek, how the hell would you know what a pussy looks like?"

Man, how I wished I'd thought to say that.

The sand we were using came from the bank upslope of the path, and we uncovered some burrows inhabited by scorpions. These were the first I had seen in the wild, and I was properly respectful as the old hands traded scorpion lore. The animals came in a variety of sizes, and three colors: shiny black, shiny red, and white verging on translucent. Roland and Switek agreed that the stings could be fatal, but Emerson and Kish took the view that it was no worse than a bee sting, Kish maintaining he knew a guy who had been stung and suffered no ill effects. Switek sort of ended the discussion by spraying insect repellent on the critters and lighting them up.

CHAPTER 4

Walking in the Jungle

Shortly after I graduated from the battalion training, Lai Khe caught a couple of mortar rounds, and we had our first company-sized overnight mission to search the area from which the rounds may have come. We just walked through the wire and into the jungle a couple of kilometers (klicks) and milled around. This mission included some firsts for me, including digging a foxhole, finding an old mortar emplacement surrounded by jungle, and sleeping in the rain.

At that time we dug standard foxholes, with three men on a position, and no overhead cover, sleeping positions, or other fancy stuff: just a five-foot hole in the ground big enough for three guys. The ground was sandy, the digging was easy; the steady rain was warm and there were no hints of hostile action. I thought sleeping in the rain would be improved by taking the helmet liner out of the steel pot and putting it over my face; eventually the sound of raindrops bouncing off the fiberglass liner became impossible to bear and I just wrapped my head in a towel.

At some point in the last stages of twilight a critter which seemed to have many legs ran through my area. I couldn't identify the species, but it was big enough so that, when it ran over the top of my steel pot which was on the ground, the front end was going down the back slope while the hind end was still going up the front slope. The water that collected around me was close to body heat, and in retrospect I had a pretty good night's sleep, though at the time I felt like I was living at the very edge of survival. At least I was too miserable to be afraid of whatever hazards bigger than a centipede might be sharing the jungle with us.

The next day we started walking through some truly dense jungle, cutting through the foliage on a compass heading. We were to avoid trails or paths at all costs, as these were likely to be mined, booby-trapped, or ambushed. Somebody would take the point with a machete, and right behind him another somebody would have a magnetic compass and direct the point man to go left or right, to stay on the compass heading, and several people behind those two would be counting footsteps, so the guys further back with the map could figure out how far we had come on that heading. On this day I had only the tiniest sense of all this, and was mainly trying to keep my footing on the slippery path as it avoided giant trees and impenetrable thickets. My stateside combat boots might have been roller skates for all the traction they provided, and I was using three times the energy of the guys with jungle boots just keeping up. In this dense terrain maximum visibility was about three meters; I could see a couple of guys ahead of me but the rest of the column was invisible. My pack and equipment made every step a contest between discomfort and agony, and every slip of my boots threatened to pitch me on my face. Although technically I suppose we were marching, most of the time we were standing still, as the line of troops could only move with fits and starts as the invisible point man, somewhere up the line, struggled to cut through whatever impediment presented itself, or go around, or, worst case, back up and find a new course of lesser resistance. Standing was usually worse than moving, because of the treacherous and uneven footing that required constant adjustment just to stay upright. Sitting, which would have provided some relief from all this discomfort, was not an option for a couple of reasons: there was no place to sit except in the middle of the muddy rut the guys ahead of me had carved through the vegetation, and the process of sitting, strung about with gear and encumbered by a rifle, and then getting up again, took several minutes, which could allow the GIs in front to get out of sight and draw the ire of those behind. I could not see the sky, or even see anything that had sky above it, no wind blew, though spatters of drops fell from time to time. Everything was green, though dozens or hundreds of shades of green, with here and there a bit of greenish brown.

Did I mention it was hot? It was hot.

A couple of hours into this venture I heard my first explosion in anger, the not-too-distant crump of an explosion coming somewhere more or less in the direction we were going. After a few beats of silence someone began screaming, a grown man screaming in agony and fear. From ahead came the shouts of "Medic!" while at the same time I was pushed aside by our platoon medic, running up the line of soldiers with his bag towards the screams. I saw then the singular expression on the face of an army medic, a unique combination of determination, fear, and love, moving as fast as he could towards the casualty, and, of course, the point of maximum danger in any combat environment. After a couple of minutes the screams diminished and ceased, and a while later four or five GIs manhandled a poncho used as a litter, with a silent, still, and bloody soldier hanging in it, along the twists and turns of our line. This was difficult, as the path cut through the jungle was nowhere wider than a single man and rarely straight for more than a meter or so, and there were no verges or shoulders, just a solid wall of green on each side. The grim-faced guys carrying their buddy had to move through this narrow path and maneuver around those of us who could only squeeze a little further into the jungle to let them by. I barely recognized the guy in the poncho, as he was from another platoon and hadn't been in my little training cohort. His eyes were shut and he wasn't moving; his arms were wrapped in field dressings which were soaked with blood. Our medic was holding a plasma bag attached to an IV line and trying to keep it going and not impede the guys carrying the poncho. Amidst all that endless green, the bright red blood was like a neon sign on a dark night. I briefly felt a burst of pity, followed by a shiver of mortal fear. I found out the next day that Freddie, the guy in the poncho, had died on the medevac chopper. With that, he moved into my head, or my heart, or something, standing there bareheaded, holding his helmet and with a shy smile.

Freddie Lee Kleckley, Gainesville, Florida, age 21. Alpha Company, 1/16 Infantry. Died August 10, 1966, as the result of metal fragment wounds to both arms and traumatic amputation of left hand when hit by fragments from hostile booby trap.

CHAPTER 5

Why Walk When You Can Ride?

A few days after that patrol we were lined up in front of the company hooch and loaded up with several days' worth of C-rations. The C-ration process was fraught with peril, as there were 12 varieties of these, each in a cardboard box labelled on top with the name of the main course. Inside each ration box were four olive drab or OD tin cans and sealed OD foil bags containing condiments, cigarettes, matches, plastic spoon, and a small roll of toilet paper. Four of the main courses were in large cans: Meatballs and Beans, Beef and Potatoes, Beans and Franks, and, *gasp*, the dreaded Ham (with Water Added) and Lima Beans. None of the rest of the items were truly vile, although the Chopped Ham (with Water Added) and Eggs had some adherents for that distinction. But the tell-tale ingredients only appeared on the top of the boxes, and the different varieties were distributed randomly within the carton, though each carton had exactly one of each, so a savvy noncom would dump the boxes upside down out on the ground, and force us to pick the requisite number of boxes blind. At this time no one in my platoon would trade for Ham and Lima Beans, so there was no recourse if that turned up. I still hadn't figured out that the only practical way to carry C-rats was in the long wool GI socks, black or OD, which could each hold the contents of a box plus a little more, leaving enough slack to tie around the shoulder harness of our web gear or a carabiner attached to some convenient piece of equipment so the yard-long socks hung down the back. This was the first time we had drawn more Cs than I could stuff in my pack, but by the time I had figured that out, and made the connection between all the ugly socks my platoon-mates were stuffing and attaching, there was no opportunity to get socks of my own, as we were loaded onto trucks and driven to the airstrip. Although I still hadn't gotten jungle boots ("maybe next week"), I had managed to get some jungle fatigues, so I stuffed the last cans and packets into the cargo pockets on my pants, further reducing my mobility and comfort level.

There are two distinct sounds produced by a flying Huey—the deep *thwocka-thwocka* of the rotor blades cutting the air, the generic noise which all choppers make, and the brutal whine of the turbine which powers the blades. Even one Huey has a distinctive sound, but 30 or 40 of them approaching in a dense gaggle create an environment which cannot be adequately described simply as noise. Sitting on a baking PSP and laterite airstrip, surrounded by trees, the first impression is an almost subliminal deep bass beating, like a giant heart; could those specks in the distance be producing that sound? The sound gets louder, and an angry buzzing starts to weave around the bass. As the intensity grows, the bass notes can be felt as well as heard; the specks disappear, and a few seconds later the first elements appear right over the trees; the pitch of sound changes, the turbine shriek almost overpowers the deep notes of the rotors, and the dark, deadly snouts of the beasts float over the airstrip, noses in the air. The blast from their rotors creates a storm of sand and other debris, which stings and gouges unprotected skin and can be felt through cloth. The first elements float to the end of the strip, followed by the rest, in two parallel lines. It is impossible to look at them in the face of the sand-storm created by their passage. The noise changes and abates a bit, as does the quantity and velocity of debris; looking up, a Huey rests a few meters to our front, the rotors continuing to beat, but not pitched for lift, the tail rotor a deadly circle. Speech is impossible. Two shadowy, helmeted, and visored heads are just visible in the nose, and a gunner likewise helmeted, visored, and tethered by cords stands in a niche behind the open side of the craft, alongside an M-60 machine gun on a swivel mount, now pointed down.

The sergeant who had collected us in our pod waves his clipboard to send us forward, the air still filled with sharp particles. I end up heaving myself into the middle of the floor of the craft, surrounded by others behind me on nylon sling seats, and to either side, sitting on the edges of the open, doorless space with their feet resting on the skids. The gunners, one on each side, give us quick looks and speak into their headsets; after some indeterminate period of time the noise changes again, as the rotor blades are pitched for lift. The vibrating box we are crammed into lifts, shifts from side to side, then goes nose down, and up like an elevator and forward, it seems within inches of the craft ahead of us, which I can see through the windscreen over the pilots' heads. It is not smooth, it is not graceful, and I have no reason to believe that I am not about to die in some horrific manner as this impossibly complicated machinery sets about defying the rules of reason and takes to the air. One of my veteran buddies, sitting with his feet out the door and lounging so the weight of his gear is mostly resting on the metal floor, flashes me a grin. Much as I would like to flash him one in return, I cannot overcome the paralysis of fear which has frozen my face into an expression with which I later became familiar, watching new guys on their first chopper ride. And that was before I saw we were headed directly into the trees at the end of the runway.

The ride continued, nonetheless, the Hueys forming two lines abreast a few hundred feet above the intermittent trees and clearings. I learned later that the object of the pilot of a "slick,"—a troop-carrier as opposed to a Huey gunship—was to avoid attracting the attention of the Viet Cong long enough to become a large, slow-moving (by airplane standards) target. This was best accomplished by either flying high enough to avoid the machine guns and RPGs, or low enough so that anyone on the ground was denied a sight line for as long as possible. For a terrified grunt on his first air assault, however, the logic of this was not apparent. After a few minutes up in the blue sky, my Huey, along with its brothers and sisters, dropped to a meter or two above treetop level; when the trees ended at a clearing or paddy, the Hueys dropped yet again, to a meter or two above ground level, rising at the last second to just barely clear the next oncoming treeline. The ground speed of these craft was probably not more than 120 mph, but it was fast enough to create the moral certainty of imminent death in at least one rookie passenger.

The ride ended, finally, as the Huey shot up over a narrow treeline and down again almost to the surface of a vast, water-filled rice paddy.

The right-hand door gunner leaned into the passenger area and screamed, "Hot L-Z! Hot L-Z!" The left door gunner opened fire, along with all his counterparts in the other Hueys, and red tracers laced the treelines and the paddy berms, or dikes. The nose went up, and the craft stalled and hovered over yellow-brown water of indeterminate depth, the rotors creating complicated waves and spume. The right door gunner shouted and gestured, and the guys in the door jumped out into the paddy. I scooted over to the door feet first, and teetered for a second looking down—way down—into choppy water with a few GIs moving through it towards the treeline. My fear of the chopper and my fear of what awaited me below struggled for a moment, and were resolved by my legs pushing me off from the skid and launching me gracelessly into the void.

The Huey was probably less than two meters above the surface of the paddy, but still far enough so that I have some memory of the actual time I spent in the air. I hit the water, and I, and all my gear, struck the muck beneath it. My boots were perhaps ankle deep in the paddy bottom, but my head was still above water, when I was hit from above by another GI. This time I went completely under, my helmet and rifle going in opposite directions, and my GI glasses disappearing forever, as someone walked over my back. My eyes were open, and while I considered the likelihood of drowning, not one of the fates which I had lately feared, I peered through the murky water and located and grabbed my rifle with my right hand and my helmet with my left. Kneeling and then standing, I found myself in water somewhat above my waist, but otherwise intact. The blast of wind from a departing Huey blew me into the water again, but I was able to hang on to my gear, get to my feet, and start slogging towards the berm in the wake of several other guys. Dumping the water out of my helmet, I gratefully covered up, as the machine-gun fire from the Hueys continued over our heads, the tracers disappearing into the paddy and the berm. Debris was flying and splashing all around me, and so much firing was taking place I had no idea if any of it was directed at me. I really wanted to get out of the paddy, and did my best to move swiftly, but not only was I carrying all the gear with which I had started the trip, I was also shipping a few gallons of paddy water and mud.

Finally I reached the shelter of the black mud berm, which rose more than a meter above the surface of the paddy. The whole paddy was like a huge rectangular pond within the berms which ranged in height from less than a meter to massive structures rising maybe two meters above the water level. The one I had reached was of that height, with mostly bare dirt sides sloping down to the water. Small trees and other vegetation grew along the top, and I could see a dozen or so GIs who had hauled themselves out of the water and were clinging to the gentle slope of the berm. Somehow, with help from a couple of the earlier occupants, I managed to pull myself out of the water. Maybe it was the water and mud that were still streaming off me, from head to toe, or just my rookie confusion, that was making the world blurry and noisy. But as I caught my breath and started to look around, there were lots of loud, complicated engine sounds coming generally from upwards, which were punctuated by the intermittent crackle of both distant and nearby small-arms fire.

From time to time one of the GIs would hitch himself up to peer over the berm and maybe fire a few rounds. Nothing made any sense to me, and whether there were incoming rounds I had no clue. I saw that the berm stretched maybe 60 meters to my left, and to my right ended in another berm after maybe ten or 20 meters. Dozens of GIs were by now clinging to the berm or standing in the paddy water just below. No more choppers were discharging troops. I noticed some dense yellow smoke rising here and there through the trees and brush which ran along the top of the berm, but it meant nothing to me. I was safe, whole, and had survived an air assault! For a couple seconds I was mightily pleased with myself.

But, as I learned, in that environment such moments tend to be fleeting. From the jumble of aircraft noises overhead a particular sound emerged, and suddenly blotted out the rest; from the whining, racing, thumping of a speeding helicopter came a tearing, roaring, crackle, punctuated by *booms*. The brush and trees covering the berm directly above me exploded into a cloud of flying debris which peppered us and hit the mud and the water with explosive force. A half dozen impossibly loud concussive explosions, somewhere on the far side of the berm, sent mud and water flying through the air and down on us.

"Throw smoke! Throw smoke!" someone shrieked.

It seemed like dozens of small dark canisters went flying from GIs up and down the berm, mostly behind us into the paddy water. I stared bemused as the objects sank immediately into the opaque water just behind me; seconds later thick billows of smoke, red, yellow, and green, rose out of the water. The angry whine of aircraft diminished a bit, and all around me I saw GIs exhaling with relief.

"You shit yourself, soldier?" a grinning sergeant asked me.

I took a mental inventory of my recent bodily functions, and was able to report that, no, I hadn't. "Well goddammit, if you didn't, you never will, then," he laughed.

I didn't have the nerve to ask him what there was to be so upset about, but it was dawning on me that maybe this wasn't like the usual ending to a chopper ride.

After a bit an officer with an RTO (Radio Telephone Operator) and a sergeant splashed down the line, telling us to get up on the berm. Slipping and cursing, the GIs started pulling themselves up the bank and spreading out in single file along the top of the berm. With some help from other GIs and some handy saplings I was able to take my place on the top, looking across another flooded paddy to an actual treeline and higher ground a hundred meters or so to our front. After a considerable period kneeling in place, nervously watching and listening to artillery rounds landing amongst the trees in the near distance, the officer, or a similar one, moved us down the berm and lined up across the paddy. The water in this one turned out to be barely ankle deep, and the ground under it was firmer. Spread out with maybe three or four meters between each guy, our line splashed across the clearing.

As we neared the opposite berm and treeline, details began to resolve: on the rising ground behind the berm, among low, leafy vegetation that I later learned were banana trees, and some taller trees, were thatched structures which had from a greater distance blended into their surroundings. As I was gaping at this and trying to make sense of the noise—aircraft, explosions, and other incomprehensible sounds—someone shouted, "Incoming," and started shooting into the treeline. I flipped off my safety and started putting rounds where I saw other tracers entering the bushes, and noticed the blackness of a hole dug into the berm. I concentrated on the opening, and emptied my magazine in that direction. At this point so many tracers were flying I have no idea if any of mine entered the hole. The firing stopped and we moved cautiously towards the berm and the treeline, when a hand appeared in the hole and a woman's voice started yelling in Vietnamese. A couple of the closest GIs reached the mouth of the hole and pulled out a woman in black pajamas, who was hysterically crying and shouting. She appeared injured, though it was hard to tell because the blood barely showed against the wet black pajamas. Another GI carefully looked in the hole and, reaching in, pulled out the body of a younger woman or girl. One of the medics came and started to examine the woman, who broke away and threw herself over the body of the young girl, who appeared dead. She cradled the girl's head in her lap and wailed while the GIs stood around. I would like to say I felt bad, or guilty, or remorseful, or even sorry, but all I can remember is feeling numb.

Some lieutenant moved us out at that point and we walked up through what revealed itself as a village, with simple structures of bamboo and thatch or tin roofs, littered with the detritus of rural life—tools, baskets, and handmade adaptations of tin cans or containers fitted with wood or wire handles. Viet Cong had been in the area, and we found several packs they had dropped during the course of the fighting. I took possession of one of these, and the lieutenant said that I could keep anything that didn't have intelligence value. Most of the contents were unremarkable, but I did obtain a large rectangle of camouflage-pattern parachute silk, maybe two meters wide and three meters long. This I kept.

Later in the day, as it began to get dark, the second platoon was guided back to the same area. I remember walking along the berm in the dusk and seeing the body of the dead girl, lying on her back. She seemed tiny, utterly still, and in the moonlight her skin was almost luminescent against the black of her pajamas and the mud of the berm in the gathering darkness. My first thought was amazement, that someone would have put such a lifelike dummy here in this primitive place. Slowly I processed the reality, and again can't recall anything that approached a feeling. As it happened, we were told to lie down on the berm in pairs, one to remain awake, and spend the night. My buddy—I forget now who it was—and I hunkered down a couple of meters from the dead girl and waited for darkness to close us in.

At some point in the middle of the night my buddy woke me up and whispered, "I hear something, someone is moving out there."

"Should we fire them up?" I asked.

No one was visible on either side, there were no stars or moon, and the darkness was profound. I thought I heard something as well. "Let's fire them up," I said, and we both opened up on what I at least thought was the treeline. Watching the red tracers arcing into the darkness, the bright muzzle flash and definitive noise of the gunshots was comforting. After a few rounds each we stopped and waited, but nothing moved, and nothing came back at us. Somehow the night passed.

In the morning, as daylight seemed to seep up from the ground, I noticed that blood was running from the mouth of the dead girl. For an instant I wondered—I hoped—that she was only wounded. I got up and walked closer, and saw that what I thought was blood was a double line of ants, one line going in, the other coming out. OK, she's dead, I remember thinking; I don't have to do anything.

Later that morning a sergeant came around and addressed a bunch of us who were sitting and eating or smoking. "Some of you were firing last night, and I don't know what you think you saw, but your rounds were going over that treeline." He gestured towards the 50- or 60-foot-tall line of trees further up the slope. "When you shoot, make sure your rounds are staying low. If that had been Charlie, he would've walked up and wasted your ass while you were shooting up the fucking treetops. And another thing. Who took a shit up there?"

I allowed as how I might have done that.

"When you take a shit, take your entrenching tool, dig a little hole, and cover it up," he said. "We might have to deploy up there and I don't want to have to lie down in your shit." He actually said this in an almost kindly way, recognizing me as a rookie. And for the rest of my tour I fired low and covered my shit.

We spent the next day walking through jungle, accompanied by what I was beginning to understand were the usual explosions and buzzing aircraft, the drilling of rounds passing overhead, and the occasional scream of a low-flying jet on a bombing run, followed by the substantial blast of a big bomb somewhere in the jungle. Whenever we moved through the countryside, usually in one long line, or perhaps two lines moving parallel to one another and staying within sight, flankers were set out on each side. The flankers were a fire team consisting of two or three riflemen. Their job was to stay just within sight of the main column and warn of, or trigger, contact with any enemy lurking on the edges of the main body's line of march. In open country, this wasn't a big deal, and I had seen flanking troops moving about on previous marches. This time, Second Platoon was ordered to provide the flank, and I was one of a couple of riflemen chosen, along with a team leader, to take the right flank of the company. I was told to take the point of the flanking unit, or point flank. At first I thought this was kind of cool, as it seemed less onerous than trudging along the muddy track in the wake of dozens of other troops. Also I got to use a machete, which had seemed to me a symbol of the competent jungle warrior as I had observed my more experienced comrades wielding it. Soon I discovered that keeping up with the moving column, barely visible to my left through the brush, was no easy matter. When the column was moving, I was hard pressed to get through the jungle without falling behind or losing sight of the one or two visible guys who were all of the line I could see. The column, which had seemed to move so slowly when I was in it, now seemed to slide with uncanny rapidity through the brush; when it halted, of course, I had to halt as well. Again and again I was confronted with an obstacle which I could not go through, or over, and had to scramble left or right in an effort to find a way around, and this effort often ended up putting me far behind the place I should have been relative to the main column. Quickly I became exhausted, my arms barely able to lift the machete, which more often than not bounced off its target rather than severing it cleanly. I was practically blinded by sweat, and unable to spend an atom of attention on the possibility of encountering an enemy, as every bit of my energy was focused on keeping up and getting through. At some point the team leader grew sufficiently disgusted to replace me on point, and afterwards we rotated through that position.

By the time we reached our destination, I was as tired, dirty, dehydrated, and generally useless as I had ever been. I remember a dustoff coming in to our front at one point, but little else about the rest of the operation. It isn't listed in the division's official history as a "battle," and I never knew where we were or why we were there. And even mentioning the sadness and guilt I've carried over my role in that operation seems indulgent, considering the much greater losses others have borne.

There is no record which I can find of the death of the little girl, but if there were, I would put it here. Jeffrey W. Smith, Hillsboro, Alabama, age 23. Alpha Company 1/16 Infantry. DIED on 16 August 1966 in Vietnam as the result of metal fragment wounds to chest and right leg when hit by fragments from hostile mine. Death is the result of hostile action.

CHAPTER 6

You Will Suffer

Back in Lai Khe for a few days, we lived the quiet life, pulling perimeter duty, day and night, and performing necessary chores. Sanitation was provided by ramshackle wooden outhouses, one for officers and another for enlisted men, which consisted of a few stairs up to a wooden platform with crudely carved holes over 55-gallon steel drums. Every morning a few of us would roll the drums out from under, pour in a quart or so of diesel fuel, and burn the contents. We had a shower made from a discarded aircraft fuel pod raised on a wood framework, which we filled by emptying buckets into the top. The water quickly reached the pleasant temperature of the air.

During my year of stateside training I had prided myself on the seriousness with which I approached the business of soldiering. Others slacked off and avoided duty, but I sought it out. I wanted to be the best soldier I could be, and had contempt for those of my colleagues who did their best to be unmilitary. Thus, on my first night ambush patrol, just a few days after the company returned to Lai Khe from wherever we had been, just a few hundred meters in front of our lines, I fell deeply asleep when I should have been awake and alert. My squad leader, a small, wiry, black man I'll call Pettengill, a career E-5 sergeant, discovered me sleeping. Since our position required us to be prone, the transition from awake to unconscious was so fast as to be imperceptible; I surely did not decide to go to sleep, I just found myself emerging from that condition with the face of my sergeant two inches from mine.

"I cannot believe you are sleeping. Are you sleeping?" he hissed.

I was washed in shame and must have said yes, for his next words were: "You will suffer. I promise you that you will never, ever, sleep on my ambush patrol again, you hear me?"

This sergeant for whatever reason did not resort to profanity, but he had no need. Never thereafter did I fall asleep on duty; I learned to take a canteen of GI coffee with me on night patrols. But the next day, back in the base area, Sergeant Pettengill came to me with a steel can containing 500 rounds of 5.56 ammo, which weighed about eight pounds, and an M-16 bipod in a canvas holster.

"You are now the squad's designated automatic rifleman, private," he said. "I will never see you without this can of 5.56 and this bipod." He did not smile when he said this.

One of our missions during this time was a road security operation to the north of Lai Khe, on Vietnam's National Highway 13, paved, if that's the word, with the usual red laterite. Rather than going to our destination on a chopper we were loaded onto tracks, box-like vehicles designed, like so much of our gear, for combat against the Warsaw Pact on the plains of Europe. The vehicle was armored with thick aluminum panels, which would offer some protection against Claymore shrapnel or small-arms fire, and could carry eight or so combat-equipped troops in its passenger compartment. Unfortunately a remote-controlled bomb or mine pretty much turned anyone riding in the enclosed space, designed to be sealed tight to protect against gas and radiation, into red Jell-O. As a result of hard lessons learned before I arrived in-country, the floors of these vehicles were now covered with a couple of layers of filled sandbags, and the top hatches were removed or tied down open, so the force of a blast from underneath would be vented up. The exposed .50-cal. machine gun, originally mounted on an anti-aircraft ring around the vehicle commander's turret, was now inside a neat wraparound steel shield; on each side of the open bay behind the .50-caliber turret was an M-60 machine gun on a swivel mount protected by a smaller version of the shield. These were field improvisations, but they turned the ungainly, box-like track into a pretty warlike beast. Usually the sides of the individual tracks were festooned with rings of concertina wire, which would be pulled open and stretched around the vehicle when it laagered at night. Of course the forbidden interior space, deadly to soldiers, provided ample storage for C-ration cartons, water, bedrolls, and other luxuries usually denied to us footsloggers.

Lai Khe was home to the 1st Squadron of the 4th Cavalry Regiment, written 1/4 and nicknamed the Quarter Horse, the equivalent of an infantry battalion, and so these guys plus some of their friends gave our whole battalion a lift up the highway. We, of course, didn't ride in the tracks, but on top. Here was where I learned the valuable lesson that a comfortable seat when the track is sitting still, on the edge of the top hatch, facing forward with legs dangling, is not the place to be, as the operation of one or more of Newton's Laws during the constant stopping and starting tended to pitch me forward into the hold, and there was nowhere to brace my feet that was comfortable. Nonetheless our column of around a hundred tracks, stretching forward and back as far as eye could see, and accompanied by M-48 tanks and overflown by patrolling Huey gunships, was a sight to cherish for a kid still in love with the machinery of war.

On the second day of the operation the Second Platoon was on the point of a company patrol moving through flat country, with spotty brush and small grassy open areas. I was somewhere in the middle of the platoon, happy to be walking on relatively level and firm ground in my slick-soled boots, but still not able to carry the added burden of my can of 5.56 ammo with anything approaching comfort, when a couple of shots from up ahead woke me up. Kneeling, I dropped the ammo can and hefted my rifle, along with all the other guys visible to me. Switek was to my immediate front, and Emerson's gun team was a couple of guys behind me. A few more shots came from up ahead of the column, but there was nothing to see. After a minute or so, though, a guy I'll call Sherman, a tall, thin kid with tight, ashy-blond hair and large, pale eyes, came back down the line. Sherman was one of the GIs who had come over from the States with the whole 1st Infantry Division in 1965, and had been in country almost a year. He was quiet and nervous, and I hadn't hung out with him. He looked scared as he moved past me. He was followed by his sidekick, a short, dark, square-built kid I'll call Marozzi, who had also come over with the division. They quickly disappeared down the column.

"Where are they going?" I asked Switek, who had his M-16 at his shoulder, and his finger on the trigger.

He didn't take his eyes off the brush to his front. "Fuckin pussies," he muttered.

A little later Sergeant Pettengill appeared, crouched over with his rifle held at the ready. He knelt down next to Emerson and his team, and told them in a whisper to move up the line. Emerson led the way, walking fast but as low to the ground as possible, followed by Kish and Wilson. Pettengill looked at me and Switek, and hissed, "Follow me," and took off up the line. A few more shots from the front gave me all the incentive I needed to imitate the veterans, trying to keep low and move fast. A few meters along we came to the lieutenant and his RTO, kneeling behind some brush. Emerson and his team has gone to their left, and Pettengill followed them. Another sergeant was crouched down nearby, and directed Emerson to set up behind a low grassy hillock. Pettengill put Switek next to them, and me to Switek's left. He then went down himself on what must have been the left flank of the platoon. For a couple of minutes I knelt there, two or three meters between me and Pettengill on one side, and Switek on the other. I could see nothing, except the ground rising gradually to our front. The brush was thicker and higher in that direction.

Another shot came from the right front about then, and this time I heard the distinctive *whickering* sound of an incoming rifle bullet passing overhead. Answering fire came from GIs somewhere to my right. Without conscious thought I found myself prone behind my rifle, peering through the brush ahead. Emerson opened up with his M-60, firing short bursts into the brushy slope, followed by Switek and a few others with their M-16s. Not knowing what else to do, I fired a few rounds into the undergrowth to my front. The M-16 is a satisfying weapon to fire in many ways, as the response to pulling the trigger is immediate, but after a few rounds my pressure on the trigger didn't produce the desired result. After a few seconds of bemusement I ejected the magazine, but there were still rounds in it. Pulling back the charging handle revealed a shell

Sniper (Peter Clark; July, 1967). Kind of a generic sketch of the response to getting some incoming sniper rounds.

stuck in the chamber. I tried a few times to get the bolt to engage, but despite my efforts, including banging the so-called forward assist button, nothing helped. Fortunately the firing died down, and no live targets appeared.

I turned to Pettengill and brandished my rifle. "It's jammed," I whispered.

He gave me a look of disgust and produced a cleaning rod assembly from somewhere about his person. "Gimme that," he snarled, and, grabbing my rifle, deftly screwed a couple of sections of cleaning rod together, inserted it into the muzzle, and tapped out the offending round. He thrust the weapon back at me, muttering something about keeping it clean henceforth, and returned his attention to the now quiet foliage to our front, as the first artillery rounds started impacting on the hillside.

The company eventually formed up and moved out. Whoever had been shooting at us faded into the jungle, and though we swept the area that had been subjected to the artillery barrage, we found nothing indicative of an active enemy presence, as far as I know. On the plus side, we had no casualties, either. I worried some about my rifle jamming, because this problem had become endemic, and the upper echelons had decided that the lazy, shiftless grunts were causing the problem by refusing to keep their weapons clean, or using too much oil, or not using enough oil. Much time was spent scouring, oiling, and wiping rifles and cartridges, to the point where we were told that the sides of the M-16 bolt needed to be lightly oiled but the face of the bolt had to be dry, a condition impossible to achieve outside the laboratory, as far as I could tell. The old M-14 had jammed with some regularity, but could always be cleared, if necessary by kicking the operating rod handle. The M-16 was designed in a way that didn't permit a stuck round to be cleared without sticking a ramrod down the muzzle, and of course ramrods, or rifle cleaning kits, were rarer than hen's teeth at that time. This failing did dampen the average infantryman's affection for an otherwise effective weapon. Many years later the army acknowledged that the problem was caused by incompatible powder in the cartridges, and was unrelated to GI misfeasance, but we spent a lot of time in base camp bent over drums of gasoline, scrubbing already clean rifle parts with toothbrushes.

I also wondered about Sherman and Marozzi, the first time I had seen GIs deliberately avoiding danger. Nobody talked about them, but they were held in quiet contempt, and the rest of Second Platoon was happy when they DEROSed in late August. (DEROS was army for Date Eligible for Return from Overseas, pronounced "dee-roas.") Their conduct put into perspective what to me was the most amazing fact, that the overwhelming majority of us, whether drafted or enlisted, would put ourselves in harm's way as a matter of course. If battle was a test, then almost everybody in Alpha was getting straight As.

Later that day the company emerged from a patch of woody jungle and was halted along a sandy road. Word was passed down the line that a company of South Vietnamese soldiers were going to be coming down the road and pass by our front. Second Platoon was on company point so I was near the head of our column as we knelt at the edge of brush and waited for the encounter. Before too long the head of the column appeared. ARVN, pronounced Arvin, was the acronym for the Army of the Republic of Vietnam, our allies, or friendly gooks, as they were known to us. I didn't know whether the troops moseying down the trail were actual ARVNs, or were local militia called RF-PFs, or Ruff-Puffs, the regional and provincial part-timers. They were dressed in green fatigues, mostly tailored so that they fit snuggly around slight, graceful frames. Probably the average height of the soldiers was about five feet, and none was showing any surplus fat. Headgear ran the gamut from comically oversized GI steel pots to berets and baseball caps, and some were bareheaded. Most of them were wearing shower shoes or sneakers. The unit was armed with the basic U. S. infantry weapons of the Second World War: M-1 Garands predominated, with a few .30-caliber M-2 carbines and M-3 grease guns here and there. Browning Automatic Rifles were carried, usually by the smallest of the Vietnamese, while others toted a version of the Browning M1919A6, an air-cooled machine gun fitted with a shoulder stock and bipod. Except for the M-2 carbines, the large and heavy weapons dwarfed the soldiers bearing them. The contrast with the robust American GIs, carrying the six-pound M-16, and the tiny and fragile appearing Vietnamese carrying ten-pound Garands and 20-pound BARs, was startling. The Vietnamese didn't seem to mind, though, as they flashed us grins and greetings in fractured English as they passed, their outsized weapons slung over their shoulders or balanced behind their necks. They may have seemed doll-like, and almost absurd under the burden of their armament, but they were tough cookies, the same stock as the Viet Cong. Underestimating these soldiers would be easy to do, I thought, but not smart at all.

During that mission we moved through an abandoned Michelin rubber plantation near Dau Tieng, much larger than the experimental plantation which we inhabited in Lai Khe. The plantation had been the scene of heavy fighting earlier in the year, about which some of the Alpha Company old-timers had regaled us new guys. Today it was quiet, with a slow rain dripping from the trees, glistening on the webs of gigantic spiders which spanned the six- or eight-meter corridors between the rubber trees. This plantation included many permanent buildings, including dormitories for the absent workers, a dispensary, a chapel, and others of less obvious purpose. Constructed of stone and cement blocks, many were neatly stuccoed or plastered, with tile roofs and extensive open areas under the eaves. Any furniture or equipment was long gone, and most bore the marks of both Vietnamese and

American military occupation. Curious, several of us explored them as we moved through the buildings towards our Rest Over Night location, RON in army speak, sometimes also called a Night Defensive Position, or NDP. One of them, perhaps a refectory, had a mural which ran the length of the building, primitively painted in once-bright colors. On the left, a gaggle of small Vietnamese figures in pajamas and conical straw hats, many of them carrying tools or agricultural implements, appeared to be gazing at and welcoming a gigantic, manically grinning Michelin tire creature, whose bulbous arms were outstretched to greet or embrace the throng of little Asians. This figure occupied most of the right half of the wall. On the left, behind the peasants, were crudely painted huts, while behind the Michelin Man were substantial white buildings, with signs in Vietnamese; one had a red cross, another a crucifix. Probably meant to be reinforcing of the corporate ethos, the painting seemed to me a chilling and surreal vision of exploitation and oppression. I wondered if in the next frame the giant Michelin Man would scoop up handfuls of Vietnamese and cram them into its maw; I don't think the mural had reached its intended audience any better than it did me, as witnessed by the endless rows of untended rubber trees through which we walked.

We ended up a few hundred meters downhill from the built-up area, where I was delighted to find a nice slab of concrete near our position on the perimeter, which I staked out for sleeping. There is nothing like slightly sloping concrete for sleeping in the rain, as there is no risk of ending up in a heat-sapping puddle of water. I had also discovered that the rectangular sheet of parachute silk I had found in the VC pack on the previous operation made a light and compact bundle in my butt pack and a warm and comfortable covering at night. Unfortunately I was too openly enjoying this windfall, as a lieutenant from another platoon heard about my treasure and confiscated it, to make spiffy helmet covers for an honor guard for some incoming general. At that time we hadn't been issued the fitted camo helmet covers which became commonplace a few months later, so his excuse for this larceny was just barely plausible. But the process served as a reminder that an infantry private was at the mercy of more than the armed foe.

CHAPTER 7

August 25

August 25, like any other August day in Lai Khe, dawned hot and dry, even though the sun was barely at the treeline. We were conducting a company-sized day patrol just outside the base camp, trudging down the sandy paths through the rubber, past the sandbag bunkers along the perimeter, and out through the wire. Cutting across the shallow rice paddies to the northwest, we entered the jungle in two parallel lines, following a compass heading that the point guys were given. As my squad's newly designated automatic rifleman, I carried the folding bipod for my M-16 in a canvas sheath and the steel box of 500 rounds of 5.56 ammo. Lugging the bipod was no big deal, but the box of ammo was a constant torment due to its weight and the difficulty with securing it to web gear. I had a narrow fabric sling which enabled me to drape the box over a shoulder, but the weight and the hard angle of the box edges as they banged against flesh and bone made that so uncomfortable that I ended up mostly carrying the thing by its handle, using whichever hand wasn't carrying my M-16. We were forbidden the use of our rifle slings in the field, so carrying the ammo meant that neither hand was available for other tasks while slogging. Going through whippy, ant-infested brush no-handed did not improve the journey, but I was still pretty much humiliated by having fallen asleep on ambush and considered the punishment appropriate.

The area around the Lai Khe camp was semi-pacified, meaning the Vietnamese civilians had been removed, and the only signs of the enemy presence we encountered were the intermittent hit-and-run mortar attacks and permanent booby-trap concentrations. After a hot, sweaty, buggy, but uneventful, couple of hours, with everybody following the guy in front through jungle with no more than a few yards of visibility in any direction, we abruptly changed direction. Word was passed down the line to hustle our asses. An hour or so later we emerged at the edge of a waist-deep rice paddy, a klick or so west of Lai Khe. We waded the paddy and scrambled up a two-meter red laterite berm. While I was waiting for the rest of the column to get across the paddy I noticed my squadmates were checking for leeches. After rolling up my pants legs I found a big one on my inner thigh. A quick touch with a lit cigarette caused the leech to drop to the dusty red path along the top of the berm. I was about to stomp on it as it wriggled helplessly, but then had a weird Ancient Mariner moment: the damn thing just wanted to be back in the cool, brown water, doing what it was made to do. Dying in the hot dry dust seemed like a harsh fate, so I kicked the leech off the berm into the water, where it swam away at a good clip. Probably this was a coincidence, but I never had another paddy leech while I was in country. Maybe I had spared the King of the Leeches.

The paddy berm ran into a red dirt road, and a bunch of trucks rolled in from the left. We loaded up and were driven back to Lai Khe. I was pleased as punch: what a great deal, a free ride. Our lucky day! Nobody had told us anything different at that point. In a few minutes we pulled up on the company street, and were ordered out of the trucks. A big pile of C-ration boxes greeted us in front of the barracks.

"Three meals each, move your asses, fall in by platoons." Sergeants buzzed around us, overseeing the distribution of the Cs. By now I had figured out that the only way to carry Cs was in the black or OD GI socks, which I tied securely to my web gear. After I had gotten my chow squared away I realized how uncomfortable my wet pants and socks were, and, being near my tent, I ducked in and started stripping off my web gear and shucking my wet boots and socks. I was just pulling delightful dry socks on when the trucks pulled up. Sergeant Pettengill stuck his head in the tent and, in classic fashion, provided additional motivation for me to get my ass on the truck; it is not easy to get dressed and tie combat boots and re-apply the 60 or so pounds of gear, to say nothing of the box of 500 5.56 rounds, and get on a truck which was already moving. I don't remember how I did it, but I must have managed, as I remember the next stop was the Lai Khe chopper pad.

Once off the trucks, we were chivvied into chopper loads and lined up along the tree line parallel to the PSP airstrip. We sat down, smoked, ate some C's, and maybe some of us dozed. I still didn't have a clue as to what was going on. I didn't have much interest in the destination, figuring it would be the same old shit—and there wasn't anything I could do about it, anyway. With almost a month in-country, I'd been down this road before, and my native curiosity was reduced, if replaced with a glimmering anxiety about the coming chopper ride. But we'd find out when we got there. Sergeants came by and told us to fasten our chin-straps, so the steel pots wouldn't blow off in the prop wash or when we un-assed the chopper.

The first birds appeared over the treeline at the left end of the strip, one after the other, nosing up to lose speed and moving down the line of the PSP. Dirt and debris stung our hands and faces as the sergeants got us on our feet and moving towards the right bird. Avoiding the deadly tail rotor, we climbed over the skids and scrambled into the body of the Hueys, either sitting on the floor in the middle or on the edge with our boots on the skids. I got a place in the middle and wedged the ammo can between my legs. After a minute or two the whole row of choppers rose up, put their noses down, and took off for the treeline, clearing the tops of the rubber by a couple of feet and swinging to our left. Looking out the open doors on both sides, I could see lots of Hueys before and behind us, and another flock coming in to pick up more troops. Wherever Second Platoon was going, it was going to have lots of company.

The chopper ride was uneventful, but for the damn ammo can. With one hand holding my M-16 and another bracing against the swerving of the chopper, the ammo needed to be gripped between my legs to keep it from sliding out the open doors. We landed on a cold LZ some minutes out of Lai Khe, in a typical open area surrounded by bamboo and low jungle. The ground was dry, sandy, and covered with clumps of grass and shrubs. We exited the chopper from both sides and knelt hunched over as the debris of the prop wash stung and bit.

After the choppers left, sergeants and officers got us moving and into positions along the woodline, where we knelt again and stared into the silent jungle. Another flight of choppers came behind us, and we moved out in two parallel columns through the brush. Both columns were on opposite verges of a sandy, rutted trail, almost a road, and were moving pretty quickly. This was strange, as I had almost never moved out on a marked trail before, and if we had flankers out I didn't see them. We could hear artillery landing some distance ahead of us, and hear the rounds going overhead. A stream of close support aircraft was circling in the same direction: F-100 Super Sabres, Canberras, and Phantoms, as well as Hueys, Forward Air Controllers in little Bird Dog aircraft like Piper Cubs, and Light Observation Helicopters, either Hillers or Hughes. As we moved along we could hear the tearing-fabric sound of the Huey gunships' miniguns and the occasional detonation of a large bomb, as well as the drumbeat of artillery battery missions. No question there was some heavy shit going down, and that was where we were going.

After about a klick I started to hear the *whicker* of small-arms rounds going overhead, first just an odd one, then a couple or three, then lots at a time. I had heard a few incoming rounds in my month in-country, so I recognized the distinctive sound, but nothing prepared me for the reality that passing somewhere really close to me were a lot of bullets. I hunkered down and tried to make myself as small and low to the ground as possible while still keeping up with the guy in front, a Second Platoon SP4 named Martinez. I could see Sergeant Pettengill ahead of me and Emerson, Kish, and Roland were about even with me on the left-hand side of the trail. Switek and a couple of his buddies and some other Second Platoon guys were here and there, interspersed with some folks from other platoons. In another few meters I spotted a couple of GIs lying in the bamboo thickets by the side of the path. Their heads were bare, and I couldn't see any weapons near them. They were alive, not visibly wounded, but seemed apathetic, barely glancing at us as we hurried by. They had the black scarves which the 1st Battalion, 2nd Infantry wore as a battalion marker. More of them appeared as we went further, including some guys either dead or badly hurt, with bloody field dressings. By now the sound of small-arms firing was constant.

At some point the two columns separated, and mine went to the right. I emerged around a curve in the path into a small clearing. The jungle was higher now, with some substantial trees as well as the ubiquitous bamboo and brush. Off to the right was a downed, wrecked LOH, and ahead and to the left, some 30 or 40 meters, was a wrecked Huey. Half a dozen or so Viet Cong bunkers were visible, some of which had GIs in them, but most of the GIs in the clearing were lying on the edges, mostly helmetless and without weapons. The sandy, bowl-shaped central area, which was scored by a shallow trench and some small excavations, was littered with the detritus of war: weapons, helmets, packs, boots, first aid packs, and entrenching tools. That was the most shocking thing, after seeing the bareheaded troops without weapons: all this stuff that we were supposed to keep track of, that we would get in serious trouble if we lost, was just lying around. Just a few minutes earlier, I couldn't have imagined anything more important than keeping track of my rifle, and then my other gear. Jesus, I had signed for this stuff! And now stuff somebody had signed for was just lying where it had fallen. It dawned on me that maybe there were things that were more important than staying out of trouble with the army, and I was about to find out what those things were.

An APC had driven through the clearing and was parked against the treeline a few meters ahead and to the right of where the platoon was emerging. So far no one had issued any orders, so I just continued moving into the clearing, tending to the left and ahead. When I was about even with the track the guy in the turret opened up with the .50 cal, and right away a bare-headed GI who looked like an officer jumped up on the track and pounded the guy in the turret.

"Cease fire! Fucking cease fire!" The guy in the turret stopped shooting and the officer yelled, "Don't shoot unless you have a fucking target! I don't want to take any more dead GIs out of there!" Just as he finished the track exploded in a fireball and the guy in the turret went flying through the air.

I found myself near one end of the clearing, with the downed Huey to my left, and a small trench or depression to my front, and beyond that a solid wall of dense jungle with some bamboo. The burning APC was

Dutch (Peter Clark; July, 1967). A sketch for a painting that didn't survive. This is me coming upon the body of Dutch Miedema, with the blown track and the other bodies to the right.

to my right, and I think another APC a few meters beyond that. The ground was dry and sandy and littered with leaves and branches as well as army gear. A couple of dozen GIs were lying under the brush around the sides of the clearing, many of them without helmets or weapons. Most had the black bandanas of the 1/2.

Soon after the track exploded a heavy machine gun opened up on us from somewhere nearby, just beyond the wall of jungle to my right front. The shallow bowl we were in provided a slight defilade from that direction, and the rounds were cutting through the trees and brush overhead. Our platoon sergeant jumped up and yelled, "Let's get that fucking gun!" and ran into the jungle towards the sound of the firing. Oh shit, I thought, but got to my feet and followed him, along with several other guys from Alpha. I left the can of ammo behind at this point, figuring that whatever trouble I'd get in for not having it would be less onerous than having to claw through jungle and fight one-handed.

The machine-gun and other small-arms fire increased, and several Alpha guys went down. The guy next to me, Martinez, was hit in the left arm above the elbow, shattering the bone and leaving a nasty mess. He collapsed, and I dragged him back to the relative safety of the clearing.

"Oh God it hurts, it hurts," he said.

I yelled for a medic but got no response, so I put my field dressing over the wound, covering the protruding bone as best I could. An abandoned aid bag was lying a few feet away. I crawled over and dragged it back to Martinez, and rummaged through it, finding some morphine ampules. I gave him one in the right shoulder and stuck the needle through his collar, and bent it like a safety pin. I was too squeamish to write the time on his forehead with blood, which I remembered from training as the proper next step. I never saw Martinez again, and I've worried for the last 40 years that maybe he didn't get his next shot because some medic saw the ampule and didn't know whether he was due because I didn't write the time. But at that point Martinez was saying "Don't leave me, man, I'm so cold." I figured he might be going into shock, and covered him with a poncho.

"Hey, this is a million-dollar wound, you're going home, you're going to be all right."

"You think so?" He asked. "Please stay with me."

But the training kicked in: leave the wounded for the docs, get on with the mission. Attractive as the little pocket of apparent safety was, I grabbed my M-16 and took off after the rest of the platoon, all of whom by now were either wounded or had disappeared into the jungle.

The sarge and the other guys had charged somewhat to the right, I thought, so I ran towards the jungle where I thought I would be on their left flank. Just a few steps over the little depression, the jungle became too thick to penetrate on foot. I got down and commenced the low crawl, straight out of basic training, but within a couple of meters the vines and brush were almost too thick to crawl through. I had my little civilian sheath knife which I used to cut the vines and stems that were holding me up. Somebody from the platoon said later they saw me "flat fucking doing the low crawl with a knife in my teeth" and, while I don't recall biting the knife, it could have happened.

I managed to work my way a few meters into the brush, but couldn't see any GIs—visibility through the brush was maybe two meters at best. The heavy machine gun was still firing intermittent bursts, the rounds cutting through the jungle growth right overhead, and I tried to steer towards the sound of the gun. After a fair amount of crawling I could see a thinning of the brush to my front. A few more meters and I could see the body of Matt Miedema, lying on his stomach and facing me. His right leg was gone below the knee and he had multiple wounds from a high-caliber weapon. He was a handsome, blond kid from another platoon, and his nickname was Dutchy. I crawled a little closer and saw that Dutch was lying in a path partially cleared through the jungle by an APC, which I could see stopped at the end of its path about ten meters to my right. A couple more dead GIs were lying between me and the APC, but I couldn't see either of their faces. I found out later they were from another battalion. For the first time I experienced the quality of stillness which surrounds the dead. Even at a glance there was no question that these guys were gone.

The machine gun was continuing to fire sporadically from somewhere close by in the thick brush, just on the other side of the path made by the APC, which was exactly as wide as that vehicle, maybe three meters. I couldn't see a muzzle flash, but the rounds were definitely incoming and I could hear them going through the foliage over my head. At that point I figured that crossing the APC path was going to make me a target for that machine gun, which had already got Dutch. I switched to automatic and fired a magazine in short bursts towards the brush where I thought the machine gun was located. The firing stopped but a grenade landed a meter or so away from me. The explosion kind of lifted me up, blew a lot of dirt and debris on me, but otherwise I didn't seem to be hurt, although my ears were ringing. I reloaded and fired another magazine into the brush at my front. Another grenade landed further away, and exploded again without doing me any harm. I still had not a clue as to the whereabouts of the guy chucking the grenades, except that he had to be somewhere in front of me and pretty close. I put in my third magazine and started to fire when a third grenade landed about two feet from my face. It was just out of reach. I could see the grain on the short little wooden handle, which looked like bamboo, and the scoring on the otherwise smooth metal business end. It was hissing and a thin stream of smoke was coming out of it. Oh shit, I thought, turned my head so my helmet was facing the grenade, and pushed my face into the dirt. There was a little pop, and when I peeked out the grenade was sitting quietly—a dud. This was the point at which I decided discretion was the better part of valor, and tried to back up in the direction I had come.

That turned out to be easier said than done. My entrenching tool was fastened to the back of my butt pack, and a tough, woody vine had wrapped around it, underneath the cover, and was preventing me from backing up. I tried to ease forward but found I couldn't get enough slack to slip the tautly stretched vine over the handle of the entrenching tool. Nor could I reach the vine to cut it. Finally I was able to detach the entrenching tool cover from my pack, and slither backwards. No more grenades were thrown. Whether the Viet Cong were out of grenades or simply chose to disengage at that point I will never know. Rather than dragging my entrenching tool back with me I abandoned it at that point, adding to the list of government property which I failed to conserve during my tour.

Although I tried to retrace my path back to the clearing, when I did emerge from the jungle I was in a different location, similar in character to the clearing I had left, but without any Alpha soldiers in evidence. Neither the burning APC nor the wrecked chopper was visible. A handful of 1/2 troops and other elements, including some artillery and track crewmen, were occupying a series of VC bunkers and trenches. By now the day was winding down, and the firing had become sporadic. I asked the GIs if they know where the 1/16 was, but nobody knew anything. "Goddam, you still have grenades!" was the dominant response. I shared my grenades and my ammunition, as most of the guys had pretty much used theirs up. While I wished I had my box of 5.56 ammo, I wasn't going to go looking for it, or anything else, in the rapidly falling darkness. There was no obvious leader in evidence. I was invited to join three other GIs in a VC bunker, perhaps a meter and a half deep and three meters square, which had a kind of roof made from bamboo and leaves. As the jungle became as dark as only nighttime jungle can, we traded stories. The others included an older E7 from the 1/2 and a couple of younger guys. We established that we pretty well represented the United States geographically and the sergeant gave us a pep talk about how Americans together could handle anything the VC could throw at us. The sergeant had heard that Alpha's captain had been killed, and most of his officers were dead or wounded. I pushed away the thought that Captain Knight was dead. The sense all of us had was that we had had our asses kicked and that we could expect an attack during the night or at dawn. There was a determination to defend ourselves in place, though there really was no alternative. We shared a couple of cans of Cs, set up a guard rotation, and spent an anxious night. Other than artillery firing H&I, which was often close enough to send shrapnel spinning over our heads, the night was uneventful.

As the details of jungle began to emerge from the opaque darkness, we prepared for a dawn attack. A chorus of what must have been insects or frogs made me think of the clickers the VC were reputed to use to pass signals at night, but in the event there was no incoming fire from the enemy. Almost as scary was the artillery which started to become a pretty constant and close barrage. This was followed by the scream of jet aircraft coming in at treetop level. Five-hundred-pound bombs and napalm fell all around us. One napalm canister landed behind us and we were literally roofed over with fire. I deeply regretted the loss of my entrenching tool as I used my helmet to improve the depth of my corner of the bunker as we cowered under the friendly fire. I later read accounts of this incident, which was about the only part of the battle that got press coverage. The napalm had landed on or near an area where a large bunch of dead GIs had been laid out, and those deaths were initially blamed on the napalm. As far as I know only a couple of GIs were actually killed or wounded by the Air Force.

At some point the explosions dwindled and ceased, and we emerged from our holes. I collected most of the remaining water from my bunker mates and made a canteen cup of C-ration coffee, which I warmed with some heating tablets and, in an episode of clumsiness that I will regret forever, spilled most of it when I climbed out of the bunker. We did all get a couple of bracing mouthfuls. By this point some officers were checking on the survivors, and I discovered some Alpha troops who had spent the night nearby. While I was looking for somebody from Second Platoon, I noticed that none of the dead GIs covered with ponchos was Dutchy—they all had two feet. I asked a lieutenant if anybody had found him, and apparently no one had. I said I could try to find him, and with a couple of guys from his platoon I went around the clearing and found what looked like the track of an APC. Just a few meters up the track we found Dutch, and a bit further along the bodies of the other GIs I had seen, as well as the APC. The First Platoon guys went back for some ponchos and we carried our brothers back to the clearing. At about that point some guys from the Second Platoon appeared.

Switek, who didn't seem to like me much, started giving me a hard time: "Where the fuck was you? Hiding your ass somewhere?"

I kind of lost my temper and braced him: "I was where Dutchy died, and I didn't see you there, asshole." That shut him up. Not very grown-up, but it felt good at the time.

As I was leaving the bunker area I saw two captured VC, who looked like nothing more than skinny old men. They were kneeling with their hands tied behind them, in dirty pajamas, and surrounded by officers and RTOs and gawking GIs. Somebody told me they had been in a tunnel which had collapsed when an M-48 tank ran over it. They were the only VC, dead or alive, that I saw during or after the fight. Probably the ARVNs killed them later. You could tell they were scared but calm. I hope they didn't suffer.

One of Alpha Company's last remaining sergeants, an E7 from another platoon, showed up and had us gather around. He said he was acting First Sergeant, confirmed that Captain Knight was dead, and then explained how each swinging dick was going to wash up, shave, and get their gear in order. This did not go over well, but with some grumbling we found a bunch of five-gallon cans of water that had been brought in by chopper. This was the purified ditchwater from the water plant at Lai Khe that was supposed to be safe but smelled and tasted like stale cooking oil. Yet it probably smelled better than we did. After getting a couple of quarts in my steel pot, I washed my hands and face and torso, used some deodorant and shaved by feel with my injector razor. As we toweled off I could feel the morale improving, despite our bitching.

A little later the sergeant had us line up for inspection. I was chewed out for losing my entrenching tool and gas mask, which had gotten buried in the bunker when I was trying to get very deep very quickly after the napalm strike. Fortunately for me no one remembered the can of 5.56 ammo and, since Sergeant Pettengill had been wounded and never returned to the platoon, the issue never arose. I learned then that Jim Emerson and Mike Kish had been killed, along with Captain Knight and Dutch Miedema. I'm still amazed Alpha only had four dead, as we had many seriously wounded guys. Pretty much half the company was gone. The day was overcast and some light rain was spitting down. I helped police up army gear until the sergeant collected us and we walked to an LZ and choppered back to Lai Khe.

James Emerson, South Bend, Washington, age 22. Died on 25 August 1966 in Vietnam of a gunshot wound to the head received in hostile ground action; Matthew Miedema, Grand Rapids, Michigan, age 21. Died on 25 August 1966 in Vietnam as the result of gunshot wounds to the chest and abdomen received in hostile ground action; Cary Michael Kish, Detroit, Michigan, age 21. Died on 26 [sic] August 1966 in Vietnam as the result of gunshot wound to the neck received in hostile ground action; Peter Knight, Key West, Florida, age 31. Died on 25 August 1966 in Vietnam as the result of metal fragment wound to the forehead received in hostile ground action.

Captain Knight was posthumously promoted to major. Here's his DSC citation:

> The President of the United States of America, authorized by Act of Congress, July 9, 1918 (amended by act of July 25, 1963), takes pride in presenting the Distinguished Service Cross (Posthumously) to Captain (Infantry) Peter Stanley Knight, United States Army, for extraordinary heroism in connection with military operations involving conflict with an armed hostile force in the Republic of Vietnam, while serving with Company A, 1st Battalion, 16th Infantry, 1st Infantry Division.
>
> Captain Knight distinguished himself by exceptionally valorous actions on 25 August 1966 while serving as a company commander during a combat mission near Binh Duong Province. When Captain Knight's company was directed to assault a fortified base camp of an estimated Viet Cong battalion, he immediately

deployed two of his platoons, held one in reserve and began to advance through the dense jungle and bamboo thickets toward the insurgent complex. As the assault elements emerged from the jungle, Captain Knight learned that the platoon on his right flank had received intense Viet Cong fire and sustained numerous casualties.

Realizing the seriousness of the situation, he rushed to the stricken platoon, reorganized his men and called his reserve platoon for assistance. As Captain Knight led his reinforced unit on a renewed assault against the Viet Cong stronghold, the Viet Cong again opened with a suppressive barrage of fire. Although his company was staggered by the intense hostile fire, Captain Knight fearlessly exposed himself and rallied a small group of men in an attack on a Viet Cong emplacement. Inspired by this courageous attack, the remaining elements pushed forward in a final determined drive to rout the Viet Cong.

Although he was wounded while exposing himself and encouraging his comrades to continue the assault, Captain Knight, with complete disregard for his safety, continued to lead his company until he was mortally wounded by Viet Cong fire.

Through his courage and outstanding leadership, he inspired his badly stricken company to continue the attack until the determined Viet Cong force was completely routed from its base camp. Captain Knight's extraordinary heroism and devotion to duty, at the cost of his life, were in keeping with the highest traditions of the military service and reflect great credit upon himself, his unit, and the United States Army.

CHAPTER 8

You Walked in, You Will Walk out

A couple of days after we choppered back to Lai Khe the Second Platoon pulled a day patrol to the north of the company wire. Most of Second Platoon's noncoms had been wounded on the 25th, and we only had one sergeant on that patrol, an E-5 who had been a squad leader but was now acting platoon sergeant whom I'll call Miller, a youngish career-army country boy from the deep South, along with the new platoon leader, Lieutenant Harden, and what was left of the rest of us. To get to the line from our hooches we walked down sandy trails through a couple hundred meters of rubber, crossing over the broken gravestone set flush on the ground, carved with the name, dates and a French epitaph, belonging to a Vietnamese sergeant who died in the 1950s. When I arrived at Lai Khe the stone was pristine, but a year later it was in fragments as foot and vehicle traffic had taken its toll. By that time, neither I nor anybody else knew or cared too much about it.

We then snaked through an access path in the wire, moving a couple of rolls of concertina aside and replacing them after we had passed through. We walked single file down the shallow paddy, waded across the Soui Ba Lang and up into the jungle on the other side, maybe 20 of us all told. Besides the lieutenant and his RTO, we had a medic and a machine-gun team. As far as we could tell, this patrol was for training purposes and based on the notion that if you're throwed you need to get right back up on the horse. At the time I thought it was probably bullshit and just a waste of a day that could be better spent doing nothing, which was pretty much what I was yearning for after the 25th and 26th. We passed

Booby Trap (Peter Clark; July, 1967). Inspired by my close encounter with a booby trap. Not a good likeness, but I got the gear down, anyway.

the strange ruined stone tower that sat just within the treeline. Two or three stories tall, it was constructed of random-sized cut hexagonal stones laid in an ascending spiral, not in parallel ashlars. I was fascinated by the structure, which looked ancient, and longed for an opportunity to explore it, but that never happened.

We threaded our way into the jungle along an azimuth a little east of north. I was maybe four or five guys back from the point, mostly bored from having been in this area before, and because there hadn't been much VC action from this stretch of country during the month I'd been here. We were so close to what I thought of as home—my dry, screened tent with a bed and a wood floor—that it was hard to get up much enthusiasm for this patrol.

As usual, we didn't follow any of the numerous paths or tracks running through the jungle, but steered on a compass azimuth provided by Lieutenant Harden. The plant cover here was not particularly dense, and showed some evidence of cultivation, so the point guy didn't need to use his machete much and we were making pretty good time. Everybody just wanted to get the hell back to the base camp.

After about a klick, the point guy, I forget his name, stopped cold and hissed "Mine!" He backed up slowly, visibly pale and shaky. "God damn it, I almost walked right through," he kept saying.

We all backed up very carefully and put some distance between us and the booby trap, which was a metal cylinder about the size of beer can taped to the base of a sapling, with a trip wire about ten centimeters off the ground running a meter or so through the undergrowth.

Lieutenant Harden and our designated demolition specialist gingerly inspected the device, and decided to blow it in place. The demo guy carefully placed a wad of C-4 next to the booby trap and cut a length of fuse. The rest of us went another 20 meters or so back the way we had come, where we hunkered down, most of us lighting up. I wasn't bored by this point, just scared. I looked around anxiously while we were waiting, not exactly knowing what to look for, but figuring I would know it if I saw it. We were trying to be quiet as well, as the existence of a booby trap implied the presence of Charlie, and although we knew it could be anywhere from an hour to a month or more since the trap had been set, the possibility that folks with black pajamas and AKs were watching us was significant.

"Fire in the hole!"

The lieutenant and his RTO, and a bit later the demo guy, hustled back down the line of troops. A few seconds later came the *whump* of a small explosion, followed by the familiar whiz and patter of shrapnel and debris. After checking out the site, the lieutenant waved us forward. Leaving the scene of the demolition, we were still pretty bunched up. I ended up right behind the point guy, who was walking very slowly and carefully through the low brush.

Whump!

A flash, nasty little whizzing noises, and a bolus of dirt and debris bloomed a meter or two to my left. I felt like somebody had slapped my leg and thrown sand in my face. The point guy was down, with a bunch of growing red splotches on his side, and four of the guys behind me were down as well. We had been close together as the point guy was going so slowly, and the column was still closed up from our wait for the demo. I found myself prone on the ground. Was that another booby trap, or an incoming round or grenade? Nothing else happened in the next ten seconds, so it was likely a booby trap. The guys who were down started moaning, and the medic came up through the line and started checking them out. I helped carry the point guy back a few meters. I stayed prone after that, with my M-16's safety off, peering into the brush and trying to process the likelihood that Charlie was out there waiting for us, or, worse, coming for us. Behind me the medic worked on the guys. The point man was the worst hurt, but all of them had multiple wounds. The doc had to collect field dressings from us as his got used up. The lieutenant and his RTO located a suitable LZ in a nearby grassy clearing, which we carefully checked for traps, then carried or assisted the wounded guys to it while the sound of the approaching dustoff grew louder. We set up a perimeter around the LZ and waited for the chopper to home in on the green smoke the lieutenant had thrown.

Once the dustoff chopper had departed, we gathered in the LZ and took a new azimuth. I was on point. Just before we moved out Lieutenant Harden asked me if I was hit. I grinned and held up my left elbow, which had been grazed by a piece of shrapnel; my left ear also had been grazed. Other than leaking a little blood on my left thigh I was in great shape, and feeling pretty good about it considering how badly the guys near me had been hit. I got the direction from the guy behind with the compass and headed into the brush. I was being careful and wasn't particularly concerned, still probably high on the survivor's adrenalin rush.

After a few uneventful minutes I came to a line of scrubby trees and bushes which bordered an old field of some sort. I stepped between two six- or eight-foot bushes. I felt safe as I knew I wasn't on a path, the gap was pretty well filled in with brush, and it didn't seem like a traveled way at all. As I lifted the leaves and branches so I could slide through I saw a bright silver braided wire in my hand. In what must have been a fraction of a second but seemed like a couple of minutes, I processed the significance of this shiny wire in the midst of all this vegetation in the middle of an innocuous gap between the bushes. Having done that, and reached the most likely conclusion, I then asked myself the next question, which was, have you already triggered the booby trap, in which case you have x seconds to get some distance between you and the explosion? And the quickest way to get distance is to keep going forward. But if the booby trap hasn't been triggered yet, going forward would certainly trigger it, but if I back out, with luck it won't go off. Hard to believe, but there was plenty of subjective time to work this out. What I did was take a gentle half step back, disengaging from the wire, and then gasped, "Mine!" and tried to set a new speed record for running backwards.

It didn't explode. The lieutenant came and checked it out, and sure enough the trip wire ran through the undergrowth to a metal canister taped to the base of the sapling to my right. Right then I was starting to truly shake with terror. Nothing I had been through up to that point had touched my sense of mortality like the vision of that silver wire in my hand, and nothing that happened since has either. I really hate minefields.

At this point Lieutenant Harden called Captain Howley, the new CO who had replaced Captain Knight, and suggested to him that we should chopper out of the area, given the prevalence of booby traps. This seemed like a great idea to me and I am sure the rest of us, but after a brief exchange the idea was nixed; Captain Howley said we had walked into the minefield and we could walk out, or words to that effect. Regardless, we all wanted to get the hell out, but what had been a typical, boring second-growth landscape became the literal stuff of nightmares.

I was shaky and fearful enough to ask not to take the point, and the lieutenant chose our only noncom, Sergeant Miller, to take that burden. By the time we moved out I felt so ashamed of my cowardice that I took the compass and stayed close enough to the point so that if Miller hit a trap I'd get hit as well. We didn't blow the trap that I had found, or any of the several more that Sergeant Miller discovered, which we noted and carefully walked around. We just gingerly stepped in each other's tracks and followed the azimuth through an increasing drizzle towards what the lieutenant's map promised was the most direct practical route back to the wire. The sky was gray and spitting rain, and a lot of time had elapsed since we had crossed the wire that morning. We really—really—didn't want to try to get through that countryside in the dark, but we had to go so slowly. Anyone who doubts the subjective flexibility of time should spend an afternoon walking through a minefield. Part of me will always be 20 years old, standing in the warm rain, and longing for the impossibly distant horizon just a few hundred meters across that green valley.

CHAPTER 9

New Guys

Our new company commander, Dennis Howley, was a recovering Special Forces veteran who had been flying over the battlefield on August 25 as an observer. When Captain Knight was killed, rumor had it, Captain Howley volunteered to take command of Alpha Company. He was a man of average height and build, but decidedly not of average temperament. From the beginning, he injected the company with the zealous ethic of the commando. Discipline, which had seemed pretty strict before, was now ferociously applied, although not always by the book. The Army's Table of Organization and Equipment (TO&E) specifies in numbing detail the equipment which each soldier will be issued and use, depending upon his functional role within his Military Occupational Specialty (MOS). For example, the TO&E requires that a soldier serving as a Radio Telephone Operator (RTO) is armed with a .45-caliber pistol. Captain Howley, reasoning that the .45 automatic was about useless in a firefight, decreed that every such soldier would instead henceforth carry an M-16 with a basic load of ammunition. He also reasoned that an M-16, if slung over the shoulder or back, was useless as well. All the canvas rifle slings in the company were duly confiscated. At the assembly where that particular rule was announced, he shared with us the vision of a column of ARVNs, rifles slung, being gunned down by Charlie from ambush. "Those weapons," he said, "were no more use to those sorry ARVN sons of bitches than teats on a boar hog, and they stayed right on their sorry backs until Charlie came and policed them up off their dead asses," or words to that effect. "You will not leave C-ration cans or foil wrappers in the jungle," he told us. "Charlie will take those Cs and fill them with nails and rocks, put a little C-4 and a grenade fuse in the bottom, and make a booby trap that will take your goddam foot off. He will take the foil from your cigarette packs," he continued, "and use it to make the contacts to build a pressure activated switch, powered by the radio batteries some RTO dropped, and mine the trail which you should not be, but nonetheless will be, walking on."

Captain Howley was relentless at the beginning, prowling the line when we were on guard duty, moving up and down the line of march, and appearing at odd times and places, usually with a nervous platoon sergeant or lieutenant in tow, bearing a notebook and a Bic pen. As punishment for disregarding these suggestions, some of us ended up burying our carelessly discarded trash in a hole six feet wide, by six feet long, by six feet deep. All of us learned to stop leaving stuff around, an early inculcation into the anti-littering movement. "Charlie will find your cigarette butts," said the captain, "and he will determine just how long ago you were on that trail, and he will run ahead and pass you up, because he knows where the booby traps are, and ambush or mine your sorry asses." We learned to field-strip our butts, peeling off a strip of paper, scattering the tobacco, and, when present, burying the filters. "You will not smoke on ambush patrol, even under a poncho," he said, "because Charlie will smell that smoke a klick away, and will creep up on your smoking ass and blow it away." We stopped smoking on night ambushes and LPs. "You will wear that steel pot at all times, whether you are walking the bush or behind friendly wire," he said, and eventually we did that as well, though with some whining amongst ourselves about how come the Green Beanies didn't wear steel pots at all, and they were so great, huh.

Shortly after August 25, and Captain Howley's arrival, during the first weeks of September, we got a bunch of replacements for some of the dead and wounded. There had been about 130 men in the company before the battle, but a bunch of the folks who survived the battle had DEROSed, and we were down to 60 or so afterwards. Among the new men were the guys with whom I forged the closest bonds, and shared the remaining nine months I had in-country. The young men assigned to Second Platoon, or Alpha Mike in RTO parlance, included Greg Murry, a tall, lanky, SP4 with glasses; Alan Roese, a stocky dark-haired guy from upstate New York, also with glasses; José Garcia, who told us all to call him Joe and was another PFC like me; and Rod Floutz, another tall young man. All five of us were a little older than the usual draftees, being 20 or 21, and had been around, with either some college or other life experience besides high school. Looking back, what we had in common was an interest in what we were doing, and something like a shared desire to do well at whatever that happened to be. Maybe we were a little smarter, and a little more mature, than some of other new guys, and maybe than some of the older career soldiers as well. One of the other guys assigned to Second Platoon was a career-army SP5 named Mallonee, whose MOS was helicopter mechanic and who complained bitterly that he wasn't supposed to be in the infantry. Because of his grade, he was made a fire-team leader, but his attitude wasn't positive. We got several other new noncoms, including an E-6 I'll call Butler, replacing Pettengill as my squad leader, and an E-7 I'll call Floyd, who replaced our wounded platoon sergeant. These noncoms had many years in the army, but no prior combat experience; of course none of the new lieutenants had combat experience either, but their competence didn't seem as critical to those of us at the bottom of the food chain as that of our sergeants.

A day or so after the patrol that ran into the booby traps, an area of my left thigh which had been hit by booby-trap debris became infected and I got sick enough to check with the platoon doc, who sent me to the battalion aid station, where the infected area was scrubbed with what felt like, and may have been, a wire brush. I was dosed with antibiotics and given a couple of days of light duty, and threatened with a skin graft if I didn't report back once a day for more debridement. The company was out on some local operation, but I was grateful for the chance to catch up on my sleep and goof off. I skulked around the company area, mostly avoiding the imposition of any duty at all, but from time to time pulled perimeter guard or a shift in the commo bunker, or rode shotgun in a truck convoy to and from the laterite pits a couple of klicks south on Route 13. The commo bunker was essentially a hole in the ground walled and roofed with multiple layers of sandbags, with a sort of wainscot and floor made of artillery ammo boxes. A makeshift table held a couple of PRC-25 radios hooked up to speaker boxes that were connected to antennas strung on poles outside the bunker. These antennas enabled us to send and receive messages to the company in the field; with standard back-pack antennas, the radio only had a range of three or four klicks. Standing watch usually just meant listening in and being prepared to relay any important messages to battalion headquarters or Alpha Company folks who usually worked out of Lai Khe, such as the cooks and company clerk. I spent my time reading or doodling on the walls, or taming the local rats with offerings of C-ration fruitcake, a canned confection that was the dessert equivalent of Ham (with Water Added) and Lima Beans.

During this sojourn I befriended Greg Murry and José Garcia, who were going through the brigade training as new replacements before going out with the company. José and I spent some time on the Lai Khe bunker line and had a chance to swap life stories. Greg and I bonded over a graffito I'd penned on the wooden wainscot in the commo bunker. As an aspiring soldier I'd read every English translation I could find of the French Indochina War novels of Jean Larteguy, who used Horace's phrase "*Dulce et decorum est pro patria mori*" in all seriousness. Maybe also I was channeling Erich Maria Remarque. But I thought it added a touch of ironic class to the standard GI anti-army graffiti, and Greg had been bemused enough to point it out to me when I was sharing a commo watch with him. I was pleased to take credit for the effort, and doubly pleased to have an appreciative audience.

Rod Floutz was sort of a hipster, and we shared some tall tales regarding marijuana consumption back in the days. I was personally too worried about non-performance issues when faced with deadly peril to indulge in the evil weed while in a combat situation, which I had learned was anywhere, anytime in Vietnam. I guess not all my buddies were as frightened as I was, as a fair number of folks smoked the ubiquitous Vietnamese weed, which was supplied as American cigarettes, with most of the tobacco replaced by a strong local product, and repackaged, complete with cellophane seals, in all the popular brands. Ironically some of my stateside friends had gone to considerable trouble to smuggle me a handful of joints in a care package, which when I received it a month or two into my tour, was totally redundant. But after trying a couple of the local smokes, and realizing that, even in the relative safety of the base camp, and even being nominally off duty, I would have been useless in any sort of emergency, I abandoned those pleasures for the duration.

One of the folks I hung out with was Sergeant Miller, who had light duty for some reason. Miller had been in-country almost a year, and had a good reputation in the Second Platoon as a conscientious soldier. He had come through August 25th with that reputation intact. I was impressed by his stories, which he was happy to share.

"Ah never call him Victor Charlie," he said of the enemy. "He is just plain too good for that kind of disrespectful talk. He is always Mr. Charles to me."

I was impressed by this viewpoint, which showed a level of reflection not common amongst the soldiering class, but my admiration was mitigated by some of Miller's other ideas.

He spent a lot of time during this interval lounging around the company area in a bathing suit, seeking out sunny spots and working on his tan. When I expressed bemusement he explained.

"Gettin' a good, all-over body tan is the best defense against sunstroke or heat prostration," he said. "Also it reduces the body's need for water. Ah can go all day without drinkin' if I have a good body tan."

This didn't make sense at the time, and still doesn't. But after a few days of dogging it the skin on my thigh healed enough to return me to full duty. By then the company had returned from their mission and, bolstered by the replacements, we were back up to a hundred or so troops, about average for an infantry company during my tour, and about half the authorized strength according to the Army TO&E.

All too soon we headed back to the chopper pad after stocking up on Cs and ammo. Second Platoon was mostly new faces, both PFCs and SP4s, and sergeants and an SP5; by virtue of my having survived a month in-country, I was no longer the new kid, if not quite a veteran. Due largely to the many casualties on the 25th, I briefly became a fire-team leader, the first step up the chain of command. A nine- or ten-man squad consisted of two fire teams, plus the squad leader. The TO&E for fire-team leader was Sergeant E-5, and I was still a PFC. I had passed the 30-day mark in the company, however, and received orders allowing me to wear the coveted Combat Infantry Badge, a device with an infantry-blue enameled bar containing a flintlock musket with a silver oak-leaf wreath around it. Black embroidered cloth versions of the CIB were sewn over the left pocket of our jungle fatigue shirts, over the U. S. ARMY patch, when we had a chance to get them to a local Vietnamese tailor shop.

The geography in Vietnam's III Corps, around Saigon, was hugely varied, in ways far beyond anything my North American childhood had offered. Much of the land was cultivated, and I had experienced close encounters with rice paddies both flooded and dry, and with other types of fields and plantations. This terrain was not what I was used to, but it was comprehensible. The jungle was something else: indescribably various in its components, each few meters presented a new challenge. At its most impressive, giant trees reached over a hundred feet unto the air, including the kapok tree with gigantic buttresses which created fantasy spaces begging for exploration. Smaller trees also abounded, and from all of them vines and creepers, sized anywhere from string-like filaments to sinuous, surreal lianas thicker than my thigh, descended and looped around and among the vertical stalks and trunks. Shrubs and bushes grew singly or in thickets; here and there the carcasses of giant trees, in every state of decay, lay across or along our direction of travel. Trails and tracks, ranging from a yard or two across to just wide enough for a single person, unbearably tempting with their sandy pathways, appeared at random, as did small clearings or gaps, whether manmade or natural often impossible to tell. The jungle was a presence, which grudgingly permitted us to pass through, but surely closed behind us. No one doubted that it could swallow us whole. Traces of earlier adventures appeared from time to time. Once we found the bones of a long-dead elephant, and once the rusted remains of a howitzer from some long-forgotten battle. Sometimes thickets of bamboo created impenetrable barriers; a variety of ants, all of them fierce defenders of their territory, built nests in the trees out of living leaves and nests on the ground of dirt and debris. To get through this jungle, we were equipped with a map, a compass, and a machete; it could take 12 hours to go two kilometers. Line-of-sight visibility was often measured in the low single digits of meters.

I was ambivalent about chopper rides at this point. I knew where the good seats were, and was used to the sometimes violent motions of getting up and setting down and the way the sounds of turbine and rotor changed in volume and pitch. My limited experience had taught me that a ride from Lai Khe was likely to end up somewhere I did not want to be. On the other hand, when choppers appeared to extract us from an operation, the reverse occurred, and we were whisked from dirt, danger, and drudgery back to the relative comforts behind the wire. The romance was fading: helicopters were becoming another form of transportation and, while getting there was not half the fun, the destination was more important than the means of arrival. As it happened this chopper ride took me and the rest of Second Platoon, along with Alpha Company and most of the rest of the battalion, a few klicks south and west of Lai Khe. There we landed in a dry, relatively open clearing, free of incoming fire, and formed up along the woodline while several more flights of choppers dropped their troops.

By now I had pretty much mastered the art of packing my gear and my Cs, so that items were unlikely to fall off at odd times, and had learned to use an OD towel as a kind of muffler, to absorb sweat during the march and, wrapped around my gas mask in its canvas case, to serve as a pillow at night. I had learned that any dry or at least well-drained bit of flat ground would serve as a sleeping place, and that a dry T-shirt, carefully kept in my butt pack, would provide warmth and comfort under my fatigue shirt at night. Dog tags worn on a chain around the neck collected dirt and abraded skin, but the chain could be looped through the top buttonhole on the fatigue jacket and the tags stowed in the left breast pocket, always with a P-38 can opener threaded on the chain in case of emergencies. I knew that underwear was otherwise an invitation to crotch rot and other forms of discomfort, that no water was too stinky or opaque to drink after treatment with a couple of iodine tablets, that fatigue pants stayed up without need for an uncomfortable GI belt, and that I really wanted to have some jungle boots, but wasn't getting any this week. I could spend the day humping my gear without gasping for breath, my mosquito bites no longer became swollen and festered, and menthol-flavored cigarettes reduced the symptoms of thirst.

That night we set up in thick jungle, with closely spaced positions: if the perimeter for which we had responsibility was small enough, we could have three men per hole, rather than two. Not only did this dramatically reduce the time and effort to dig the hole, it permitted as much as five and a half or six hours of sleep, instead of four or less. I could function on five or six hours, but was seriously sleep deprived after a couple of nights of four hours or less, so this was a treat. We put out trip flares and Claymores, rigged a hooch with a poncho behind the hole, and passed an uneventful night. At dawn, we took in our flares and Claymores, filled in the hole, and I at least buried my shit and made sure no dangerous C-ration cans were available for the enemy's use.

The day was spent patrolling in thick, humid jungle. Several times we stumbled across bunkers and huts, some of them pretty good sized. The bunkers typically were neatly constructed, with closely spaced bamboo poles supporting several feet of earth, some with carefully sited firing ports and others which seemed more like dormitories or shelters than fighting positions. Some were actually dug under and around the roots of large trees. Above ground we encountered well-made bamboo pavilions, some partially excavated, which still contained furniture, also artfully constructed of bamboo. While what we found was in good repair, there was little evidence of recent use, and at first nothing much worth destroying, although some eager officers experimented with using demolition charges to disrupt a few bunkers, and we tried to burn the few banana-leaf roofs we found. The jungle was damp if not wet, though, and nothing much would burn. I think we were doing platoon-sized, clover-leaf patrols at that point, though a troop in the line, like me, was rarely apprised of the details of the mission. I followed the guy in front; when he stopped, I stopped, and when he walked, I walked, trying to keep the right interval. Constant artillery fire was being directed to map coordinates ahead of our point and to the flanks, so the whiz of shells going overhead and the crump of rounds landing in the trees was always with us. From time to time a round would land too close and a whickering shrapnel fragment would cut through the vegetation over our heads. At some point I heard some small-arms rounds, but nothing that I could identify as incoming.

By late afternoon, exhausted by the heat and the slogging/standing/slogging non-rhythm of jungle travel, we were digging holes again. That night I learned that Sergeant Landers, from another platoon, had been shot and killed by a sniper. I didn't know Landers except by sight, but he was one of the old-timers, a tough, wiry, career noncom who seemed old enough to be my father. He hadn't been in Alpha more than a couple of weeks when he was killed.

Billie Dwaine Landers, Everett, Washington, age 40. Alpha Company, 1/16 Infantry. DIED on 17 September 1966 in Vietnam as the result of gunshot wound to chest.

Next morning we did more patrolling as we marched and, while we found no Viet Cong we did discover a lot of rice. Hundreds of cloth bags, many of them imprinted with USAID logos and cheerful slogans in English and Vietnamese, were cached in raised-platform and leaf-thatched hooches, well hidden from above by the thick jungle canopy. Early in the day some of us were detailed to carry bags of rice to a clearing, where they were dumped on cargo nets and eventually flown out by Chinooks. I was lucky enough to be pulling security for these folks and didn't actually have to hump much of the rice, though I did carry a bag or two. Everyone in Alpha wished we had slings for our rifles at that point, but Captain Howley cheerfully pointed out that with some assistance we could balance a rice bag on our left shoulder and still have our right hand free to carry the rifle and engage any hapless gook who tried to take the rice back.

Near the end of the day Second Platoon discovered a rice cache in deep jungle, and for a bit I was sure that I was going to be carrying rice through the jungle at night. At the beginning of the project a large, terrified, gray rat dashed from underneath the hooch and darted between the GIs who were standing glumly around estimating how many trips to the LZ would be needed to move the rice. I was fearful for the safety of the little guy, but I needn't have worried. Not even the nastiest of my buddies was going to spare the energy needed to stomp on a rat. It ran within inches of Switek, who was leaning back with his pack against a tree.

"See that rat?" I asked him.

His gaze met mine. "Fucka buncha rats," he said.

It was a measure of our collective exhaustion that even Switek couldn't get it up to kick at the rat in passing. Fortunately by then the last Chinook had departed and we were told to destroy the rice in place. We hacked the rice bags open with machetes and entrenching tools, then threw a couple of white phosphorus grenades on top of the pile. This process demonstrated that rice does not burn, at least not in a damp jungle climate; the WP burned brilliantly, created satisfying clouds of thick, white, smoke, but only scorched the top of the rice. Finally Lieutenant Harden convinced somebody higher up that we could render the rice inedible with CS gas, so we trudged back towards Alpha Company's line of march with the acrid smell of tear gas following us through the jungle. A few of us put on our gas masks, and I did for a minute, but decided I preferred the irritation to the heat and discomfort of the mask, especially since my goggles immediately fogged up and essentially prevented me from seeing where I was going without lifting the mask up every couple of steps.

Once again, back at the perimeter, I learned an Alpha guy from First Platoon, an SP4 named Nichols, had been killed by a sniper. The event, and whatever our response to it had been, had been subsumed in the general background noise of artillery and airstrikes and random small-arms fire, and had simply not registered. Fucka buncha snipers.

Sometime in the middle of the night a loud explosion to the left of my foxhole was followed by cries of "Medic." A few tracer rounds arced into the jungle, as three of us crowded into the hole, which suddenly seemed inadequate protection, and tried to make sense out of the blackness of the jungle a few feet to our front. Artillery began to fire, and a few parachute flares drifted down over our positions, creating brilliant light and swiftly pivoting shadows as the flares descended while drifting in the wind, leaving the jungle even darker and more impenetrable. I don't recall hearing a dustoff. In the morning, rumor was somebody had put in a Claymore pointing the wrong way, or Charlie had snuck in and turned it around. A kid named Duffett from Third Platoon had been killed.

Next day we did some more sweeps, and I had my first chance to walk point for the company as well as the platoon. By now we had plenty of sergeants, so my days as fire-team leader were over and I was back to being just a rifleman. To my delight company point was easier than walking point flank, mainly because I could choose when and how to go around the impenetrable bits. About midday we emerged at a clearing and waited until choppers came to take us back to Lai Khe. I had seen no enemy and had not fired my weapon, but had survived three days in the field with the new guys in the Second Platoon, and with our new officers and noncoms. I actually enjoyed the chopper ride back, sitting with my feet on the skids and looking forward to a night inside the wire.

McArthur Nichols, Durham, North Carolina, age 24. Alpha Co., 1/16 Infantry. DIED on 18 September 1966 in Vietnam as the result of a gunshot wound to the head received in hostile ground action; James Henry Duffett, Jr., Baltimore, Maryland, age 21. Alpha Co., 1/16 Infantry. DIED on 18 September 1966 in Vietnam as the result of metal fragment wounds to the body received when unknown explosive device detonated.

CHAPTER 10

Dead Man's Boots

Shortly after that operation, in late September of 1966, we moved from our tents into our new barracks, humping our iron cots and tin lockers up through the rubber trees. Each barrack had room for about 20 standard stateside-issue steel bunks, in two long rows; I had bought a tin locker and a mattress from the Vietnamese, rather than use a GI air mattress, most of which didn't hold air overnight in any event. During previous sojourns in base camp I and other Second Platoon guys had spent some time leveling the laterite floor of the barracks. While we had been out on the last operation, other folk had installed a floor of wood planks made from artillery shell cases. Second Platoon's new home was dry, clean, and luxurious; the corrugated-tin roof was impervious to water, and the screened sides let in the maximum amount of air and kept out many of the flying insects. And the wood floor made it easy to spot centipedes and cockroaches. We killed one centipede at least eight inches long and an inch wide; after chopping it in half with a machete each piece took off in different directions. The walls rapidly became the territory of large, brightly colored gecko lizards, universally known amongst GIs as "fuckyou" lizards because of their loud eponymous cries. Tolerated because of their eating habits, a gecko could devour a giant cockroach almost as big as it was in a couple of crunchy bites. On one of the jungle hikes I'd seen a pitcher plant that had a six-inch pod, clearly hoping for giant insects; the golden orb spiders spun webs six meters across between the rubber trees. The country began to unfold to me, strange and beautiful in the main. That notwithstanding, my slick-soled stateside combat boots continued to remind me that I wasn't a real jungle soldier yet. I checked with the supply sergeant every time we were in Lai Khe, but unless I wanted a size 13 wide I was SOL. The worst of it was the knowledge that if I expressed my unhappiness even slightly, my chances of getting jungle boots, if and when they arrived, were even more remote.

We also heard a rumor about this time that Captain Howley might be leaving us, but no one had any idea why that might be. Despite the early grumbling and complaining over the new regime, after a month we (or at least some of us) were calling ourselves Howley's Howling Commandos and maybe moving with a bit more *élan* than we had before.

On October 2 Second Platoon did another day patrol north and west of Lai Khe, going over much of the same ground (though not using the same routes) as we had in August and September. This close to Lai Khe the terrain was more open, again showing signs of recent cultivation, although whoever had farmed this country and hadn't been killed had been relocated for at least a year by now. We passed by the strange ruined tower of irregular hexagonal stones in a spiral ashlar, and eventually came to a narrow, swift-flowing stream which required a safety rope to cross. Although it was no more than five or six meters across, it was over our heads, and filled to the brim with the monsoon rains. While crossing, I was able to float horizontally in the current, despite my gear. The water was cool and refreshing, but 20 minutes of walking later I was dry again except for sweat. The patrol itself was uneventful until near the end, when I heard an explosion ahead. There was a moment of silence after the blast and then the screams started. SP5 Mallonee, walking flank, had tripped a booby trap. After a bit he was carried past me to a clearing for dustoff. He was hit in the legs and looked pale and worried, but he was conscious and I figured he'd be fine. The chopper came in and took him away with no problems.

Next day we had a company formation and Captain Howley told us we were going on a real mission, starting the next day, north up Highway 13 to the vicinity of Bau Bang, where the battalion had seen action in the past. He also told us that Mallonee had died of his wounds. This was kind of a shock, as I figured that if you were awake when they put you on the chopper you were going to be OK. Mallonee, perhaps understandably, had a bad attitude about being stuck in an infantry company and was not somebody I felt was reliable in the same way as Murry or Garcia, but his death provided me an unexpected benefit: sometime after the formation, I was walking into my barracks when the platoon sergeant, who was going through Mallonee's foot locker, noticed me.

"Hey, Clark, what size boot you wear?" he asked.

I could only stare at the jungle boots he was holding. "That size," I said. Damn, they weren't new, but they still had some miles on them and they were already broken in.

So next day we had a chance to show our stuff on this road-clearing operation near Bau Bang, a village seven or eight klicks north of Lai Khe on Highway 13. We had a short chopper ride out of Lai Khe into a cold LZ. By now I had learned the basic rhythm of being in the field on an operation. We got dropped somewhere, we walked around, with more or less difficulty depending on the terrain, we stopped walking, we dug foxholes where the lieutenant said to dig them, it got dark, maybe we went out on an ambush patrol, or maybe we just took turns sleeping and watching from our foxhole, it got light, we filled in our foxhole, and we walked around some more. Sometimes shit happened, but usually it didn't. Eventually we got picked up. And so it went. But having the right shoes did make things better. Man, I loved my new boots. I had feared I was innately clumsy, or worse, after two months of slipping and sliding while the old-timers effortlessly climbed steep banks and danced along narrow berms, but at least some of that problem turned out to be solved by wearing the massively treaded rubber jungle boots instead of the slick leather-soled GI combat version. I found I could not only keep up with the veterans, but offer a hand to the new guys who were still wearing their stateside boots. And another guy joined the little group making its home in my head.

Kenneth A. Mallonee, Ottumwa, Iowa, age 24. Alpha Co., 1/16 Infantry. DIED on 3 October 1966 in Vietnam as the result of multiple metal fragment wounds to both legs when hit by fragments from a hostile booby trap.

CHAPTER 11

Settling in

After an uneventful day trudging along the treeline bordering the highway, we dug in on a gentle slope facing relatively open country. That evening my squad was selected for an ambush patrol, reinforced by Greg Murry's newly constituted M-60 team, which in addition to Greg included Roland, formerly Emerson's ammo bearer, and now assistant gunner, and a new guy called Mac. For some reason Mac wasn't around, so Murry and Roland provided our fire support. The squad leader, Sergeant Butler, called us together and gave us a briefing on the patrol, showing us on the map where we were to end up, maybe a klick northeast of our rest-over-night position. This was a long haul for a squad-sized ambush, but the country was so open that it was feasible.

After full dark, we headed out of the perimeter in single file. I was on point, following the whispered directions from Sergeant Butler, a few steps behind. There was some muttering by a few of the more experienced troops, and after going about 400 meters down a grassy slope and up a little hill, Butler hissed at me to stop. He was visibly, and audibly, nervous; this turned out to be his first ambush patrol, and he had only been a couple weeks in-country.

"How much further?" he whispered.

Although I knew we were only about half way to our designated area, I had no great desire to keep stumbling around in the dark. But we were out of sight of the perimeter, and the terrain was dry and open, with a few clumps of low brush, and pretty good visibility to our front.

"We could just set up here," I whispered back, expedience (and sleep deprivation) trumping character.

We quickly distributed ourselves in two-man positions. I and a buddy were on the far left flank; I set a Claymore to my front and was just hunkering down when I heard loud whispers coming from my left: "They're out here, I can hear them moving," followed by some inaudible murmurs, then "They're coming!" I couldn't hear or see anything suggestive of enemy presence, and was pretty confident that somebody was having a case of nerves when—*whump!*—a flash and a loud explosion to my right front was followed by the whistle and patter of post-explosion debris. I glimpsed a GI running hell-for-leather back towards the perimeter, followed by several other shadowy but definitely GI figures headed quickly in the same direction. I saw one of them throw something over his shoulder as he ran, followed a few seconds later by another flash, explosion, and the whistle of shrapnel and dirt. That one sounded like a grenade.

"What do we do?" my buddy, one of the new guys, whispered.

"Oh, shit," was my response. Clearly we couldn't stay where we were, but I didn't think there were any VC around. There was no incoming fire or anything else beyond the normal night sounds, once the debris had settled. "You might as well go," I said. "Don't run into the perimeter or they'll fire you up."

He quickly departed. I stayed put for a few seconds and tried to pierce the gloom, but nothing was moving, and there was nothing to shoot at. Training dictated that, when leaving a position, one either recovered or blew one's Claymore. No way, I thought, am I going to go stumbling around in the darkness recovering that Claymore with who knows what trigger-happy GIs around, so I blew the sucker and, after waiting for the dust to settle, prepared to follow the departing guys. I could see some distant figures disappearing into the gloom, and heard some voices near the perimeter, but the count of departing GIs seemed light to me. I thought there might still be some guys around.

I moved quickly down the line to my right, and didn't see anybody at first, but then heard a whispered "Help me, anybody." A couple yards ahead of me, lying prone in the grass, was Greg Murry behind his M-60, and another GI next to him. "He's hit," Greg whispered. "I can't leave him."

"I'll get help," I replied, and started off towards the perimeter. When I got within shouting distance of the positions I hollered, "We got somebody down, we need a stretcher!"

"How about the VC?" someone shouted back.

"There are no fucking VC!" I yelled. Pretty soon after that several guys with a stretcher came out and I led them back to Murry and the wounded GI. Before long we were safe in the perimeter, and then the night started to get interesting.

First, a night dustoff was called in, and a bunch of guys made a perimeter outside the foxholes for the chopper, and the wounded guy was on his way. Second, Captain Howley quickly discovered we hadn't been where we were supposed to be. I did mention to the captain that Murry had stayed behind to cover our "retreat" and protect the wounded guy. Murry had lost his contact lenses and had no GI glasses yet, and as a new guy probably thought the darkness was teeming with VC, so his conduct showed me true courage. Howley may have been amused at some aspects of the situation, as he looked at me, shook his head, laughed, and said, "No fucking VC, huh?" Yet his basic response to us was remedial: get your collective asses back out to where you were supposed to be, right now. And so we went. Butler must have had a piece chewed off in private, as he was really pissed at me, which is understandable. He also appeared to be still nervous about the possibility of ground combat, which made for an unpleasant night. I had point again, and he kept snarling at me to go faster, in a muted sort of way. We finally reached what looked like our originally designated location, a streambed among grass and low brush. We set up along the banks and spent a restless remainder of the night. As usual, half of us slept while the other half remained alert. Butler snored, and at one point I awakened him and suggested he change sleeping positions, as I couldn't listen for creepy-crawlies over his exhalations. This was not meant as harassment, but he took it badly and kept waking me up during his awake time. All in all, it wasn't one of my better ambush patrols.

We kept getting missions with no apparent purpose, but I was aware that I was getting better at soldiering and learning more about myself at the same time. Around midday on a platoon patrol we were approaching a village, coming over the crest of a low hill in relatively open country, with low brush, banana groves, bamboo thickets, and cultivated fields. I was near the point when I heard the crump of a small explosion behind me. The platoon leader, Lieutenant Harden, and Sergeant Reeves, a wiry, red-headed, career noncom, had been hit by booby-trap shrapnel. Down below, in the village, small figures were scurrying about. A couple of them jumped into a jeep-like vehicle and took off, away from us. I had them in my sights with the safety off, and shouted, "Do I fire 'em up? Do I fire 'em up?" I really wanted to pull that trigger, but Harden came quickly up the column, with his face bloody and a fist-sized chunk of his left calf missing and dripping blood. He took in the scene, and said, "Put down that weapon." Reeves had also caught a bunch of shrapnel in his face, and ended up losing an eye.

We set up around a nearby clearing, and Reeves and Harden were dusted off. Harden I never saw again, but Reeves showed up back in Lai Khe a few weeks later, on his way home. He had an eye patch but otherwise looked pretty good considering. Second Platoon eventually got a new lieutenant, Fred Denton. For now, though, Floyd, the platoon sergeant, took over the patrol, and we continued down towards the village. Along the way we saw a couple of middle-aged men working in the fields, and Floyd had us round them up.

"Make them walk the fucking point," he said.

I felt a fierce pleasure in putting one of the men in front of me, my rifle in his back, and following his footsteps into the ville. As it happened, we reached the village without incident, and released our hostages. Nothing of interest was discovered, and eventually we looped around back to our perimeter. But as the adrenalin rush faded, I realized that a single syllable from Lieutenant Harden, or actually anybody in authority, would have had me putting 20 rounds into the people below. I figured out that what Harden showed me was what the army instructors called moral courage, and his action, among other things, probably saved me and the rest of the platoon from doing some bad things.

During another patrol, company-sized this time, I was walking extreme left flank through rolling, grassy hills interspersed with regular treelines and thickets, when, coming out of one such thicket, I saw a single older guy in black pajamas with a hoe in the middle of a field. Because the country was open, we were spread out with 50 or so meters between flankers, so I was pretty much alone. The guy saw me, dropped his hoe, and took off running down the hill away from me. I had the rifle on my shoulder, safety off, and was leading the guy while I shouted, "Do I shoot him? Do I shoot him?" Once again the adrenalin was pumping, and if somebody had said "Shoot him!" while he was still visible I think I would have pulled the trigger. By the time somebody came around close enough to see the guy, he had disappeared into a treeline. Yet I had processed the fact that he was old and unarmed, and maybe I wouldn't have shot him. As it happened, we followed him into a village, which yielded a bunker with couple of old rifles: an American M-1 Garand, the stock of which was half eaten away by rot or termites, and an ancient Japanese bolt-action Arisaka rifle. How long these implements had been hidden away was anybody's guess, but they didn't suggest an active Viet Cong presence. Nonetheless, as the village was being searched I was put on perimeter guard, near a small animist shrine which was constructed around carefully tended topiary birds and animals, with dozens of small ceramic dishes and cups on miniature bamboo structures. None of the command structure was around, just another rifleman from the Second Platoon. I was seething with frustration. I had really wanted to shoot that old guy, although I didn't really have any idea if he was an enemy or not. So I took my machete and tried to decapitate some of the topiary, but the plants were surprisingly tough, and mostly my blade just bounced off. I smashed a bunch of the ceramicware. All in all, I felt ashamed after doing it, and even while I was doing it, but I probably spent ten minutes trashing that beautiful, peaceful, place. Later I thought about those ten minutes, and the earlier incident with Lieutenant Harden and the village, and tried to make some sense of it all, which I wasn't quite able to do. But I figured out I was OK with not shooting the villagers, and not shooting the old guy, but not so much with chopping up the topiary.

Road security missions could be easy, when we weren't aggressively patrolling in the jungle. We followed an armored unit with a Rome plow, which dug a furrow in the shoulder, hopefully severing any wires leading from command-detonated explosives buried under the laterite to a concealed position in the distant treeline. Flanking units in the treeline meanwhile worked their way along our line of march, and small observation posts, basically just a couple of guys, were placed here and there along the route to intercept any attempts by the VC to approach. On one such mission, another kid and I were placed as an OP around 100 meters from the road. No other GIs were within sight. The terrain was flat, and the vegetation was partly open, but with enough thickets of random brush so that there were no clear sight lines of more than a few meters. My foxhole buddy, I'll call him Wohlford, was a young, white-blond city kid who had come in sometime after August 25. We lucked out right away, finding a meter-deep depression at about the right spot, open on the road side, and with fairly thick brushy cover in the area facing away, where any VC would be coming. Best of all, the brush around it provided deep shade over the declivity itself. As the slightly senior guy, I convinced Wohlford that we should clear firing lines through the brush on our respective sides of the hollow, clipping enough of the five or six feet of vegetation so we could observe our sectors but would not be visible from outside. We did this, though his firing line, to my left, was more like a tunnel, but it still was a good position. We settled down in our snug little hole, and I started a letter to Sheilah Rae Bernstein, a high-school classmate for whom I carried a serious but unrequited case of longing. As I composed, sitting on the right-hand side of the hole, I checked my brush tunnel every few seconds. Well into page two of this letter, *bang!* Wohlford fired a single rifle round, causing me to basically do a back somersault into the hole, scattering paper, pen, and assorted C-ration goodies. Crouched behind my rifle, safety off, I saw nothing through my tunnel.

"Whaddid you shoot at?" I whispered to Wohlford.

"I saw a gook, right there," he stammered.

"Didya get him?"

"Dunno. I think so, he just disappeared."

I peered through Wohlford's tunnel, but saw nothing. No unusual sounds or movements in the brush were apparent. "Did you get off a good shot? Did you get off an aimed shot?" I hissed.

Wohlford shook his head. "I just looked up an' saw him, and shot," he said, his voice shaky.

I doubted he had hit anyone, but somebody was out there. Whoever it was knew where we were, and had either hauled ass back the way they came, or was slinking through the brush looking for a way to drop a grenade on us. We had no way to contact anybody, so for now we were on our own.

"OK, recon by fire," I said. "Put a few rounds out." I shifted back to my tunnel, switched to full auto, and put a couple of three- or four-round bursts into likely thickets. Then my rifle jammed. "Holy shit," I said as I turned to Wohlford.

He was staring at his M-16. "It's stuck," he said.

I started pounding on the charging handle of my rifle, but of course that accomplished nothing. Once a round was stuck in the chamber, the only way to clear it was by inserting a cleaning rod down the muzzle. But there was still a shortage of cleaning rods, and at this point only squad leaders had them. Probably the same folks in the rear who had all the new jungle boots had plenty of cleaning rods as well, but that didn't solve our problem: here we were with maybe a bloodthirsty VC sneaking up on us, and we were without a functioning firearm between us.

"I'm going to throw a grenade," I whispered. I unsnapped a fragmentation grenade, pulled the pin, and threw it over the brush to our front, figuring that was where any low-crawling gook would likely be approaching. We both hunkered down in the hole, and waited … and waited. Nothing. I looked down and confirmed that the pin ring was still around my finger. The grenade was a dud. By now I was probably not thinking too clearly. I unsnapped another grenade, pulled the pin, and threw it. This one wasn't a dud, and produced a satisfying explosion and cloud of debris to our front. I had another grenade in my hand, and still had one left on my belt; these were my only weapons, and I didn't want to waste them. We listened a while.

"You throw one," I said to Wohlford, who threw one of his grenades, which detonated.

After that, silence. We were crouched in the hole, gripping our grenades, when the platoon sergeant called to us from the direction of the road.

"We shot a gook," Wohlford said.

The sergeant darted across the open space behind us and slid into the hole. A couple of other GIs followed him and, after we explained our predicament, they cautiously explored the front area in front of our position. They found nothing: no body, and no evidence of injury, although they did find a well-worn path leading back towards the treeline at the point that Wohlford had seen the VC. While producing a cleaning rod, the sergeant gave us a snarly lecture on not firing aimlessly and wasting grenades with no visible target, and causing unnecessary inconvenience amongst the folks back at the road. I didn't argue, but I was pretty sure Wohlford had seen a gook, as he was spacy but not that spacy, and that my recon by fire wasn't a bad tactic given that our position was already compromised by his first wild shot. I wished I had seen the VC and imagined that, if I had, I would have dropped him with a careful aimed burst, but wishes aren't horses. The grumbling sergeant and the troops left and I, at least, had a new appreciation for the M-16 rifle: the only round you can count on is the one in the chamber. From then on I was much slower on the trigger. At least I was able to finish my letter to Sheilah with a good war story.

Soon after that incident Lieutenant Denton's RTO went on R&R. Since the primary function of an RTO was to speak and understand English, my somewhat undeserved reputation as one of the platoon intellectuals came to the attention of Sergeant Floyd, who designated me as the interim RTO for the lieutenant. While I had trained on the Army/Navy, Portable, Radio, Communication 25 (AN/PRC-25, or Prick-25) and occasionally used the sets in their sessile configuration back in the commo bunker in Lai Khe, or intermittently during OPs or ambush patrols, I had never carried one on a regular basis. The device weighed about 23 pounds with battery installed, plus of course antenna, hand-set, back-pack, and spare battery, bringing the total package up to around 30 pounds. Although the TO&E called for an RTO to carry a .45-caliber automatic pistol (with a couple of extra magazines) as a weapon, Captain Howley meanly (and correctly) required RTOs to carry an M-16 and a basic load of 5.56 ammo. While I could forego the four fragmentation grenades typically carried by riflemen, and the trip flares, Claymore mines, and other odd weaponry, RTOs were expected to carry copious amounts of smoke grenades for the use of whatever nearby officer was inclined to throw smoke. And of course the need for all the items of personal consumption and comfort remained the same. The net gain in weight to carry was probably in the order of ten to 15 pounds. And, while the RTO never would walk point or flank, his antenna made him a visible target for any VC capable of taking aimed shots at the column. But nobody asked me what my preferences were, so for about a week I humped the radio. Each platoon had one or two radios, depending on platoon strength at the moment, all of which were on the company frequency, or net. Captain Howley had two RTOs, one who carried a radio on the company net and the other with a radio tuned to the battalion net. So as a platoon RTO, my call sign Alpha Mike Kilo, I got to listen to all the company chatter and consequently had inside knowledge that was not normally vouchsafed to the mere riflemen. Though nominally I had to help dig the foxhole for the lieutenant (which I would share if we were attacked), often I had to follow him on some errand or other during foxhole-digging time, which was good. Sometimes there were three of us pulling watch, as the platoon medic and the platoon sergeant's RTO would share that duty, as neither the lieutenant nor the platoon sergeant pulled regular watches. This meant a chance for more sleep, also good. So while on balance I was happy to relinquish the radio when the regular RTO returned, I had been exposed to the calculus of costs and benefits involved.

Back at Lai Khe, we were chivvied into formation one morning, in full field equipment, and marched to a corner of the base camp where I had never been before. There we were halted beneath an enormous jungle tree, from which depended a ladder-like contraption consisting of ridged metal rungs about the diameter of a broomstick attached to steel chains. A couple of strange sergeants were standing around, never a good sign. I couldn't tell exactly how high the thing went, but it was more than seven or eight meters, maybe more than ten. Maybe way more than ten. As the guys looked apprehensively at this device, one of the strange sergeants explained that we were going to be trained in techniques of extraction via hovering Chinook helicopter. If the jungle was too dense to permit a chopper to land, he explained, the Chinook would dangle a ladder such as the one we were observing down into the jungle, so that we could scamper up to our ride. We were going to climb this ladder for practice, so when the real thing occurred we would be ready. Each of us was to climb the ladder, in full combat gear, touch the barely visible limb from which the ladder dangled, and then, and only then, return to the ground. We were permitted, as a special dispensation, to attach our slings to our weapons, and use them for the climb. This would have been bad enough, in ordinary circumstances, but as chance would have it I was still the acting RTO for Lieutenant Denton, so I was carrying more weight than usual. Well, OK, I guess I can do this, I thought. Many of the guys went up pretty easily, tapped the limb, and were down in minute or two. Others were obviously struggling, and needed repeated threats from the sergeants to complete the climb. My turn came soon enough, and I quickly regretted that I had not paid more attention to the details of the ascent. I came to understand Newton's Third Law, as it applied to chain ladders: when you push with your leg to go up a rung, rather than pushing you up, as on a rigid ladder, your leg pushes the rung out and away from the perpendicular, leaving you, and your 60 or so pounds of equipment, essentially hanging from the upper rungs by your hands. After a bit of trial and error I figured out how to keep the rungs more or less under my feet, but most of the work was still being done by my arms, and it was painful and scary. Had there been an honorable way to stop short of the top I would have taken it, but unable to think of one I continued to the point where I could graze the top with a finger, and gratefully begin a fortunately uneventful descent. Back on the ground, sitting with my buddies, I could contemplate the struggles of my comrades with some compassion, but was basically grateful that the ordeal was over. That was before I detected the sound of Chinook helicopters in the distance.

So we were marched to a clearing not that far from the tree ladder, where, in the midst of a storm of dust and debris, a Chinook hovered a dozen meters or so in the air, with chain ladders dangling from both its front and rear cargo doors. Although the roar of the engines and the chop of the rotors made speech impossible, the sergeants didn't need to spell it out: we were to climb up the up ladder, enter the body of the beast, and climb down the down ladder. I was one of the first to attempt the climb, all the while whingeing inside over the unfairness of having to do this with the damn radio when I wasn't even a real RTO. Quickly I realized that the exercise on the tree ladder was at best a poor approximation of the difficulty posed by the real thing. While to a disinterested observer the Chinook appeared to be stationary in mid-air, in reality it was moving constantly in every dimension to keep itself, on average, in the same place. Each movement, of only a meter or two, perhaps, created a new challenge to the dangling GI. The worst of all occurred when I was a third of the way up and the damn Chinook dropped about four meters, leaving me back on the ground, mocking the considerable effort I had made to that point. Gripping the ridged rungs like death, I somehow made it to the open cargo bay where an aircrewman gave me a hand as I stepped onto the blissfully horizontal floor. He did a double take and looked at my hands, which were bloody. Apparently the corrugated rungs, and the intensity of grip, fueled by my desire not to plummet to my death, had caused the calluses on my hands to tear off, and rivulets of blood were running down my palms. Speech, of course, was impossible, but he motioned me to the side of the aircraft, and I happily obeyed, sitting against the side of the hull while my buddies, one by one, emerged in one cargo bay door, traversed the shuddering aircraft, and disappeared down the other, giving me curious looks on the way. Last up from Second Platoon was Lieutenant Denton, who noticed me and came over. I held up my hands by way of explanation, and he gave them a look, then shook his head and motioned me towards the down ladder. I suppose I could have refused, but actually I was starting to feel ashamed of not finishing the climb, plus my arms had had a chance to recover. I nodded, wiped my hands on my pants, and did the down ladder without much trouble. Down is actually much easier than up, when it comes to chain ladders. Later, on the ground, when we had moved away from under the Chinook and speech was possible, Denton came to me and explained that he thought it was best for me to complete the exercise, for the benefit of my own confidence. I was impressed that he had taken the time to give me an explanation, which he didn't have to do. I had realized up in the Chinook that he had made the right call, and I was proud of having finished the exercise, bloody hands and all. But I fervently hoped I would never have to climb a goddam chain ladder again.

Most of the ground we walked over was flat, at least from a map-maker's perspective. For us on the ground, of course, otherwise insignificant ridges and hollows could assume monumental proportions when we were trying to get over them in a hard rain carrying 70 pounds of stuff. But as we moved from October to November we had a brief experience walking over some of the handful of steep hillsides that dotted the countryside. The largest of these was Nui Ba Den in Tay Ninh Province, the Black Virgin Mountain, an extinct volcano rising about 1,000 meters over the surrounding plains. The much smaller hill we climbed was probably volcanic as well, as it was strewn with boulders and steep enough so that some of the time at least I was using my hands as well as my feet. The heat was intense, but it wasn't raining, and we reached the summit around midday, where the column halted for a brief rest before starting the descent. I was sitting comfortably in a pile of rocks and had just opened a prized can of C-ration sandwich cookies, like vanilla Oreos, when Sergeant Floyd came clambering down the line of seated troops towards the front of the column. Those cookies had been hoarded for just such as moment and I had intended to savor every bite. As Floyd passed me he stopped and grabbed the can of cookies out of my hand and grinned at me in a nasty way. I at least was starved for simple carbohydrates, as most elements of the C-ration diet, designed for the winters of North Korea and northern Eurasia, were concentrated fat and protein. While I did not actually decide to shoot Sergeant Floyd right then, I was tempted, and I would have been delighted if someone else had. He may have read some of this in my expression, as he stopped grinning and moved on smartly down the line with my cookies. I would have shared those cookies without a thought with any of my buddies, and would have shared them with Floyd if he had asked, but stealing cookies from an armed 20-year-old was not on balance a wise thing to do. I thought at the time that Floyd's luck would not last forever if he kept this up.

Sometime during the next day we were pulling security on a section of roadway when a Huey came in for a landing in a small clearing just outside the area where I was standing. The passengers included Captain Howley and another officer I didn't recognize. I was only mildly curious until it hit me: this chopper, with the Old Man in it, was about to land in an *unsecured area*. Without conscious thought I yelled to a couple of guys nearby, "Spread out into that woodline," and hustled over the clearing in front of the chopper and took up a position inside the brush on the far side, thus technically at least moving the perimeter out to include the chopper. I didn't think anything of this at the time, but later learned that Captain Howley had recognized me and, because of that, along with other misdeeds, put me in for SP4, the next step up from PFC.

CHAPTER 12

Sneaky Petes

Next day the company was due to walk out of the perimeter on a day patrol; we got one meal of Cs each and set out lightly burdened and enjoying only moderate heat and plenty of sunshine. The terrain was more open than not, with a lot of clearings and only moderately dense jungle, so we moved right along at first. Second Platoon was somewhere back in the column, so I just dawdled along, thinking about the usual stuff 20-year-old guys think about. Around noon we started running into some old bunkers and, as we entered higher and thicker jungle, crossing some well-travelled trails. We were eventually placed in a big circle, and Second Platoon went out on a clover-leaf patrol, so called because the platoon would walk out for a few hundred meters, then send out squad-sized patrols in three directions, each looping around and returning to the platoon. I had point for a while, and found an old VC sandal made out of a section of automobile tire and rubber straps, and a few more well-travelled trails through the jungle. This information was combined with similar observations by the other squads, and was duly reported to the lieutenant, who relayed our findings in turn back to the Old Man. The platoon then returned to the company area by completing another loop; we never retraced our steps, as lurking VC might have booby-trapped our trail.

At some point I had eaten my C-ration lunch, and was looking forward to dinner back at the battalion perimeter, but that was not to be. After we arrived at the company perimeter, the lieutenant and the platoon sergeant with their RTOs were called over to the company command post. They returned with news: due to the prevalence of well-travelled trails through the jungle, Captain Howley thought there were good odds a bunch of VC would be moving through the area tonight. We were going to set up a massive company-sized ambush along the most likely of these trails. And in order to make sure the gooks didn't figure out we were there and go around us, we wouldn't dig in, but just sort of hunker down in the bushes. No foxholes to dig! That was the good news. The bad news was that a few empty Hueys were going to land in the clearing. Some GIs would be lying down on the floor of these Hueys when they landed. When the Hueys took off, the GIs would sit upright so that it would appear to any watching VC that we had been extracted. Since any offloading of C-ration cases would have been inconsistent with the total extraction of the company, we would have to tighten our belts and do without dinner tonight. This was seriously depressing news, indeed. So a hundred or so hungry men with an average age of about 19, who had been doing pretty vigorous exercise all day, were arranged by the officers and noncoms in as sneaky a manner as possible along the targeted trail. Just before darkness fell, the phony extraction took place and, despite our fervent wishes, no C-Rations were delivered. Small knots of grumpy GIs pooled their resources. Greg Murry, I recall, had a C-ration can of Ham, Sliced, With Water Added, and I got one of the four slices. It was indescribably delicious. I had some jungle chocolate bars, and various other folks chipped in, so we didn't exactly starve, but morale could have been higher. Whether from incipient starvation or just bad attitude, some numbnuts in another platoon had, against a direct order, not only put out a trip flare, but had accidently set it off just at dusk, which may have compromised the whole plan, or maybe Charlie just wasn't travelling that night. Probably that was to his great good fortune, as we were all pissed over our lost supper and would have taken our ire out on any legitimate targets, but none appeared. An offshoot of this experience is that never again did I have less than one more meal than I expected to need stowed away amongst my gear, a habit I suspect that most of the guys who lived through that dreadful night adopted as well.

Next up was a bigger operation which for us began with a chopper ride to a cold LZ north of Lai Khe near the Cambodian border. We spent the next few days walking through dense jungle some of which had been defoliated with what we now know as Agent Orange. From a grunt's perspective the defoliation didn't accomplish much, as most of the leaves stayed on their respective branches, albeit turned dead and brown. Sightlines weren't much improved, and the leaves that did fall made a crunchy carpet which prevented any sort of stealthy movement. The feral ants which plagued our lives in the field certainly seemed angrier and more numerous in defoliated areas. The diminished shade made the sun seem even fiercer.

We had a new member of Second Platoon, an E-5 sergeant I'll call Fellowes. He was short and quite fat, which made him unique among Alpha Company. Rumor had him previously in an artillery unit in Germany, where he had a reputation as a fuck-up and had been sent to Vietnam as punishment. His MOS reportedly was 11C40, Heavy Weapons Infantry, and he had been first assigned to our weapons platoon where, again according to rumor, he had continued to fuck up and so had been reduced to the lowest level of all, the one we occupied. On one of our company patrols, midway through a blisteringly hot day of scuffing through the ant-infested defoliated jungle, the column halted for a bit and offered the opportunity for a brief sit-down. I spotted a single small tree, which had somehow remained foliated enough to provide a patch of shade perhaps two feet square. José Garcia spotted it at about the same time and we both headed for it. Believe me that unless you have carried 60 pounds of gear for half a day in 100 degree heat and not much water, under a baking tropical sun, you cannot truly understand how utterly inviting and blissful sitting for five minutes in that spot of shade would appear. A meter or so from my goal José and I noticed each other and our eyes met. I gestured that he should take the spot, and he shook his head and wordlessly offered it to me. There was no way that tiny patch of heaven could be shared, nor was there any objective basis to allocate it clearly to one or the other of us. While we stood there equipoised, Fellowes scuttled, there is no other word for it, past us, pivoted, and plumped his butt under the tree. He then looked at us with a smile and took out a canteen. José and I shared a look and a grin: both of us had just taken a test, and each of us had aced it. Fellowes appeared oblivious to the fact that he had achieved about the opposite result. He hadn't been in the platoon very long, but he was making a strong impression nonetheless.

That incident occurred on November 13, my 21st birthday; that afternoon the company moved to a clearing where we boarded choppers which took us to an airfield, from which we marched to a large perimeter well-guarded by other units. For the first and only time outside of a base camp, we were given the night off, although I was picked to pull a shift of platoon radio watch which consisted of responding to hourly requests for status from the company HQ. I managed to get the first shift, and sat down with my back against a tree and the radio handset cradled between my head and shoulder, and without conscious thought fell into a deep slumber from which I was awakened at dawn by a call from Captain Howley's RTO, telling us to rise and shine. If anyone had called and been concerned about not getting a response, it wasn't apparent. I was mildly concerned that I had slept through five or six watches and that somebody, somewhere, would be pissed, but the only reaction I got was from one of the guys that should have taken the shift following me on radio watch.

"Why didn't you wake me up?" he asked.

"So I took care of it, you're cool," I told him, and went to wake up the lieutenant. Best birthday ever.

Near the end of November we got the news that Captain Howley would indeed be leaving Alpha Company. Rumors centered upon compassionate leave due to a family emergency. In three months the Old Man had gone from being a feared and hated zealot to a respected and admired zealot, and in the process the company had changed in an organic way, recovering from the wounds of August 25, assimilating the dozens of replacements, and learning war from someone we all recognized as an expert practitioner of the art. Given that at least half of the company consisted of drafted kids who didn't want to be there at any level, I thought that this was a pretty substantial accomplishment. So when we had a moment of inactivity in Lai Khe, the collective feeling was receptive to the idea of a going-away party. Each platoon was charged with coming up with some entertainment, and Second Platoon decided to perform a comedy skit. We had barely a day to organize this effort, but pretty much everybody contributed to writing a script, obtaining props, and casting the parts. Probably because Captain Howley and I were of similar height and complexion, I was cast as the Old Man. As a chance to play broad comedy before a friendly audience, this role was the stuff thespian dreams are made of.

The party went off as scheduled the next afternoon. The Old Man and the other headquarters staff, including the XO, first sergeant, FO, and the various RTOs, medics, cooks, and clerks, were the nominal audience, along with the platoons whose performances were concluded or pending. Maybe a few people from the rest of the battalion were there, but pretty much it was an Alpha Company affair. All told, over a hundred GIs clustered around the dirt area in front of the company orderly room, with Captain Howley and a few other dignitaries seated on camp stools or other odd pieces of stuff, and the rest of us sitting on the ground. A few clouds kept the temperature down, and no rain fell. First Platoon had a bunch of guys, mostly black but with a couple of white and Hispanic additions, who had fooled around for some time doing improv musical numbers, mostly the romantic hits of 1964 and 1965, and they were really good. Their *a cappella* "Tracks of My Tears" was brilliant. They were a hard act to follow, but we did our best. The essence of our script was contained in the following sequence: A couple of GIs are sitting and bullshitting and one of them drops a miniscule scrap of tinfoil from a cigarette pack. Captain Howley, who is lurking behind them, leaps out, grabs the scrap, and berates the cowering GIs. "Charley will find this scrap of tin foil, will use it to fashion a detonator, and attach it to a Claymore mine, and blow your sorry asses to Hell! Now dig me a hole six feet deep and bury this!" Our platoon medic had fashioned huge captain's bars for my helmet, and I was carrying several M-16s and other weapons as well. At one point, when all of the GIs are pantomiming digging new foxholes, after I've ordered them moved three feet from the existing foxholes, I dropped my trousers and turned my butt to the captain, and scratched my ass, saying "Goddamn it feels good to command an infantry company!" Our medic had also fashioned giant captain's bars in white tape for the seat of my OD boxers, never worn in the field but donned now as part of my costume. The climax was a revolt by the oppressed troops who jumped on me in a classic pile-on. We never had a chance to find out what the Old Man really thought, though he gave us a goodbye that seemed sincere, saying how proud he was to have been our captain. This was just about the only time during my service that I ever witnessed or participated in an overt act of collective and mutual affection and respect. I knew I was lucky to have had two outstanding company commanders, so far. And I'm pretty sure my recent promotion to SP4 would have gone through even after the skit.

For an infantryman, the platoon is the family, the company is the clan, the battalion is the tribe, and the division is the nation. After that it's samo-samo, except for Marines and sailors, of course. As we waited to meet our new company commander, and busied ourselves with the pleasures and problems of sleeping in bunks, eating hot chow, visiting the ville, and avoiding work details, I at least from time to time did some math. We'd been almost two months without a death in the family. Our last KIA had been SP5 Mallonee, back on October 5. So when we did meet our new commanding officer, I had some hopes that our lucky streak would continue. But first impressions were not comforting. Captain Williamson was a very tall, very slim West Pointer with piercing eyes under black brows. He came to us, rumor had it, from a stint as a staff officer in some higher echelon, and was here to get his six months of combat command, a necessary ticket to be punched on the way to an eagle or star. He didn't say much, and didn't try to fill the void left by Captain Howley's departure. But our quiet time was over, in any event. We weren't going to see Lai Khe again for a long time.

CHAPTER 13

Walk in the Dark

The first day of December brought a chopper ride from Lai Khe to another jungle clearing and an uneventful walk through the brush. We set up a company perimeter and dug in, and the next day was much the same. The area was definitely hostile, and various contacts with small numbers of VC occurred. There is a heart-stopping quality to the first few seconds of a firefight, when the initial couple of shots is followed by a sudden increase in firing: how big is this going to get? This time the firing never went beyond the squad level, although there were some different kinds of heart-stopping moments when gunships and fighter-bombers came in to support us. One of them, a navy Phantom from the sound of it, came screaming directly overhead and put a 500-pound bomb really close to the part of the column I was occupying, close enough so that I was covered in dirt and debris, bounced a couple of times by the concussion, and had my ears ringing for a few minutes. Fortunately the thickness of the jungle protected us from much of the force of the blast and absorbed much of the shrapnel, as I doubt the impact was more than 50 feet from where I was crouched. In fairness, I guess it is pretty difficult for a Phantom pilot coming over at 400 miles per hour to put a big bomb in just the right place, when all he can see is the top of triple canopy jungle. At the time, though, my thought was that if I could see the fly-boy rat-fuck bastard I would have fired him up. The incident also provided a lesson in the limited effectiveness of big ordnance in jungle warfare. A bomb that size that close to an infantry column in the open would have likely been devastating, killing and wounding with blast and shrapnel, instead of just scary and annoying, because of all the dirt and jungle bits that covered us.

Most or all of the battalion was involved in the operation, although we had been operating as a company so far. The third day began with another patrol, uneventful until near the end. We had been moving through an area which was slightly less dense than the day before, and were expected to join the rest of the battalion for what we assumed was a battalion-sized RON. At some point in the mid-afternoon, Second Platoon was in the middle of the column as we moved towards our destination. We had been moving fitfully, with more than the usual stops and starts, when the word came down the column for me to go to the point. I was bemused—this wasn't something that had happened before. Was I in trouble? When I got near the head of the column a lieutenant told me that we were moving too slowly and the Old Man had said to put Clark on point to speed things up. This was, to date, my finest hour. I was pleased as punch, and proceeded to show off my point-walking skills by taking us through the brush at a good clip. The essence of walking point is not to focus on the obstacle ahead, but on the more distant ones, planning a route that reduced the possibility of ending up facing an impenetrable barrier with no alternative but going further off course to the left or right, or, worse yet, backtracking. As I was doing this for the next few hours, I glowed with the feeling of competence. It was as if my pack had shed 20 pounds. I understood my mission as not only being speedy, but also being savvy, so I was vigilant as well as swift.

All went well until late in day, when my senses picked up disturbing vibrations. I slowed down, and focused on my surroundings. There, ahead of me in the underbrush, was a smoldering cigarette butt, unfiltered! I crouched down, and signaled the men behind me to get down as well, took my weapon off safety, and peered into the jungle, all my senses straining. In a couple of minutes, the Old Man and his train of RTOs came striding up the column, and passed me despite my hissed warning. I got up and followed them through a screen of brush and into a clearing occupied by the rest of battalion, in the process of organizing the RON. Would have been nice if somebody had told me we had reached our objective. Nonetheless, I still treasure the moment the call came for me to go forward and take the point.

Once we entered the battalion perimeter, which had already been secured by Bravo and Charlie companies, we were grouped by platoons but not placed on line. Soon Lieutenant Denton and Sergeant Floyd appeared and briefed us on our next mission: a night march by the entire battalion to provide a blocking force for an ARVN operation. The ARVN mission was to roust a village for Viet Cong sympathizers or other bad guys who might be lurking there. Because we would be leaving at moonrise, we wouldn't have to dig in, which was an unexpected treat. After the lieutenant gave the platoon briefing, we got some more details from Sergeant Floyd. We were going to walk all night, exercising extreme noise and light discipline, which meant no talking, no cigarettes, no rattling gear. We were to march without rounds in the chambers of our weapons, to minimize the risk of an accidental discharge. Switek asked what if he had to fart, which drew snickers from many of us, but just pissed Floyd off. According to Floyd, there would be no dustoff if some sorry son of a bitch broke his fucking leg; we would have to carry the sorry motherfucker. When we got to our position, before dawn, we were to scrape ourselves prone shelters, the least demanding of the field fortification emplacements. Basically it was a shallow gouge in the earth, just wide and long enough to lie in prone; whatever spoil was collected was pushed to the head end to provide some cover for the occupant to fire over. Some of us would be facing out, and some in towards the ville we were blocking. So far so good; at least we weren't going to have to dig in at the end of the march, either.

Around 10 p.m. we were formed into parallel columns and moved out under a rising moon which illuminated a few wispy clouds. The air was relatively cool and the terrain was easy; for most of this trip we followed a valley largely covered with dry rice paddies and open areas punctuated by small groves of trees. On either side of our line of march the ground rose gently into denser treelines. Although I was tired, coming off a couple of days of strenuous activity with a maximum of four hours sleep a night, the march was easy. For a change the pace was fairly even, without the stop-and-go quality of jungle travel. I was near the middle of our file and the other file was visible a few hundred feet away on my right, so there seemed little need for vigilance. I found myself in a walking trance, day-dreaming, if that is the proper expression on a night march, about girls and such things. After a few hours of uneventful semi-sleepwalking, I was startled awake by a flash and boom from the treeline to the left. I halted and knelt, trying to get the cobwebs out and peering into the dark lines of vegetation which now appeared like black and ominous shadows rising above the moonlit fields. A team including Greg Murry was detached from the column and disappeared into the treeline. That scurry of activity in the direction of the explosion produced no further detonations or small-arms fire, and my heart and respiration returned to normal.

Soon Greg and his guys rejoined the column and we took off again, moving smartly now. Before long the columns were split, and the left-hand column, which included the Second Platoon, moved to our left, while the other column disappeared into the darkness to my right. Although clouds had obscured the moon, there was enough ambient light to pick out the loom of a village on high ground ahead. The area we moved into was mostly hard, packed dirt with a few scrubby plants here and there. We moved to the left of the village and were placed a few feet apart in two lines, one facing out and one in towards the ville. I was facing in, and scraped out a few inches of the hard soil, lay down with my rifle pointed at the ville, and concentrated on not falling asleep. As usual now, after my disgraceful ambush-patrol sleeping incident, I carried a canteen of C-ration coffee which helped me keep me awake, despite the temptations of darkness and the prone position. I was facing just south of east, and as the horizon lightened behind the village we heard the rumble of engines and an amplified voice speaking Vietnamese. Shortly thereafter a shadowy form streaked out of the darkness surrounding the ville a dozen meters or so to my left. A few shots and red tracer rounds followed. Now fully alert, I continued to peer into the slowly resolving cluster of hedges, groves, and buildings, from which nothing more than a growing chorus of shouts, crashes, and wails emerged.

Eventually the sun rose on what promised to be a clear, hot morning. The shots had been fired by Rod Floutz, and had mortally wounded a young man who was probably a draft dodger or deserter. He had been unarmed, in any event, and now an older woman, probably his mother, was wailing over his body. Rod was not happy about this killing.

"Man, he's just a fucking draft dodger. That could have been me," he was muttering.

After a while we were formed up and started to move out. I was desperately tired and assumed we were going to some nice clearing where friendly choppers would take us to a safe place to sleep for about 20 hours. And while no one told me any different, after a couple of hours of walking through brush and cleared areas, many of which would have made dandy LZs, I began to have some doubts as to our ultimate destination. Second Platoon was around the middle of the column. Around midday, as we approached a settlement, a couple of explosions in the direction of the lead elements of the company woke me up a little. The column stopped, and we remained in place for a while, while a couple of choppers landed and took off. Later I found out that we had taken a couple of RPG or mortar rounds and a kid from another platoon, whose tour was almost over, had been killed.

William D. Robbins, Hapeville, Georgia, age 19. Alpha Co., 1/16 Infantry. DIED 4 December 1966 in Vietnam as the result of metal fragment wounds to chest received in hostile ground action.

While we were waiting to move on I noticed Sergeant Floyd and the lieutenant coming down the line. Floyd had something in an OD canvas case that was roughly cylindrical and about two feet long. He noticed me and, without interrupting his conversation with the lieutenant, walked over and started fumbling with my butt pack.

"That'll do 'er," he said, giving something a couple of tugs.

I turned to look at him, and saw he didn't have anything in his hands, and my load felt a bit heavier.

"That's a new starlight scope. Give it to me when we get to the RON, Clark," he said, and continued on with his conversation.

What the hell is a starlight scope, I wondered briefly, and then forgot about the whole incident as we moved out again. Throughout that long afternoon the column was periodically sniped at, and friendly artillery was more or less constantly falling ahead of and on our flanks. I was too tired to care, my energy pretty much absorbed by the immediate task of keeping up with the guy in front. Fortunately I didn't need to walk flank or point, so I could sort of drift most of the time. Late in the afternoon we approached a village and spread out to sweep through it. We were told we were looking for evidence of Viet Cong presence, which to me was a no-brainer, as we had been taking fire all afternoon. As I walked between bamboo and thatched structures, I saw a young woman standing in the open. She was dressed in the traditional white blouse and black trousers, her black hair tied in a tight bun. A conical straw hat was slung over her back; her hands were clenched in fists at her sides, and she was staring into the middle distance. Shrapnel from the nearby artillery concentrations was littering the area between the structures, and I tried to get her to seek shelter. She was beautiful as only the Vietnamese can be, and I truly wanted her to get under cover. She turned to look at me as I tried with pidgin Vietnamese and hand gestures to get her inside, for although the houses offered no shelter themselves, most of them had dugouts excavated in the sandy floors and that's where I thought she should be. The look she gave me was an elegant combination of utter hatred and disdain which held no trace of ambiguity. Clearly she would rather die than submit to any direction I could offer her, and had she the power and I the vulnerability she would have killed me in an instant. Nonetheless I picked up a piece of spent shrapnel that was still smoking and, waving it around, herded her into the closest dwelling and pointed to the shelter in the floor. She continued to stand and wish me dead, so I left her there and continued the sweep of the village. She was the only person I saw above ground. Most of the families were crouched in their little bunkers. Of course there were no weapons or obvious signs of enemy presence, but I suspected that if we were going to win the hearts and minds of these folk, we had a ways to go.

The sweep completed, the company moved out of the village a few hundred meters and halted for a bit. I was able to sit down under a shady bamboo thicket. Nobody was talking much, as we were punchy from the cocktail of adrenalin and sleep deprivation. Soon enough we were on our feet and moving down a sandy road to a relatively bare hilltop where another company had already dug in. After some standing around we were told that we were going to occupy the half-dug holes our predecessors had left in what turned out to be hard, laterite-laced soil. I was assigned to a position on the forward crest of the hilltop, along with an M-79 gunner I'll call Shelley. Shelley was a sandy-haired draftee from somewhere in the Midwest and, like Wohlford, was not a bad kid but also not looking to win any good soldiering contests. As we were trying to improve the half-dug hole by hacking at the hard, stony laterite, Sergeant Floyd came up with Lieutenant Denton.

"Clark. Gimme the starlight scope," he barked.

I stared at him stupidly for a moment, truly having forgotten that whole transaction, which seemed to have receded into the distant past.

"Oh, yeah, it's on my pack, right?" I went over to where I had dumped my gear, and pawed over the pile of webbing, weapons, and oddments that I had shucked as soon as we were assigned a position.

"Geez, I don't see it," I said. I walked over the area around our hole, but it was nowhere in evidence. "Maybe it fell off," I suggested.

Floyd turned red and Denton turned white.

"That was a top-secret prototype we were supposed to test," the lieutenant said. "I'd better tell the Old Man you lost it." He glared at Floyd and took off.

Floyd turned to me and hissed: "I don't know what you did with that fucking scope but you better find it before the Old Man gets here."

Like I needed this. As best I could in my be-fogged state, I tried to remember where in the course of the last four or five hours the damn thing might have come loose. Throughout the day I'd been walking pretty much with somebody following behind me, so if something as substantial as the scope had fallen off my pack it would have been noticed. The only thing I could think of was when we had rested in the bamboo grove just before we started up the hill to the RON. It could have come off while I was sitting and not have been noticed among the foliage. So I grabbed my steel pot and my M-16 and took off back down the sandy path, stopping to tell the guys digging in nearest to where the track left the perimeter that I would be coming back soon, so don't fire me up. Dusk was falling, the shadows were long, and as I loped down the track I swear I could hear the snick of breech bolts and muttered conversations in Vietnamese from the thickets. But getting shot to death seemed preferable to dealing with having lost some valuable piece of army gear. After a few hundred meters I came to the bamboo grove, and searched the area where I had been sitting, but found nothing. For a few seconds I contemplated continuing my search into the village, where for a time no one had been behind me. But, even through my haze of sleepiness, I figured that the folks in the village would have found the thing if I dropped it there, and were unlikely to return it even if I asked nicely.

I didn't actually run back to the RON, but I walked pretty fast. I gave the bad news to Sergeant Floyd and Lieutenant Denton, who were highly displeased, and didn't appear to take much comfort from the fact that they could blame a SP4 for the actual loss. We all went to the command CP to face the music. We got a surprisingly bland reception from Captain Williamson. It seems Bravo Company had followed us into the RON, and the Bravo Company commander had radioed Captain Williamson that he had 'found a little something you might be missing" and would return it after trying it out tonight. Sergeant Floyd still wanted to punish me, but I pointed out that I hadn't even touched the thing and Floyd had fastened it to my pack. The Old Man looked thoughtful and allowed that, as the scope only weighed a couple of pounds, and given our general levels of fatigue, I couldn't be expected to notice it dropping off. He admonished us in general to keep track of the things, pointing out that if the VC got them they could pick us off at will at night. We were then dismissed. My extreme dislike of Floyd was reinforced by the incident, and a budding sense of respect for Captain Williamson began to take hold. But mainly I just wanted to rest. That wish, however, was not going to be fulfilled any time soon.

Back at the hole, Shelley had gotten it a bit deeper mostly by breaking up the hard soil with the pick end of his entrenching tool. Dusk was falling and, despite my fuddled brain, I was concerned about surviving the night. I took a careful look around the front of our position. We were on what's called the military crest of the hill. Though we had higher ground behind us, our position overlooked a steep, largely bare, slope of hard soil. To the right of our hole, and starting about three meters down the slope, a significant gulley cut to our left front. I walked down the gulley, and it surely made an attractive path for anyone who wanted to sneak up on our position, concealed from observation and protected on both sides. The draw was maybe four meters across at the bottom, tapering slowly upward for 20 or so meters before narrowing and finally disappearing near our hole. An infiltrator could walk upright about half that distance, but by kneeling and then crawling could get within a couple of meters of the hole without being observed from either side, or from above, unless the observer leaned far out over the lip of the hill. The good news was that our position was basically invisible to anyone crouching in the gulley.

The GI-issue trip flare was a chemical firework the size and shape of a frozen orange-juice can (or a can of Red Bull for you youngsters) that had a detonation mechanism, protected by a pin like a hand grenade's, which when properly rigged with its tripwire would provide a minute or so of hellishly brilliant white illumination, along with clouds of choking white smoke. I took our trip flares and installed one at the bottom of the gulley and the other about halfway up. The U. S. Claymore mine, as I have mentioned, was designed to defeat human-wave attacks, such as we were told happened in Korea, but rarely, if ever, occurred in Vietnam. Most of the weight in a three- to four-pound Claymore was in the 700 or so steel balls set into a plastic matrix, and the layer of C-4 explosive, both of which followed the convex, rectangular plastic case. The case consisted of two clamshell pieces that clicked together. A separate component kit consisted of a hand-held generator thingy with a lever which produced a jolt of electricity, which could be directed through wires to a blasting cap that could be inserted into a receptacle on the mine, arming the device. There was a certain ambivalence amongst the infantry over the utility of the Claymore as a defensive weapon versus the additional weight it added to our load. While we were expected to have one or two slung about our person, a moment's work separated the components of the mine into useless steel balls (discard), C-4 (keep for heating Cs) and a nice, waterproof case perfect for holding letter-writing materials. The results of this modification reduced the weight of the device without changing its visible appearance. On this occasion I was happy to have an unmodified or original version of the Claymore, and set it up right at the point where infiltrators would have to get down to stay protected. I concealed it with care, and likewise tried to ensure the wires running up to our hole were out of sight. By now it was pretty dark, and I was happy to get back to the hole, which was just about deep enough for the two of us to crouch down, and a good depth for firing over. We had a few sandbags which we filled and arranged around the front. To our left a couple of dozen meters was a similar hole, with a couple of Second Platoon GIs; after that scrubby brush and the leftward curve of our line hid the next position. To my right a small brushy thicket mostly hid our neighbor on that side, though we could see the guys when they were standing up.

Just as we were settling in, we heard a loud explosion behind us. I found out later that Lieutenant James and Sergeant Reeves, leader and sergeant respectively of a Bravo Company platoon, had been killed outright by some undetermined ordnance while sitting on the lip of their hole, the bottom of which became filled with blood that couldn't drain through the dense laterite soil. This led battalion to reinforce that sector of the RON, on the other side from our position, by stripping some of Alpha's positions and shifting folks to what was deemed the threatened sector. Sometime later the Old Man, along with Lieutenant Denton and Sergeant Floyd, came along the line. Alerted by the thicket of radio antennas, Shelley and I appeared alert and vigilant when the entourage reached our hole. We were told that the position to our right was becoming vacant as the line was being moved to cover additional positions on Bravo Company's front. After unnecessary admonishments to stay alert, the CP group departed.

Any thoughts of sleep now banished, Shelley and I tried to pierce the gathering darkness to our front. Soon enough we heard the *pop-pop-pop* of small-caliber mortar or M–79 grenades leaving their tubes to our left, seeming to come from the brushy treeline which rose across the valley immediately to our front. The rounds landed to our left, wounding one or both of the guys in the adjacent hole. Neither appeared to be seriously hurt, as after attendance by the medics they walked up the hill towards the center of the RON, but no one was moved into their hole. Shelley and I were basically on our own. I had a pretty good idea of where the rounds had come from, although by now darkness was well settled.

"C'mon, Shelley, use that M-79," I whispered.

"I can't, I don't know where to shoot," he whined.

I pointed to where I thought he should fire.

"We got to return fire, we can't just let them take pot shots," I hissed. "Goddammit, if you won't I will."

That was a hollow threat, as I had no intention of firing the one round I could trust from my rifle at a distant and unseen target, or of giving our position away with such a low likelihood of inflicting harm.

"OK, OK," he grumbled, and let off a couple of rounds in the general direction I had indicated. I wasn't satisfied, but figured that was all I was going to get.

About the time that darkness became total a C-47 started circling the RON and dropping parachute flares. Surreal under the best of circumstances, to my fatigued brain the flares completed the dreamscape we inhabited. The C-47 dropped the flares at short intervals as it flew in a circle. The flares, suspended beneath parachutes, slowly descended in a complicated spiral, pulled down by gravity, and sideways by the angular vectors of the aircraft and the effects of the breeze on the parachutes. Half a dozen or so flares were in the air at any given time, each at different altitudes, and each brighter than a full moon, casting multiple moving shadows across the stark white landscape that they illuminated while transforming the areas that their light could not penetrate into a blackness deeper than natural night. Clouds of thick, white smoke drifted from each burning flare, alternately enveloping or reflecting other flares as they descended. Really, you had to be there.

The likelihood of picking out an enemy threat any smaller than a light tank in the visual confusion was remote. Odd crackles of small-arms fire, some of which was certainly incoming, sounded around the perimeter. I could imagine stealthy gooks creeping up the gulley, or infiltrating to our right and left, where only empty foxholes stood guard. I carefully unsnapped all four grenades from my ammo pouches and, straightening the pins so I could quickly arm them, placed them in a row along the sandbags to our front.

"You got grenades?" I asked Shelley.

"No," he whispered, "I never carry them. I have the M-79."

"Well, you got your .45, right? How many magazines you got?"

Long pause. "Don't have my pistol. I forgot it."

"You got any shotgun rounds for the '79?"

"No. I had one, but I used it and nobody gave me another one."

It was shaping up to be a long night. The C-47, or another one, chose this point to open up with its Gatling gun, sending down streams of red tracer like water from a hose into the darkness across the valley to my right. I noticed that the tracer mostly burned out before the rounds reached the ground, so there was no visible sign of the impact. Greg Murry and his gun team were actually somewhere out in the gloom, part of a squad-sized ambush patrol which was now trying to direct the C-47's fire at likely targets, but I didn't know that at the time.

Then one of my trip flares went off. Gooks in the gulley! I set off my Claymore, which theoretically would have eliminated anybody creeping up on us, and certainly set off the remaining trip flare. Shelley and I hunkered down in our hole while the trip flares burned out, peering over the row of sandbags into the thick white smoke generated by the flares. Eventually the flares burned out and the smoke cleared. Nothing was visible, and I could hear nothing that suggested movement in the gulley or surrounding brush. Time went by, and the flares drifted away and the gunship's firing ceased. I must have dozed, because I remember jerking my head up when Shelley elbowed me in the ribs.

"Listen," he whispered.

Suddenly wide awake, I held my breath, and sure enough heard a scraping and rustling down the hill to our front, the sort of sound a stealthy infiltrator might make. I took a grenade from the sandbag and put my finger in the ring, straining to make sense of what I was hearing. It came in fits and starts, but I heard the unmistakable sound of someone or something moving quietly below our position. I pulled the pin and threw the first of my grenades. It detonated and a patter of shrapnel and debris landed on and around our heads, which we had pulled down below the lip of our hole. Looking down over the top of the hole, I saw a face peering up at us from near the top of the gulley. Quick as that I threw another grenade; after the blast, we looked again. The face was still there. I looked harder, and saw no movement; whoever it was, was dead.

"You see it?" I asked Shelley in a whisper.

"Yeah, yeah, dead gook," he breathed.

I had two grenades left, and at least one round in my M–16, and fervently hoped that would be enough for whatever came next. Which was nothing. The night continued its seemingly interminable journey into daylight, while I slipped in and out of a hazy, semi-awake state, trying to listen for any ominous sounds. I peeped over the lip of the hole a couple of times, and each time the frozen rictus of the dead VC greeted me: an older man in his forties or fifties, sparse black hair, stubble, high cheekbones, thin and lined. I can still see that face. Eventually the sky began to lighten and I think I fell asleep for a period.

When I jerked awake Shelley was slumped in the bottom of the hole, sound asleep. Mist was visible rising from the ground in the valley and shrouding the distant treeline when I looked over the edge of the hole, expecting to see the dead VC. Nothing. No body, nothing visible to suggest one had ever been there. I reached down and shook Shelley's shoulder.

"Do you see anything?" I asked him.

He peered over the top of the hole and stared for a while. "Nothing, where is he?"

"Did you see him last night? What did you see?"

"Dead gook. Staring right up at us."

It was too much to process. There didn't seem to be any existential threats looming in the quiet, deserted valley to our front, and so without any conscious decision we both checked out.

My next memory is being kicked in the boot by some GI, as I lay sprawled on the slope behind our hole. Shelley was likewise being roused. I looked up, and up, and up, at the tall, lanky form of Captain Williamson, who was standing several feet up the hill from me, shaved, neat, and disapproving. I scrambled up and tried to look like I had just been resting my eyes, but surely expecting to be chewed out for sleeping.

Night Action (Peter Clark; July, 1967). This is me about to throw the second grenade I write about. Great likeness of the rifle.

I realized this was not the way to make a good impression on the new CO, but my, the sleep had been refreshing. While Shelley and I were blinking and trying to straighten our clothes the Old Man allowed, in a dry sort of way, as how our hole was inadequately camouflaged, then moved on down the line trailing his RTOs and other attendants. Shelley and I looked at each other and grinned, knowing we had just been cut some major slack. But what about the dead gook? I went down the front of our position, and checked out the gulley from top to bottom. Other than the residual effects of a couple of burnt flares, and disturbances consistent with an exploded Claymore mine and a couple of hand grenades, there was nothing. Not a drop of blood, a shred of clothing, or any marks which would have supported the notion that someone was there and had either crawled or been dragged away. Nothing. Maybe the whole episode had been a stress-induced hallucination that Shelley and I had somehow shared; when I asked him after I had examined the ground what he had seen, he described the dead gook just as I remembered him. I'm leaning to the hallucination theory, as I can't imagine any other explanation for the complete lack of forensic evidence, and the improbability that the body could have been spirited away without Shelley or me hearing that happen. Of course it was a hallucination. But when I close my eyes, I can still see every wrinkle and pore of that dead face, and the brown, sightless eyes looking up at me.

Alvis Reeves, White Oak, Texas, age 34. Bravo Co., 1/16 Infantry. DIED on 4 December 1966 as the result of gunshot [sic] wound to chest received in hostile ground action; Samuel James, Jr., Raleigh, North Carolina, age 24. DIED on 4 December 1966 as the result of metal fragment wounds to the head received in hostile ground action.

CHAPTER 14

Time for a Change

Along with the three rifle platoons and the weapons platoon, Alpha Company had its own little headquarters unit, consisting of the Old Man; the executive officer or XO, usually the senior lieutenant in the company; the first sergeant; the senior company medic; and the cooks, supply sergeant, and a clerk. In addition, there was a communications section, headed by the commo sergeant and including the Old Man's RTOs. The commo sergeant was a short, thin, intense native of the Philippines named Acquinino. He was responsible for ensuring the operational status of the dozen or so PRC-25s, the odd walkie-talkies left over from Korea which still showed up from time to time, and the field telephones, World War II technology which relied on wires and bulky handsets. We sometimes used the latter on short OPs, and the bunkers on the line were equipped with them. English was not Acquinino's first language, so sometimes understanding him was difficult, and he also had a prickly personality which manifested itself as frustrated impatience when people didn't appear to comprehend his directions. On the plus side, he was intelligent and conscientious, and ensured that the commo equipment was functional and the personnel operating it were trained and capable. But he had little to do with the average grunt, unless that person happened to be carrying a radio for somebody. So when he came looking for me during a lull in an operation somewhere out in the boonies, shortly after the harrowing night march, I had no idea as to his purpose.

"Hey, Clark. The Old Man's RTO is DEROSing. You like to be his new RTO?"

I was surprised, as I certainly hadn't seen the offer coming. I'd carried the radio for Lieutenant Denton or Sergeant Floyd a couple of times as a fill-in while the regular RTO was unavailable, and so I knew my radio procedure and the GI phonetic alphabet. My skill level, for good or ill, would have been apparent to anyone listening on the company net, but I had no sense that I'd made an impression. But here it was: a reprise, of sorts, of the moment when the personnel SFC back in Long Binh had asked me if I could type.

"I got a choice?" I asked, stalling for time.

"Sure you do, you do what you want. I think you a good RTO, Old Man's OK to try you out, but you gotta want to do it. I got somebody else in mind, you don't do it."

So I had to think quickly. I did a cost-benefit in my head: the main cost was the loss of opportunity for leadership and promotion. I was getting pretty good at my job; I had just been made a fire-team leader and could look forward to becoming a squad leader and getting sergeant's stripes, which I coveted. I had lots of good buddies in the Second Platoon—Greg, José, Donnie Gunby, Floutz, Al Roese, Fred Burris—and lots of others with whom I wasn't as close but nonetheless knew well and with whom I'd gone through a lot, like Switek, Wohlford, and Shelly. Floyd was an asshole and Fellowes was a pimple on the ass of progress, but Second Platoon was still my home and family. The challenge of leading men in combat, even if it was just a fire team, was scary but compelling, and I was loath to give up that possibility. And Acquinino would not be anyone's choice as an immediate superior. Also the RTO carried more weight, which was another minus. While the risks of death or injury were pretty high in the rifle squad, I didn't think RTO was much safer, and sometimes maybe not as safe, because the radio antennas made the RTOs visible, high-value targets, so that factor sort of cancelled out. But what were the benefits? Becoming RTO for the Old Man was to enter a position of special trust and responsibility. That the Old Man would consider me was flattering and a bit surprising, as to the best of my recollection every time I had come to his attention I was losing valuable equipment, asleep on the job, or otherwise fucking up.

"How many headquarters guys for each foxhole, when we're in the field?" I asked.

"Three, sometimes four," Acquinino replied.

Right at that moment I was tired, and desperate for sleep, but I could still do the simple math. Instead of four hours of sleep a night, and that only if all went well, I could look forward to five or six hours, and no ambush patrols either.

"OK, I'll do it," I told him.

I wasn't going to assume my new duties until the next day, but after we stopped for the night Acquinino presented me to the Old Man as his nominee. I kind of braced, as we didn't salute in the field, but Captain Williamson just looked hard at me and nodded. "Welcome to headquarters, Clark," was all I remember him saying. I nodded at the guys who were going to be my new colleagues, then engaged in digging foxholes, and went back to my own excavations, hoping I'd made the right choice, but already envying those guys who would be getting a solid six hours of sleep tonight. I took some ribbing from my buddies, who seemed to mostly view my move as a promotion, and were a little envious, but happy for me, and maybe looking forward to having a contact in the CP to get useful information from time to time. Switek predicted I'd be back in a couple of weeks, as I was going to fuck it up, but even he showed a grudging hint of respect for the first time and I was almost sorry to leave him behind. Floyd, whom I had expected to snarl a "good riddance," was actually almost jovial as he wished me luck. I realized that proximity to the source of power was a kind of power itself, and folks otherwise not so inclined didn't want to be on my bad side, as I was going to be literally connected to the Old Man by two meters of cable for the rest of my tour.

So on December 8 I started humping the radio for keeps. The set I carried was the one on the battalion net, which meant I heard all the radio traffic going between the various company COs and the battalion commander, Lieutenant Colonel Rufus Lazzell. Captain Howley had required his RTOs to carry an M-16, but Captain Williamson reverted to the TOE weapons requirement, probably as a result of an order from the battalion CO, so I traded my M-16 in for a Colt .45. At the time I thought that was my great good fortune, due to having about 15 pounds less weight in weapon and ammo to carry.

As luck would have it, we were on a battalion-sized road-clearing operation a few klicks north of Lai Khe on Highway 13. Because the road had been opened, we actually had a few jeeps for the brass, and as the new RTO I actually got to ride in the Old Man's jeep for a couple of klicks. We set up in a clear area along the highway, with several companies on the perimeter, so things were pretty secure. I was reveling in the extra sleep, and had some respite from carrying the weight of full combat gear as we sent platoon patrols out from the perimeter, while the headquarters folks, now including me, stayed inside. I didn't have to carry much besides my weapon and the radio as I followed the Old Man around the perimeter. December 10 was rainy but quiet during the day. I had a snug hooch near the Old Man's tent, and it seemed like a vacation, lazing around listening to the reports from the guys in the rifle platoons running their patrols.

In the course of the day's patrolling, fresh footprints were found on a sandy track near the highway, a klick or so up Route 13 from our RON. In order to exploit this discovery, Second Platoon was sent on a night ambush patrol along the likely VC trail. After dark had fallen, the platoon lined up inside the RON and was inspected by Lieutenant Denton and Sergeant Floyd for noisy accoutrements. As quietly as possible, the platoon filed out of the perimeter and faded into the brush, following an azimuth to the ambush site that had been determined during the day patrol. After reaching the ambush site, the platoon settled down into the brush along a likely stretch of the trail. Of course no one dug in or set up trip flares. José Garcia and Donnie Gunby had the left-most position, and set up a Claymore facing down the trail. Late that night José and Donnie heard movement on the trail, coming from their right. To their amazement an oxcart and a gaggle of shadowy forms appeared out of the gloom, having passed the front of the rest of platoon. Donnie blew his Claymore, hitting the ox and three of the VC. A number of other VC started running down the trail, past the wounded ox. Not knowing how many adversaries they faced, Donnie and José followed up with grenades rather than give their position away with rifle fire. Their

Donnie Gunby (José Garcia; 1967)

grenades expended, José crawled to his right and reached Sergeant Floyd's position. Floyd hissed at him to be quiet, but José refused to leave until he had collected more grenades. He returned to his position, but the VC who were capable of flight were long gone and the rest of the night was uneventful. For whatever reason, the remainder of Second Platoon hadn't engaged the enemy to their front. While my heart was with my buddies during this encounter, my ass was warm and dry in my hooch. I had a bit of envy for José and Donnie getting some action, but on balance I was content to listen to it on the radio. This encounter was duly reported to battalion HQ, which may or may not have used this information to send out Charlie Company's Second Platoon to that area on the morning of December 11.

That morning dawned sunny and hot, with a few wispy clouds. Alpha Company was on perimeter duty, as we had had platoons out during the night, and Charlie Company was running a platoon-sized patrol. Because we had the luxury of a jeep, we could carry some heavy stuff that we wouldn't bring when we were humping. Among these items was a portable radio speaker, a steel box about the size of an ammo can that amplified the voice transmission from a PRC-25. This was hooked up to the battalion net, and the Old Man and a few other headquarters folks were sitting around listening to the progress of the patrols and shooting the shit. I was sitting nearby in the shade of my hooch, reading a paperback and drinking C-ration coffee. Life was good! But then I noticed the Old Man, one of the lieutenants, and Sergeant Acquinino fussing with one of the radios. I got off my butt and strolled over. Acquinino had changed the frequency on one of the radios to the Charlie Company push, or frequency. The PRC-25 had two pre-set pushes; mine had the battalion push, which I monitored by default, and the Alpha Company push which could be quickly selected if needed. But any frequency could be dialed in. In this case Charlie Company's Second Platoon, Mike, had made contact while out on patrol. The radio traffic on the Charlie Company net was coming over the loudspeaker.

"We got three Victor Charlie, they're running," I heard.

"Mike Six, this is Devour Six," came out of the box. Devour was the battalion call sign, and Devour Six was Lieutenant Colonel Lazzell. He had come in on the Charlie Company frequency.

"Devour Six, Mike Six."

"Mike Six, you get those little bastards. You got that, Mike Six?"

"Roger, Devour Six." The guy was panting. There was a pause. Lazzell gave some instructions to Charlie Six, and then Mike Six came back on.

"We're taking fire, we're taking fire. We got some down." Small-arms fire was audible behind the voice transmission. "Oh my God, we need some help here."

Lazzell came back on. "Now, calm down, son, what do you see, over?"

"I'm hit, I'm hit."

"Now just calm down, son, and tell me what's going on, over," said Lazzell.

"This is Mike Six Kilo, Mike Six is hit, we're taking fire from the woodline," said a new voice.

We could hear a distant eruption of small-arms fire, which lasted about a minute. Then silence. Lieutenant Colonel Lazzell boarded an observation chopper and took off immediately; he continued to transmit while he looked for the battle site.

From what I observed and later heard, Charlie Mike platoon had 30 or so guys, plus an artillery forward observer, moving on a typical platoon patrol, following predetermined compass headings for a predetermined distance. The platoon had been given a ride north on Highway 13 on some tracks, and was supposed to return to the road in the afternoon after making their loop through the brush. They quickly encountered the site of Alpha Company's ambush the night before, where the dead oxen and a couple of the dead or dying VC that José and Donnie had hit still remained. The ground they were on was a combination of grassy open areas and wooded, brushy thickets, not the dense, triple canopy jungle which impeded movement and reduced visibility. So the platoon was able to move out pretty quickly along their designated azimuth. After a couple of hours of uneventful humping through the woods, the platoon encountered an open area. When the point man reached the edge of the brush and first looked across the large clearing, he saw a treeline around a hundred meters across an expanse of scattered clumpy grass with a few small bushes and saplings, some fallen tree trunks, and the odd anthill. The lead element proceeded across the open space and was surprised to find three armed VC, who took off running into the far woodline. The platoon leader, Lieutenant Starr, his RTO, and the artillery FO, Lieutenant Carter, moved quickly up the column of troops. Starr was an experienced officer, a first lieutenant and former enlisted man with ten years of service. Stepping out into the clearing, Starr decided that the fleeing VC must have crossed the open space and entered the opposite treeline. He directed one squad to his right, another to his left. When the last men in the column—Staff Sergeant Elmer Dickens, along with the platoon medic, Private First Class Vito Bruno—reached his side, the platoon was spreading out in a line a few feet into the clearing. After the dimness of the woods, the sunlight was bright and hot. In the opposite woodline, the tops of the trees and the higher branches were painfully bright green and yellow; the shade under the trees was black

José Garcia (Unknown; 1967)

and opaque. Moving out immediately, the platoon was approaching the middle of the clearing when the first muzzle flash sparked out of the dense shadow under the trees. As the whole treeline erupted in fire, the brilliant green tracers were followed by a wave of sound from the enemy weapons. Sergeant Dickens and Bruno were killed by bullets in the chest and abdomen, along with rifleman John Lawlor. SP4 Willie Walker was severely wounded. Lieutenant Carter was hit in both arms, rendering him unable to fight or use the radio; somehow the rounds missed his vital areas. A few seconds later rocket-propelled grenades or mortar shells exploded in the midst of the command group, mortally wounding Lieutenant Starr, as well as SP4 Alvin Kurtz and Privates First Class Robert Jones, Tommie Mooney, James Smith, and Bruno. The survivors by now were prone, and starting to return fire, but all they could see were the brilliant muzzle flashes and the neon green of the enemy tracers. Some of the GIs near their point of entry to the clearing backed into the woods and tried to set up a defensive position behind a machine gun; these were ultimately the survivors, though most were wounded. There was little cover on the open field. Sergeant Antonio Solis and Private First Class John Widener were killed by bullets to the head, and Privates First Class Joshua Welch, Michael McCommons, Donald Lamar, Sergeants Michael Kirby and Dennis Harper, and SP4 Jimmie Poe were killed by fragments from grenades or mortar shells.

Back in the perimeter, a relief force was being hastily organized. A dozen or so M-113 tracked personnel carriers were summoned from a laager down Highway 13, and the remaining troops of Charlie Company were throwing on their gear and running towards the road. Alpha Company was going to stay put to guard the perimeter, but Captain Williamson got a call to send the company's medics on the tracks with Charlie Company. The platoon medics saddled up and joined Bravo at the roadside. Our senior medic, whom I will call Duckwiler, and who was part of the company headquarters family, wasn't around. He was a big, fair, pudgy kid who had been the Second Platoon medic until he moved up the top spot; he had no lack of courage or skill. The Old Man was annoyed at his absence, but none of us knew where he might be. The tracks came roaring up the road in short order, and the waiting GIs clambered aboard and were gone in moments towards the now long-silent map coordinates where Charlie Mike had been. Helicopters were hovering over the area now, and artillery was beginning to whistle overhead. Before long we got the first reports from the troops entering the killing ground. Duckwiler showed up around then. He had been hanging out with some of the other battalion medics when the call had come, but he had missed the tracks. But by then we knew he wasn't needed. All of the wounded had already been evacuated by command choppers and medevac teams who had been in the area and vectored into the battle coordinates when they picked up the radio chatter. When Charlie Company swept the area they found the bodies of a handful of GIs, the rest of the dead and wounded having been flown out.

CHAPTER 15

A Little R&R

When we next got back to Lai Khe, I was officially moved into the headquarters barracks, on the other side of the company road, next to the orderly room, the officers' quarters, the commo bunker, the chow hall and the supply room. And I got my orders for R&R, which was to commence on December 22: travel on that day, five days in the R&R location, and another day for travel. Rest and Recuperation, or whatever the Rs stood for, was a highly structured program that provided troops in Vietnam with a week of uncharged leave, a cash bonus, and free transportation to and from a designated Asian city at about the midpoint of a 12-month tour. The cities available for R&R varied depending upon local political vectors, but among the ones usually available were Bangkok, Hong Kong, Singapore, and Tokyo. We got to pick first, second and third choices, and were given orders based on those choices and other factors; my first choice was Tokyo, and that's what I got. First stop after getting the orders was Tan Son Nhut airport. There was no road traffic between Saigon and Lai Khe due to enemy control of most of the countryside at that time, so local travel was by air. After getting my orders, I cleaned up a set of khaki Class As and hitched a ride to the Lai Khe airstrip, where, after presenting said orders, I got on a list of folks who needed to get to Tan Son Nhut. R&R travelers had priority, since if we missed our outgoing flight to the R&R city we were SOL. So pretty soon I was on a civilian jet bound for Tokyo. After arriving in Japan, we were bused to a depressing barracks–like structure where we saw a sappy film about proper behavior in Japan and a sergeant gave us a realistic orientation about VD and not getting so drunk we got arrested. Japan insisted that R&R troops arrive and sojourn in civilian clothes, so we ditched our khakis and had a chance to rent or buy a shirt, slacks and a cheap windbreaker jacket that more or less fit. Our black low quarter shoes were sufficiently generic to serve as civilian footwear. We were able to change our dollars for yen. We also had to pick a hotel and make a reservation before we were taken by van to the hotels of our choice, where we were checked in in the company of an R&R guy and required to pay for the five days of our stay in advance. Basically the system had been refined to prevent the most preventable disasters from befalling the intemperate or otherwise challenged young men who were about to be turned loose on the natives.

Tokyo in December 1966 was a world away from anywhere else I had been. I reveled in the strangeness. The first morning in my hotel I ordered breakfast from room service.

"You want Japanese or American?"

"Oh, Japanese, definitely," I replied. So I had my first sushi, and liked it as well. Venturing out on a grey, chilly morning, I gaped at the immaculate streets and shop windows, which were decorated with candy canes and Santa Clauses and Christmas trees. Morning rush hour produced phalanxes of serious, even dour, businessmen in western suits and overcoats, a handful of businesswomen in equivalent attire, and a few, a very few, women in traditional Japanese garb, kimonos and pattens. I saw a businessman intercept a blowing sheet of newsprint as it skittered across his path without missing a step, then deposit it in a trash receptacle as he passed. In the afternoon and evening, I saw tableaus of World War II veterans, in clean but ragged tan uniforms, their legs wrapped in puttees, the lizard-sharp peaked caps with flowing Havelocks and the Imperial chrysanthemum centered on the crowns, many missing limbs and with disfiguring scars, arrayed in perfect stillness in impossible positions of violent action. Lit from beneath by candles in bowls, and accompanied by haunting and alien melodies played by one of their number on accordion or flute, these veterans collected bills and coins from a few of the passing Japanese, most of whom did not even glance as they hurried by.

Quickly realizing that in my cheap clothes I looked like what I was, an enlisted man on leave, I located a Japanese department store which seemed a rough counterpart to Carson Pirie Scott in Chicago, and with some difficulty found a suit and an overcoat which were big enough to fit me. Tailoring took all day, but that evening I was able to feel less like a peasant while I was gawking at the big city. I was befriended, or so I thought at first, by a trio of young Japanese men who earnestly desired to improve their English. Over several days we met and explored a bit of Tokyo, ate noodles, and exchanged addresses. At some point they gave me a necktie as a present. I immediately removed the one I was wearing and pressed it on one of them, which he only accepted after great effort on my part. One of their number then told how the necktie giver had a girlfriend in Osaka, whom he missed very much, but, alas, could not afford to visit, and would I loan him the cost of a ticket on the bullet train, which would have been over a hundred dollars' worth of yen. I was mildly disappointed, but not surprised, that the whole endeavor had been a scam and declined to reunite the lovers.

During the evening, touts streamed out of the bars and cabarets, trolling for American GIs. Dressed in my finery I was able to confuse some of them, and quickly learned to respond to their bonhomie in German, which again confused some of them. I had a drink at one large club with live entertainment; an emcee came on stage and directed a spotlight to various GIs arrayed in the ascending tiers of tables.

"Hey there, where you from, my man?" he would say into his microphone.

"Texas!"

"Ah so, Texas, you cowboy, huh?" Much laughter and applause. "Where you from?"

"Chicago!"

The emcee grabbed an air tommy-gun and pretended to shoot in a great circle. "Rat tat tat tat, ha ha!"

The light landed on me. Three days ago I had been slogging through the boonies with a weapon, and was not amused by the smug Japanese.

"Where you from, friend?"

"Vietnam," I shouted. The guy deflated, clearly not having expected an uncomfortable truth, and shook his head, making disapproving noises. But he perked right up when another, more docile, GI got in the spotlight and the show went on.

The next night I ventured into another club that seemed a bit more cool, with at least some Japanese patrons and a jazz trio rather than ersatz Beatles on stage. A Japanese lady came by and asked if she could join me; delighted, I agreed and tried to engage her in conversation. She said her name was Koneko. I had a couple of drinks, but despite a buzz eventually noticed that she was tossing back shots of brown liquid with amazing rapidity. An unobtrusive waiter was plying her with these and rubber stamping a piece of paper on the table by her side. I reached over and picked up the paper, which was pretty well filled with little red rubber stampings.

"What is this?"

"You buy me drinks," she muttered.

"The hell you say," I said. Even as I started to get up the waiter appeared with a tiny glass and reached for the paper with his stamp.

"I'm out of here. I bought you one drink," I said, and as I put on my coat, furious mostly at myself, a bouncer and his buddy appeared.

"You pay!" he brandished the paper in my face, and named a ridiculous amount of yen. I was sorely tempted to pitch into the little fellow, but was sober enough to realize that I might not be viewed as innocent in the matter of ordering drinks, and that this was not my turf. I pulled out a handful of yen and dropped them on the table.

"That is it, you fuckhead. You're running a fucking scam. Get the fuck out of my way." I said this loud enough so that heads turned, and the guy and his buddy backed off long enough to let me get to the street door. Once on the sidewalk I stopped to put my coat on, and the bouncer came out behind me and grabbed my arm.

"You pay or I call MPs," he shouted. I shook him off and turned on him, absolutely ready for some cathartic violence. I was majorly pissed. I moved closer to him, in his face really, with my fists raised and shouted back, "You do that, call the MPs. I'll wait."

He paused for several beats, during which time I briefly wondered if he was some martial arts master who was going to dance on my head, but he muttered something like, "You come back with money, pay me later," and disappeared back into his doorway.

I strode off down the crowded and brightly lit sidewalk, really burned at myself for getting suckered. A minute later I felt a hand on my arm, and wheeled on what I assumed was the guy from the bar. But it was the lady for whom I had bought the many drinks. I sort of stared at her in confusion. She was probably in her twenties, older than me, and attractive, in a short, stocky, square-built kind of way. She was well-groomed, with shiny black hair put up in some fashion, dressed in simple Western clothing, and wearing a coat.

"Please, I am sorry," she said, backing up a step. "I must make you buy drinks, or lose my job."

This made some sense to me, and I felt my anger at her ebbing, though not disappearing. I was amenable to the idea that we were both victims in that transaction. I mumbled something to that effect and she brightened, putting her hand on my arm again.

"You come home with me?" she asked.

I didn't have to think about it too long. The five months or so I had been in Vietnam was the longest I had been celibate since losing my virginity a couple of years before, and I was certainly susceptible. Some discussion of money followed as we walked, and the whole transaction, despite the drink scam, seemed to work out for me. We took a subway to an apartment, which was pretty much devoid of personal touches, and may or may not have been where Koneko lived when she was off duty but it was extraordinarily clean and neat. An older woman met us at the door to the apartment, and a brief conversation in Japanese ensued, after which the older woman bowed and left. Koneko directed me to a small room and indicated I should undress and put on a light robe, which I did. Meanwhile, in another room, she drew a bath in a deep tub. Having changed herself into a similar robe, she led me to the bath and we both disrobed. The water was hotter than any bath I had taken, but it felt good after it stopped hurting, and being naked in a big tub of hot water with a clean woman was about the best thing I could remember experiencing.

So clean, relaxed, sated, I spent the night with Koneko on a futon. In the morning I offered to buy her breakfast, and she took me back to my hotel on the subway. I gave her my room number, as I would have happily spent my last two days in her company, but something occurred in the hotel lobby which made her nervous and she left abruptly, with what might have been an apology. I suspect the concierge spotted her as a prostitute, logical enough when a Japanese woman comes in holding the arm of a young GI, and some communication occurred which I missed, making her aware of his disapproval. She never tried to contact me at the hotel, and I didn't go looking for her. But, all in all, I was happy to have chosen Tokyo for my R&R.

CHAPTER 16

Back to Work

Coming back from R&R brought me a rude surprise. Someone had broken open the hasp of my cheap tin footlocker and rifled my belongings. The only item of value that was missing was my Minox camera, but that was a valuable item; the cost of the thing was equal to about two months' pay. I duly reported the theft to the XO and complained to my buddies as well. A day or so later somebody told me a guy in Third Platoon had my Minox. When I tracked him down he said he had bought it from Sergeant Miller for 20 bucks, just before Miller DEROSed. I retrieved the camera and reported this to the XO, who shook his head sadly. "Hard to believe that Sergeant Miller would do something like that," he muttered. I thought so as well, but mentally filed it away in the never-can-tell drawer.

I was getting into the rhythm of the RTO job, and mostly liked it a lot. Particularly I liked the extra hours sleeping, usually around six hours a night. All was not a bed of roses, of course. RTOs were treated by their officers as useful beasts of burden, and were hung about with extra smoke grenades, and other useful items, like trees at Christmas. In classic GI revenge mode, most RTOs carried large numbers of what appeared to be spare batteries, but in fact were empty battery boxes filled with items of comfort and convenience. The rule was batteries should be changed every 12 to 24 hours, but a good one would last for days. Some of us were adept at appearing to change a battery while in fact simply removing and replacing the perfectly good one in the radio. Or so I have heard. We all did carry at least one spare, but the damn things weighed about

Pabst Blue Ribbon (photographer unknown; January, 1967). One of my so-called buddies took this shot during Operation Junction City, after a long, hard day in the boonies. Obviously we'd just been re-supplied. That's my radio I'm using as a backrest. This is the only picture I have of me in the field in Vietnam. Fortunately it captures the essence of ground combat pretty well.

five pounds and most officers thought four or five of them looked just right on the back of an RTO.

Soon after I returned to Alpha Company we received orders to prepare for an extensive operation in the fabled Iron Triangle, a pocket of mostly dense jungle to the west of Highway 13 and a little to the south and west of Lai Khe. The army named this operation "Cedar Falls" and it was intended to enter a VC stronghold, locate and destroy the enemy formations believed to be lurking there, and eradicate the local Vietnamese villages which were thought to support the communists. The rumors regarding the fearsome nature of both the terrain and the foe caused some anxiety, especially among the folks who had arrived after the battle on the 25th of August and had suffered through many tales of that débâcle from the survivors. The loss of Charlie Company's Lima

Platoon had only increased the general level of nervousness among the newer troops. Alpha Company had been extraordinarily lucky in the four months since August 25, with little action and few casualties, so while the new guys had substantial time in-country, some of them still had some acclimating to do. The rest of us weren't inherently any braver than the new guys, but we had long since reached our individual maximum sustainable level of chronic fear and had developed coping mechanisms to live with it. By now, for me, every minute in Vietnam felt like going over the lip of the water slide for the first time, looking a thousand feet straight down to almost certain death and not having a damn thing to do about it. You get used to living in mortal terror. So for the veterans, the Iron Triangle was just another set of map coordinates that might or might not coincide with a bunch of angry gook bastards trying to kill us, just like every other set of map coordinates in Vietnam.

So on the 8th of January, 1967, we choppered in to a clearing just north of the Iron Triangle. As the Old Man's RTO, my job was just to stick close to the Old Man, a task usually physically difficult because, at about 6 feet 6 inches, Captain Williamson could move swiftly and effortlessly through terrain than my shorter stride found severely challenging, but morally simple, as I no longer had to decide, within tactical limits obviously, where to go and what to do when I got there. My RTO colleague on the Old Man's company net, an SP4 I'll call Sanchez, was even shorter than me, but though small was whipcord tough and appeared totally fearless. Fortunately Captain Williamson spent most of his time talking on the company net and focused on the direction he was going, so when I lagged a couple of meters behind he didn't often notice.

About this time we had a change in our CP family, as the first sergeant, a thin, elegant Southerner with a thick white crew cut, had moved up to become battalion sergeant major. Our new first sergeant was a sergeant first class named Toliver, a dark, muscular Filipino with deep parallel tribal scars on his cheeks and a heavy accent. The contrast was alarming, at the beginning. First Sergeant Toliver was probably in his forties, but was physically able to run rings around most of us kids and had an endless store of soldierly competences which he was happy to share as needed. When he smiled, which was often, he displayed strong white teeth, a couple of which had been filed to points.

Our chopper landed in the second wave on a cold LZ. The Old Man led us quickly toward the edge of the extensive clearing, already getting crowded with GIs. Alpha Company was lining up inside the brushy limits of the LZ and we were getting into the customary slot for the CP between the lead platoon and the rest of the company. As we moved past the columns of kneeling GIs, Sergeant Floyd came hurrying bareheaded down the line towards the LZ, holding his left hand, which was wrapped in a bloody bandage. He barely nodded at the Old Man as he moved towards the incoming choppers. We briefly made eye contact. He was maybe a little pale, and had a worried expression different from his usual smirk. I thought at the time, one less worthless pussy-ass bastard for the company to carry. Later word went around that he had shot himself in the hand, which didn't surprise me, as there had been no incoming fire that I was aware of. While it is physically possible to shoot yourself in the hand with an M-16, the chances of that happening accidently seem vanishingly small. Anyhow, he didn't come back to Alpha.

The new Second Platoon sergeant, Willie Magee, was a smart, tough Korean War veteran and a huge improvement over Floyd. So other than that little incident, we commenced what at the time was the largest operation of the war, with most of the 1st Infantry as well as elements of the 25th Infantry Division. Other than assisting in the forcible relocation of a substantial number of Vietnamese peasants, Alpha Company had an uneventful ten days or so wandering through the jungle. While we didn't do much damage to the enemy, no one from Alpha Company was killed. We did find a few old bunkers and some rice caches. So we wandered around the Iron Triangle for a couple of weeks, watching gigantic armored recovery vehicles fitted with dozer blades cut highway-sized swathes through the dense jungle and miserable peasants being loaded onto army trucks with only the possessions they could carry, while their homes were torched and their crops and orchards bulldozed. The lower air was thick with wind-blown soil, ashes, and smoke, and the upper reaches of the heavens filled with prowling tactical aircraft, looking, usually in vain, for targets for their 500-pound bombs and napalm canisters. Since tac air never landed with unexpended ordnance, at the end of each mission the pilots would choose a likely clump of greenery to dump their combat load; the ground periodically shook with detonations and the black and greasy products of napalm combustion joined the other particulate matter in the air.

On the plus side, we were able to practice foxhole-digging skills as we implemented the directive from the division commander, General DePuy, to construct elaborate fighting and sleeping positions with sandbags and overhead cover. These new foxholes had firing positions on the sides, while the front of the hole was built up with sandbags and dirt. We started carrying empty sandbags around with us, and either cutting saplings or using steel stakes to make roof joists upon which we placed a layer or two of sandbags. In theory an attacking enemy wouldn't be able to engage the occupants from the front and would be picked off by troops firing from the sides of adjacent foxholes. This theory had its merits, but in good army fashion was required to be implemented even when local terrain features called for a front-facing firing position. While the new-model foxholes were not popular with those of us at the business ends of the entrenching tools, and in many instances were not tactically superior to the old open-front holes, they did get us into the habit of constructing mini-bunkers with substantial overhead protection, for which we would later be thankful. While we had often had been resupplied by chopper each evening, that process became the norm, so we had to clear a substantial area of jungle in addition to constructing our field fortifications for the night. And of course we had to disassemble and fill in the holes before we left the next morning, except on the rare instances when we patrolled out of the same RON two days in a row.

We did usually get hot chow in Mermite containers as part of the resupply. Our company cooks really did a great job preparing hot meals that we gratefully wolfed off paper plates, often washed down with tepid canned soda and beer. The only photo of me in the field that I possess was taken during this mission, near the end of a long day. I was caught by one of my Second Platoon buddies leaning against my radio, dirty, bare-headed and sucking down a can of Pabst Blue Ribbon.

Mail call was a regular part of resupply as well, and outgoing mail was collected. Torn and raggedy uniform elements were replaced, and although jungle boots remained in short supply, I shamelessly parlayed my new RTO status into a pair of actual new boots in my exact shoe size, replacing my original set obtained from Mallonnee's estate, the canvas sides of which had by now worn through. I became adept at poncho hooch-building, an art form perfected in the jungles of Vietnam. A good hooch, made using the rubberized nylon GI poncho, provided excellent shelter from rain. This poncho was basically a seven-by-five-foot rectangle with a hood in the middle and metal grommets at the corners and along the edges. Using scavenged cord or string through the grommets, whatever local vegetation was at hand, and usually a thin stick through the neck hole and seated in the hood, an experienced grunt could make a comfortable and sturdy dwelling for two in less than ten minutes regardless of the terrain features around his position. The poncho was never worn as a garment, because it was shiny when wet and thus visible to snipers, and its size and texture made stealthy or rapid movement impossible, but the hooches it created were home to me and my buddies.

Meanwhile I was adjusting to the reality of being an RTO in a tactical situation. The biggest challenge was physical, as it took me two steps for every one of lanky Captain Williamson's. This didn't matter under most conditions as the terrain didn't permit speedy movement, but on one occasion during Cedar Falls we were moving along one of the massive, bulldozed tracks when Lieutenant Colonel Lazzell himself came on the battalion net. I was only a few meters behind the Old Man when the call came in, but just at that point Captain Williamson got a call on the company net and took off along the tumbled jungle detritus which lined the cleared area, towing Sanchez while having an intense discussion with some platoon leader and oblivious to my efforts to catch up. I suppose I could have yelled at him to slow down but that would have been a serious breach of RTO conduct, as we were always supposed to be within arm's reach, so I just sped up as best I could. Lazzell came back on the net every ten seconds, and was getting more pissed each time, not satisfied with my gasps of "This is Alpha Six Kilo, wait one."

Finally the Old Man paused and I was able to catch up, giving him the handset with a panted "Devour Six actual for you." Lazzell's first words to the Old Man were "Your RTO is flat on his ass!" but then he got to the substance of the call and didn't elaborate on how long he had been on hold, which was probably about a minute and a half. I got a look from Captain Williamson, but that was all, and there were no official consequences. But the look was enough. I was never flat on my ass thereafter, at least in that particular manner.

So Cedar Falls wound down with only a handful of Alpha casualties. Nobody was killed and that made it a pretty good operation from a grunt's standpoint. I was able to catch up with Second Platoon from time to time. Greg Murry had been in the hospital since before Christmas with a bad leg infection which had turned into septicemia, but had recovered and was back in the platoon. Greg became weapons squad leader, which was a good move for Second Platoon. Alan Roese also got his rifle squad about this time. In the interval José Garcia had taken over Greg's M-60 machine gun, with Donnie Gunby as his assistant gunner. Losing Floyd and gaining Magee as platoon sergeant, the platoon was in pretty good shape. Rod Floutz also moved up to squad leader about this time. In the not too distant future my own survival would depend on the competence and courage of Second Platoon—Greg, José, and Donnie in particular—but at the time I was just happy to see my old buddies in a position to take care of each other.

CHAPTER 17

Tet Truce

Back in Lai Khe, we had a couple of days off, then choppered north for another road-security operation along Highway 13, near the village of Bau Bang, where Charlie Company's Lima Platoon had been wasted. We had been in the same area twice before. As was usual with road-clearing operations, we were working with armored units, in this case the first squadron of the 4th Cavalry Regiment, 1/4th Cav, known as the Quarter Horse, which was also based in Lai Khe. This operation took place over the Chinese Lunar New Year, called Tet by the Vietnamese, the biggest holiday for the mostly Buddhist and animist folks who lived outside of Saigon and a couple of other larger cities. A tiny percentage of the population practiced Roman Catholicism as a legacy of the late French colonial regime, and incidentally formed whatever indigenous ruling-class South Vietnam could claim. But for 95 percent of the hearts and minds we were supposed to be winning, Tet was a combination of Thanksgiving, Christmas, and New Year's, a time for family reunions, feasts, gifts, and parties. Whoever was running the war had decided that there would be a truce over the days during which Tet was celebrated, culminating in the actual New Year's Day which was February 9. We got these facts explained to us by some officers at a formation, along with a barely veiled sub-text, which was that while we couldn't conduct *offensive* operations because the pussy-ass boys in the striped pants had made a deal with the gooks, we could naturally conduct *defensive* operations to protect ourselves from the treacherous Little Red Bastards, and we would do this aggressively and constantly. Got that, boys? Aggressive defensive patrolling was the order of the day.

So we were choppered a few klicks up Route 13 and arrayed ourselves along the east side of the highway, mostly facing east and north. Saigon was to our west and south, and the idea was that the VC would be streaming in from their Cambodian sanctuaries and jungle redoubts to spend Tet with their families in Saigon, and we would defensively kill some of them. A couple days into the operation a Second Platoon gun team, not José's, had been surprised by some VC who fired them up and took off, wounding three of our guys. The VC got clean away. Later that week a Second Platoon night ambush patrol watched a large VC formation lope down a trail and across Highway 13. This was reported on the radio and Captain Williamson alerted our mortar platoon to be ready to engage. We at the CP were poised for the sound of rifle fire, but for whatever reason the squad leader in charge of the ambush didn't engage the VC. Next morning the Old Man and his faithful RTOs checked out the area and it was obvious that a large number of folks in rubber sandals had used the sandy path that the ambush had been designed to interdict. The Old Man was pissed at the missed opportunity and shortly thereafter Greg Murry, who had been on the radio the night before, quietly but emphatically describing the enemy presence, was permanently elevated to squad leader and the incumbent went elsewhere.

So clearly the VC were utilizing the truce to move some bodies around, but all our aggressive patrolling had to show for it so far was three wounded GIs. Lieutenant Colonel Lazzell became aware of our missed opportunity and came by the Alpha Company CP. He emphasized the need to kill some of the little bastards before the truce was over and they went back to their impenetrable jungle lairs.

In aid of this totally defensive and peaceful, truce-respecting pursuit we had some exotic assistance in the form of a couple of M-42A1 Dusters. The Duster is a twin-40mm pom-pom anti-aircraft gun turret, designed for World War II warships, mounted on an M-41 Walker Bulldog light tank chassis. These bad boys, like the quad-.50 cal. anti-aircraft machine guns mounted on World War II half-tracks, which were also deployed in our general area, were designed to engage low-flying aircraft but were also useful as anti-personnel weapons. Somebody at the Pentagon must have stumbled over a cache of these relics and figured, what the hell, let's ship 'em over. I had made Renwal plastic models of these very same vehicles, not that many years before, and was thrilled to see them in the flesh, though skeptical about their usefulness. I shouldn't have been, as on the last night of our operation, just before Tet proper, around 10 p.m., heavy firing jolted me awake. Quickly donning my weapon and radio, I took off with the Old Man towards the sound of the fracas. What I had heard was mostly outgoing M-16 and M-60 fire, as a Third Platoon ambush patrol fired up a bunch of VC heading towards Saigon. Other elements spotted some VC running across the highway in the same direction, and the Dusters roared off down the highway and started firing their twin cannon into the gloom. The pyrotechnics were impressive, as the weapons produced thick clouds of white smoke which clung to the ground and reflected the yellow muzzle flashes and red tracers as they fired hundreds of rounds of 40mm into the brush. Those cannon were designed to put large numbers of shells very rapidly into the air as a battleship's last defense against kamikaze attacks, and sounded like machine guns on steroids. Of course the Old Man was checking out the various sources of firing, first the ambush patrol, which had killed four or five VC, including a young woman soldier, and then the highway next to the Duster platoon. Running around in the brush at night with only a captain and another RTO, none of us armed with anything more lethal than a pistol, was a new experience for me. At one point, when I heard somebody in the brush, I proved to myself that I could in fact draw my .45 and chamber a round in less than a second. Fortunately Captain Williamson didn't notice that, as my intended target turned out to be the Third Platoon lieutenant and his RTO. Of course, Sanchez on the company net could anticipate these rendezvous as the arrangements went through his headset; on the battalion net I was stumbling around clueless. That incident did inhibit any remaining tendency to draw my weapon in anger, which I only did on one other occasion during my tour.

We found the Third Platoon and four dead VC, including the young woman, all with weapons and packs. I had a chance to go through the woman's pack, looking for intelligence material, but all I remember finding was a tiny vial of what turned out to be perfume. I was disturbed and saddened by this discovery, but didn't have time to process this feeling before we were on our away again. Determining that there were no more VC coming from that direction, the Old Man took off back towards the highway, where the Dusters were revving up. We reached the road in time to see the Dusters and some tracks pouring 40mm and machine-gun fire into the brush across the road, which by now was a solid bank of roiling smoke lit by flashes and explosions. After the first few seconds there had been no incoming fire or any of the enemy's characteristic green tracers, and our firing tapered off. While we remained vigilant until dawn, nothing happened the rest of the night. As soon as it was light, the Old Man checked out the dead VC on the east side of the highway again, after which we went back to road and checked out the west side, which the Dusters and tracks had fired up. Despite the hundreds or thousands of rounds fired, there was only one body close to the highway, the remains of a VC who appeared to have taken a direct hit from a 40mm round. His head was not in evidence, and his torso had been opened with almost surgical precision and identifiable internal organs were arrayed like an anatomy diagram. Second Platoon was holding this part of our sector, and while we stood around, the platoon medic, not as squeamish as the rest of us, rolled the body over. He discovered the guy's head, which had been under the eviscerated torso, and a Chicom carbine. That weapon, a semi-automatic rifle with an integral bayonet attached to a swivel, was much prized as a souvenir as it could be tagged and taken home by the lucky owner, unlike the fully automatic AKs which had to be turned over to the brass, who presumably had ways of getting them home without attracting the attention of the MPs at the embarkation points. Or so I've heard. As we continued into the heavy brush to the west of the highway, we started finding more bodies. Many of them showed the devastating effects of the 40mm explosive rounds. Captain Williamson turned over the body of another woman, finding an intact AK-47 underneath, which he happily slung over his shoulder.

About this time Lieutenant Colonel Lazzell showed up to gloat over the dead VC. Somebody had located a bulldozer and dug a pit in a clearing a few hundred meters or so off the road and the bodies of the VC who had been killed on the west side were dragged into it and covered up. Lazzell had some of our guys drag the bodies of the four VC killed by the ambush patrol onto the highway and line them up along the shoulder. A considerable gaggle of buses, trucks, and smaller vehicles had backed up to the north, filled with Vietnamese families on their way south, probably to Saigon for the holiday. Lazzell had the idea of letting the vehicles go through one at a time, slowly, while grinning GIs gestured towards the dead VC. The dead, dressed in traditional Vietnamese peasant garb, and with their weapons and military accoutrements long since dispersed among the troops, looked small and harmless, and otherwise indistinguishable from the folks on the buses who were being taunted with their remains. Watching the expressions of the civilians in the vehicles, it occurred to me that we weren't winning any hearts or minds by this macabre display, and probably our morning's efforts were worth about a full battalion to the enemy. There was supposed to be a truce, after all, and I doubt the Vietnamese in the buses understood that we were just kind of operating within our rules of engagement. The Old Man and Lieutenant Denton, the Second Platoon leader, were both kind of glum, despite Lieutenant Colonel Lazzell's gleeful posturing, and I don't know what they were thinking. I kept my mouth shut, but what I was thinking was that this was a really stupid thing to do if we wanted to win the war.

Later that day we did a sweep of a village without much in the way of results, except the Second Platoon leader, Lieutenant Denton, was wounded by fragments from a Claymore mine and medevaced. His wound wasn't serious and he soon returned to the platoon. When we got back to Lai Khe, I was visiting my Second Platoon buddies, and while we were shooting the shit José told me that Sergeant Fellowes had been killed back at Lai Khe. Greg Murry had heard more details. Apparently Fellowes had been desperate to avoid our outing into the Iron Triangle during Operation Cedar Falls, probably having had his stem winded by war stories from the folks who had been there before. He had gone on sick call with some medical complaint, but the docs were unimpressed and he was returned to unrestricted active duty. But he must have been desperate, as he had then altered his sick slip to appear medically unable to take the field, and so missed the operation. Somehow his ruse had been discovered, and he was facing a court martial when, as an able-bodied denizen of the base camp, he was ordered to take part in a night ambush patrol at the laterite pit a klick or two south of Lai Khe on Highway 13. The night he was chosen the ambush was ambushed, and he took off running north up the highway as the first shots were fired. He was killed by rifle fire, shot in the back, perhaps by the VC, or perhaps not. Another kid, James Stewart, from the battalion recon platoon, was certainly killed by enemy fire in that engagement.

This otherwise mundane skirmish actually resulted in a change in the way the Pentagon reported casualties: up until then, after-battle reports listed casualties as heavy, moderate, or light, based solely on the percentage of casualties to the force engaged, but the actual numbers were not disclosed. Because the force engaged in this action was about eight GIs, and two were killed and several wounded, the Pentagon reported the engagement as one where the US suffered "heavy casualties." It must have been a slow news day, and this report made headlines in the US, for example, the *San Bernadino Sun* for February 2, 1967:

> U. S. Platoon Suffers Heavy Casualties
> SAIGON, South Vietnam (AP) A platoon of the U. S. 1st Infantry Division suffered heavy casualties when it was hit in pre-dawn darkness today by a Communist force northwest of Saigon. The platoon was on security duty in the Iron Triangle.

So it appeared that we had suffered a significant defeat, which didn't suit the folks running the war at all. Thereafter, the Pentagon generally reported actual numbers of US dead and wounded. So Fellowes in death contributed, at least incrementally, to the slow convergence of appearance and reality in the Pentagon's release of war information.

James B. Stewart, Kennewick, Washington, age 19. Recon Plt., HHC, 1/16 Infantry. Indiv was on security patrol when engaged in a hostile force [sic] in a firefight; Edward E. Fellowes, Buffalo, New York, age 24. Alpha Co., 1/16 Infantry. Indiv was on security patrol when engaged a [sic] hostile force in firefight.

CHAPTER 18

I Know I'm Gonna Die

On February 23 the battalion was airlifted from Lai Khe to a town up north called Sui Da, as part of the largest operation yet, Junction City. Instead of our usual choppers, we got to ride up on C-130 fixed-wing aircraft. Imagine a shoe box with tiny little wings and a huge tail, and a door that opens under that tail and forms a ramp. Around 25 young guys with various automatic weapons, grenades, trip flares, blasting caps, and other explosives are chivvied up the ramp and take seats on the floor of the aircraft. The sole nod to in-flight safety is a check by a sergeant that the visible weapons don't actually have a round in the chamber as the lads embark. After the last of the guys is seated on the floor, the ramp goes up and the couple of air force crewmen, notable by long cords running from their headsets, sit down on jump seats that fold down from the bulkhead that partially separates the pilots, who work up a ladder in a little cockpit that has windows and lots and lots of switches and dials, many of which we can see from our seats on the floor. That is all we can see, as the few windows in the hold of the aircraft are several feet above our heads when we are seated. After a time the engines roar, and the plane begins to shake. Dozens of sympathetic vibrations harmonically compete with the unmuffled turboprops. The crew are watching the engines out of little windows and speaking into their headsets, but of course whatever they may be saying is inaudible. The engines reach a crescendo of noise, the cargo bay fills with exhaust, and the aircraft lurches forward as the brakes are released. Bouncing and slewing, the box-like contraption accelerates on the pierced steel plates of the runway and in a few seconds the nose of the aircraft points upward at about a 50-degree angle. The GIs who had occupied every square foot of floor area before are now crammed together in the bottom third of the cargo bay, along with their live hand grenades and all, as the shrieking engines presumably are pulling the dead weight of the aircraft over the towering wall of jungle at the end of the airstrip. We find out the takeoff has been successful when we don't die in a horrific manner but instead level off as the sound diminishes from incomprehensible to merely frightful. The crew members scurry around checking wheel wells and engines and presumably reporting to the pilots on what structural components of the aircraft are still present. And almost before we get a chance to sit back and enjoy the flight, we're landing. Landing is sort of like taking off, but in reverse, in that we end up in a bunch in the forward third of the cargo bay. So finally the army has come up with a form of transportation that makes a helicopter assault landing feel comfortable and secure.

Ap Soui Da was like Ap Lai Khe, only smaller. We emerged from our aircraft onto a PCP strip not only shorter but even more tightly girded by tall trees than at Lai Khe. Trailing along behind the Old Man as he utilized the company net via Sanchez's radio to organize the platoons into their respective areas for the night, I realized that much of the new duty I had assumed was, well, boring. And with this I was basically OK. Soui Da was also noteworthy for the prepared emplacements we were able to occupy for the night, similar to Lai Khe's fortified perimeter, and for the handful of mortar rounds the VC lobbed into the battalion perimeter early the next morning, missing Alpha Company altogether. By sunrise the mortaring had ceased, as had the furious response from our own artillery, and we lined up by platoons and marched back to the airstrip, where we waited for choppers to take us into battle, or not. As it happened, the chopper ride was uneventful, and definitely less scary to me than the C-130's. The landing was treated as a full-scale air assault, with the chopper gunners lacing the treeline with their M-60s and the first wave of GIs, including Second Platoon, jumping off the choppers in mid-air and firing as they advanced towards the jungle. Although the battalion LZ where we landed had been heavily shelled previously, and was surrounded by fresh VC emplacements, there was no incoming fire.

We were greeted by the distinctive smell of freshly detonated artillery rounds and the organic matter which they had vaporized on impact, a smell both sweet and sharp, unpleasant without being foul, as we secured a section of the LZ for following chopper loads.

After an hour or so, the rest of the battalion had landed and we moved out to the north, along the verge of a narrow laterite road, Provincial Route 4. Unlike Highway 13, which was as broad as a two-lane city street at home, and cleared of trees and large brush for around 100 meters on either side, Provincial Route 4 was hemmed in by tall and dense jungle, in many places forming opaque and impenetrable curtains which reached to within two or three meters of the roadway. By now the road had been cleared of mines, although we passed a couple of recently damaged trucks which had been pushed off into the jungle alongside. The road itself was secured, more or less, by the Blackhorse Regiment, the 11th Armored Cavalry. This outfit consisted of lots of gunned-up APCs and M-48 tanks, as well as other mechanical odds and ends, and would have been formidable in open country, but the narrow road and enveloping jungle created something very like an arcade shooting gallery for the VC. One enterprising communist with an RPG launcher, which is basically a World War II-era Russian bazooka, could take out our heaviest armor with one round and be long gone before any retaliation was mounted. Whether there was only one stalwart and sneaky gook, or a bunch of them, we never knew, but something like 20 vehicles were hit during the course of the operation, including three M-48s. The $20 RPG round could and did pierce the seven inches of turret armor of these 45-ton bruisers, killing or wounding the occupants, and of course disabling the tank. As far as anyone on the ground could tell, this VC, known to us as the Mad Bomber, emerged unscathed despite a bounty of an extra week of R&R offered to any GI who could kill him. The Mad Bomber could strike at any time, but he (or she) preferred to hunt in the early evening, as the Blackhorse roared back to their laager.

Alpha Company lucked out in that we were assigned the first RON position, just a few hundred meters south down Route 4. We dug in with one side of our perimeter almost on the road, in a clearing partly natural and partly shaped by the VC, who had obligingly left us numerous bunkers and trenches which we incorporated into our defenses. The Old Man set up his command post in the middle of the southern half of the clearing, where we had the benefit of shade from some small trees. Our weapons platoon set up their 81mm mortar tubes in the middle of the RON, which was sizable enough to allow mortar rounds to clear the surrounding jungle, as well as permit a chopper to land near the road, from which we received ammo resupply and hot chow in Mermite cans. One of the perks of being an RTO was often getting out of foxhole digging, as Sanchez and I had to follow the Old Man around as he toured the company line. This RON was sufficiently compact and open that by the time we got back to the CP, the foxholes for the Old Man and the artillery FO had just been finished, but our positions hadn't been started. The ground was soft and sandy, easy to dig, so even though Sanchez and I didn't get out of doing our share of the digging, we had a pretty quiet start to the night. Of course we sent out squad-sized ambush patrols, one per platoon, not too far out because of the thickness of the jungle. A while after the patrols left, we heard the crump of an explosion to our southeast. First Platoon's ambush squad came on the company net: they had been hit while moving to their ambush site, and had a bunch of casualties. They were told to stay in place. By now the night had fallen and the jungle was impenetrably black, although light cloud cover and moonlight combined to provide decent visibility in the RON. Captain Williamson mobilized the rest of First Platoon, and sent them after their comrades. I could only imagine the unpleasantness of stumbling through the opaque darkness looking for the hunkered-down patrol, hoping that whatever enemy had struck them wasn't waiting around for seconds.

Everybody in the RON was on alert, manning their foxholes and staring into the darkness, but the jungle remained quiet. The First Platoon returned to the line, with one guy carried in an improvised stretcher and a couple of others walking wounded. The guy who was down was a kid from Philly named Kirby, who had joined the company just after I got back from R&R. I barely knew him. He was not moving and his buddies put him down under a big tree just behind the CP. His shirt was open and he had bloody field dressings taped to his chest. The platoon medic was working on him, along with Duckwiler, with flashlights and bandages. One of them had started an IV and I made myself useful holding the bag and staying out of the way. The platoon medic started giving CPR while Duckwiler rocked back on his heels and looked grim. After a while the platoon medic started sobbing, and was pounding on Kirby's chest and trying to breathe for him, but I thought the kid was gone. About this time a dustoff chopper landed in the clear area near the road, and some guys came over and grabbed the poncho Kirby was on and ran off towards the chopper, one of them taking the IV bag from me. Duckwiler put an arm around the medic and kind of signaled to me with his head that I should move on, which I did. I stepped around them and back to the CP, where the Old Man, the First Platoon lieutenant, and a couple of sergeants were hunkered down talking to a First Platoon GI. The guy had been on the ambush patrol, and hadn't gotten hit, but wasn't going to go back out with the reconstituted patrol.

"Sir, I'm sorry, but I know I'm gonna die if I go out," he kept saying.

Captain Williamson was talking straight to him, not yelling or overbearing, but trying to get him on track. "All your buddies are going out, you won't be alone out there, you've done this a hundred times," he was saying. But it didn't work.

"Oh, man, Captain, I know I'm gonna die."

Finally the Old Man told him if he didn't go out with the patrol he was going to be placed under arrest and sent back to Lai Khe for a court martial and he'd spend ten years in Leavenworth. The guy was pretty shaken up by this development, but was perfectly clear about his position.

"If I go out there I'm going to die, and I'd rather spend ten years in jail than die out in the jungle," he said.

Eventually the Old Man had him taken back to the Weapons Platoon area, and the new ambush patrol went out and spent the rest of night alone with their thoughts. The reluctant GI went back to Lai Khe on the resupply chopper the next day. I never heard what happened to him, but he never came back to Alpha Company. I didn't know the guy well, but he was an OK soldier, had been around for a while, and was definitely not a fuck-up or a coward. All of us lived with the knowledge that we could die violently at any time, but we didn't know when or even if it was going to happen, and most of us learned to live with the fear, which became kind of a background noise to life, which most of the time could be ignored as we tried to do our jobs. But living with fear is far different than walking to your own execution. From this kid's perspective, he had a choice: live or die. Once it comes down to that, subjectively, I might have chosen the Leavenworth option as well. But the Old Man had to do what he did; once going into greater peril becomes an option rather than a duty, lots of folks are going to decline that option.

The next day was business as usual for a road-clearance operation, first sweeping a section of Route 4 for mines or booby traps, sending patrols out through the jungle roughly parallel to the road, and then setting up observation posts at intervals a few dozen meters into the brush. Instead of doing all of that hot, dirty, and dangerous stuff, I strolled along behind the Old Man along with Sanchez, mostly just listening to the battalion net. When battalion called for the Old Man actual, as opposed to just checking in with some administrative bullshit that I could handle on my own, my job required that I get the headset to him within a few seconds. As mentioned, Colonel Lazzell had a habit of designating deficient soldiery as being "flat on his ass," and my object was to avoid having that sobriquet applied to me or my boss, to the extent I could prevent it. So far into my RTO experience I had been able to, except for that one time during Cedar Falls. The road was being used by all sorts of military traffic, and in addition to our efforts was being secured by the Blackhorse guys in their tanks and tracks. The Blackhorse officers often stopped to chat with the Old Man, and I got to listen in to some of these conversations, as well as conduct a few of my own with the armored outfit's RTOs and drivers. Just before we had flown into Suoi Da, a bunch of airborne units had actually jumped out of choppers with parachutes and landed in an LZ a few klicks up the road. This had been reported in *Stars and Stripes* as the first combat jump since Korea, and I was curious about it. Talking and listening to the Blackhorse, the following story emerged.

The airborne mystique was huge in the army; every infantry officer and almost every career infantry NCO expected to cycle through jump school and win the coveted airborne badge. This little silver badge consisted of a parachute surrounded by feathered wings, and next to the Combat

Infantry Badge was the most treasured proof of manly prowess that the army offered. The badge itself was awarded upon graduation from the three-week jump school, and many soldiers proudly wore it whether or not they were assigned to airborne units, but some grizzled old troopers sported a tiny gold star in the shrouds below the parachute canopy: the award for a combat jump. The Vietnam officer generation wanted desperately to add that little star to their badges, but tactical opportunities for combat jumps had not so far emerged. Somebody way high up had gotten the notion that you could justify a jump as part of the opening of Operation Junction City, which had as a featured goal the capture or destruction of COSVN, the Central Office of South Vietnam, thought to be the Commie Pentagon from which all the mischief flowed. COSVN was believed to be located somewhere north of Tay Ninh and west of Loc Ninh, the area in which we were operating. The only downside of this plan was the possibility, remote but nonetheless real, that COSVN might actually be there and take advantage of the slowly descending paratroopers in typical treacherous Asian fashion, by shooting them. But oh, those shiny little stars! So the Blackhorse was sent up the road, along with a battalion of straight-leg infantry, to surround and secure the drop zone so the only sequelae of the combat jump would be the normal quota of broken legs and twisted ankles. Thus the 173rd Airborne Brigade, and a bunch of visiting firemen, added the combat jump star to their badges.

The only untoward event of the day occurred when a bunch of loose artillery rounds was found by the roadside in our sector, probably offloaded when one of the Mad Bomber's victims was towed away. Greg Murry, who had somehow become the designated demo man for the company, was called in to blow the ordnance in place, which he did. But the winds bloweth where they listeth, and an overachieving shrapnel fragment struck Sergeant Acquinino in the abdomen as he was resting on top of one of the CP bunkers back in the RON. He was dusted off and, while the wound wasn't mortal, he was short enough that he never returned to Alpha Company, so we made do without a commo sergeant thereafter. Greg always struck me as someone who loved explosives a little too well to really be trusted with demolition work, but he continued to be the company's go-to guy for blowing things up.

A couple of nights later, during that quiet period between the end of the road-clearing and before the ambush patrols went out, while most of the company was eating chow, cleaning weapons, or finishing up a letter in the last of the twilight, a brilliant red ball of fire, the size of a baseball, looped over the jungle wall and into the middle of our RON. It struck a mortar tube and bounced into the air.

"Incoming! Incoming!"

Everybody dropped whatever they were doing, grabbed their weapons, and dove for the nearest foxhole or bunker. Some nervous troops fired off a few rounds into the gathering darkness, but after that all was still. Crouched in the CP bunker with the Old Man and Sanchez, I listened as the platoon leaders all called in to report nothing happening. Meanwhile the artillery FO was calling in fire missions based on his estimate of the direction from which the round had come. As it was otherwise a quiet night, over 500 rounds of 105mm, 155mm, and 175mm were dropped onto a patch of jungle somewhere. When a suitable interval had passed, life resumed. The round had scored a direct hit on an 81mm mortar tube, but otherwise the only casualties were minor bumps and bruises caused by collisions as the guys were diving into their bunkers. The next day we figured out that the Blackhorse was hot-footing down the road on their way to laager and, having become respectful of the Mad Bomber's prowess, were shooting up the jungle along the road as they went. We were used to this racket and weren't paying much attention to it. When one of their .50-caliber tracer rounds took a bad bounce and landed in our RON, nobody connected that to the armored column, which was long gone before we got ourselves sorted out.

The following named individual has been reported (dead) in Vietnam as the result of hostile action: PFC Steven Kirby, Philadelphia, Pennsylvania, age 19. Alpha Co., 1/16 Infantry. Indiv was on ambush patrol when hit by fragments from hostile Claymore mine.

CHAPTER 19

Count 'em Again

The errant tracer-round incident occurred around February 25. The next couple of days passed in what had become a pleasant routine, at least for the lucky RTOs who didn't need to pull ambush patrols or man OPs in the jungle. Our holes were dug, our poncho hooches were dry, and choppers brought in hot chow and mail every day. Torn fatigues were replaced, C-rations were plentiful, and, with our RON serving as a base camp to return to, we didn't need to carry everything necessary for combat or convenience while we patrolled Route 4. While the Mad Bomber continued to haunt the roadside, taking his toll of large vehicles, it seemed that Charlie had decided to leave us footsloggers alone for a time after his hit on our ambush patrol. This changed, suddenly, on February 28.

By late morning on that day, Alpha's rifle platoons were distributed in OPs in the jungle and the weapons platoon was guarding the RON. The Old Man and his RTOs were basically hanging out on the road when a call came in from battalion: Bravo Company had been on a company-sized patrol out of their RON, into the dense jungle to the east of Route 4, and had run into some shit. The Old Man called his platoon leaders, and within minutes the OPs were starting to come in. We returned to the RON and, as the rifle platoons returned over the next hour or so, we packed up the gear that had been left that morning. I added the extra batteries and smoke grenades that I had been stowing in my hooch, which I disassembled and tied to the bottom of my radio pack. Everybody grabbed a few Cs if they could and, within a couple of hours from getting the first radio call, we were lined up along the road. Artillery was going overhead and impacting in the jungle a few klicks away, and air support was buzzing around as well. So much for a quiet morning. A flight of Hueys landed right on the road and in a few minutes we were skimming the trees in the direction of the fight. The Old Man, along with me and the rest of his CP, landed in the second wave of choppers. The guys from the first wave were moving towards the treeline, firing from the hip, while artillery was still impacting in the jungle nearby. When we got off the chopper I heard the crack and whine of incoming small-arms fire, but the Old Man ignored this annoyance and moved around the perimeter, making sure the rifle platoons had formed a cohesive defensive ring. The LZ itself was on the small side and surrounded by truly towering hardwood trees. The afternoon sun was shining through the heavy foliage of the canopy, and shafts of sunlight illuminated patches of the undergrowth as we moved into the tree line. The weapons platoon was hunkered down with their mortar tubes at the edge of the clearing. As I hurried after the Old Man I heard a shot and followed the bullet flash as it passed a meter or so to my right, through one of the sunlight shafts, the only time I ever saw a bullet in flight, and watched it hit a kid from weapons platoon. Probably the sniper was aiming for the Old Man, an obvious target at 6 feet 6 inches, with his tail of RTOs. The kid from weapons was lying prone and facing away from the shooter, and the bullet hit him in the back of his leg right behind his knee. This guy was in a rifle platoon and had been wounded twice before, once by booby-trap shrapnel a couple weeks after he joined the company and then, a couple weeks after returning to duty, by shrapnel from a short artillery round. He was a nice kid, but hadn't been in the company much since he was always getting wounded. He got put in weapons platoon as an act of mercy, I guess, but the battle goddess wouldn't be denied. He didn't die from this wound, but he didn't come back to the company, either.

After Alpha Company got the LZ secured, another flight of choppers brought in another company, and they moved right through our perimeter towards the sounds of the battle zone. By mid-afternoon all we were hearing was sporadic sniping, though the artillery was still coming over with some regularity, with jets and gunships buzzing around in the near distance. Later our Charlie Company choppered in and joined us for the

RON; we dug in for the night, which was spooky, with a lot of nervous intermittent firing, but nothing untoward occurred.

First thing in the morning of March 1, we got the word from battalion to do a sweep of the battle zone and get a VC body count. We filled in our foxholes and moved off through the jungle. Charlie Company had helped take out Bravo's dead and wounded, and what was left of Bravo was sent back to Lai Khe, while Charlie Company maintained security around the area. The area where the fighting had occurred was mostly under tall trees, interspersed with smaller trees and with brush and shrubs lower down, classic triple canopy jungle. The signs of battle were all around, field dressings, scraps of clothing, and cartridge cases, though the big stuff had been policed up by Charlie Company. Here and there we found fresh VC bunkers and hooches, with a lot of their broken and abandoned gear, stuff that didn't make good souvenirs. We made a pretty good sweep of the area, going through the thickets and checking the trees. We found exactly four dead VC; the Old Man checked each one out. Charlie Company reported finding three bodies in the area they were patrolling. When we were done, the Old Man reported this to battalion, and Lieutenant Colonel Lazzell came on the net.

"Alpha Six, Devour Six, how many of the little bastards did you find?"

"That's seven confirmed."

"Seven? Goddammit, somebody's flat on his ass. Count 'em again, you find those bodies. Out."

The colonel sounded unusually tense. The Old Man didn't say anything for a while, then called the platoon leaders on the company net and told them to double-check their areas for bodies, blood trails, anything. Pretty quickly each platoon reported back that they didn't find anything they hadn't already reported. The Old Man was shaking his head, tight-lipped. He motioned for my headset and called up battalion and gave them the count again.

Again, Lieutenant Colonel Lazzell picked up. "Those little bastards always take their KIAs with them. If you found seven, they must've taken ten bodies for each one. That's 70 confirmed."

Somebody from brigade came on the net: "Hell, Devour, if you got 70 that means 140 for sure."

"Roger that, and another 30 or 40 died from wounds, they carried them off, we got blood trails all over," said Lazzell. "We got 160, 170 of the goddam little bastards."

Division came on the net. "What's your body count, Devour?"

"This is Devour Six, we got between 160 and 170 but we're still counting, sir."

"Well that's good, that's good, keep counting and make sure you got 'em all, great work, Devour, keep it up."

Captain Williamson was holding the handset, and listened to this unfold with a tight, unhappy, expression; army captains don't chime in when colonels and generals are having a discussion. I was listening with my headphones and was bemused. In 20 minutes I had gotten the fundamental lesson in American military politics in Vietnam in 1967. I didn't process that knowledge for a while, as life went on, but nothing thereafter felt the same as before I had been a fly on that particular wall. Later that day a Vietnamese interpreter went through some of the VC material we has collected, and interrogated a prisoner, then told us that the unit which had engaged Bravo Company had been a field hospital company. When Bravo's first patrol had entered the hospital area, the patients had been evacuated and a handful of VC had stayed behind as a rearguard, engaging Bravo while the others escaped. The seven bodies we found probably represented much of the enemy which was actually fighting. Bravo Company lost 25 guys killed outright, and a similar number seriously wounded, at least one of whom later died of his wounds.

This action resulted in a posthumous award of the Medal of Honor to Sergeant Matthew Leonard. The citation reads verbatim:

> For conspicuous gallantry and intrepidity in action at the risk of his life above and beyond the call of duty. His platoon was suddenly attacked by a large enemy force employing small arms, automatic weapons, and hand grenades. Although the platoon leader and several other key leaders were among the first wounded, P/Sgt. Leonard quickly rallied his men to throw back the initial enemy assaults. During the short pause that followed, he organized a defensive perimeter, redistributed ammunition, and inspired his comrades through his forceful leadership and words of encouragement. Noticing a wounded companion outside the perimeter, he dragged the man to safety but was struck by a sniper's bullet which shattered his left hand. Refusing medical attention and continuously exposing himself to the

increasing fire as the enemy again assaulted the perimeter, P/Sgt. Leonard moved from position to position to direct the fire of his men against the well camouflaged foe. Under the cover of the main attack, the enemy moved a machine gun into a location where it could sweep the entire perimeter. This threat was magnified when the platoon machine gun in this area malfunctioned. P/Sgt. Leonard quickly crawled to the gun position and was helping to clear the malfunction when the gunner and other men in the vicinity were wounded by fire from the enemy machine gun. P/Sgt. Leonard rose to his feet, charged the enemy gun and destroyed the hostile crew despite being hit several times by enemy fire. He moved to a tree, propped himself against it, and continued to engage the enemy until he succumbed to his many wounds. His fighting spirit, heroic leadership, and valiant acts inspired the remaining members of his platoon to hold back the enemy until assistance arrived. P/Sgt. Leonard's profound courage and devotion to his men are in keeping with the highest traditions of the military service, and his gallant actions reflect great credit upon himself and the U. S. Army.

That night we moved into the RON that Bravo Company had prepared the night before they walked into the meat grinder, and continued our basic chores of road security and patrolling for a few days. During the middle of the night of March 3, I was off watch and sleeping when I was awakened by Sanchez. Hastily pulling on my radio, I ran after Sanchez and the Old Man who were on their way across the perimeter, where a confused gaggle of shouting and flashing lights surrounded an M-48 tank which was sitting and belching diesel smoke in the middle of our RON, right in Second Platoon's position. The RON was close to Route 4, and the tank came down the road for some unfathomable reason around midnight, veered out of control, and overran the sleeping position of Robert Pointer's machine-gun team. Fred Burris was killed outright and Pointer was injured slightly. His ammo bearer was also injured and was dusted off for good. As a result of these losses a couple of new guys, Carl Johnson and David Ward, were added to the Second Platoon gun teams. Carl stayed with Pointer, and José traded his ammo bearer for Ward.

The following named individual has been reported (dead) in Vietnam as the result of non hostile action: Frederick Burris, Monsey, New York, age 19. Alpha Co., 1/16 Infantry. Indiv was in a night defensive position along a road when a tank went out of control and struck him.

CHAPTER 20

Down in the Ville

We continued to patrol around Route 4 for the next few days and, while sporadic fighting continued, neither Alpha Company nor the rest of the 1st Battalion were involved. Around March 12 the battalion choppered back to Soui Da and, while the other companies returned to Lai Khe, Alpha got loaded up on C-130s and sent to the Phouc Vinh base camp, the home base of another brigade of the 1st Infantry Division. That brigade was out in the field, so Alpha was tasked with guarding part of the base camp perimeter. We got to bunk in the relative luxury of wooden barracks, belonging to the 1/26 Infantry, and while the rifle platoons were busy with local patrolling in the jungle and paddies around Phouc Vinh, I was pretty much resting up, pulling commo watch and following the Old Man around the perimeter. One day, when we were down in the brigade HQ area where a bunch of officers were meeting, I ran into a high-school classmate, Craig Johnson. I hadn't even known Craig was in the army, much less Vietnam. We shot the bull for half an hour or so; turns out Craig had been badly wounded early in his tour in a rifle platoon, and on his return, still seriously banged up, had gotten a job driving his battalion commander's jeep. Craig and I had been pretty good friends during four years at New Trier, and had mutually participated in most of the ways kids got in trouble during the early 1960s. Seeing him in this new context and connecting for a few minutes, while the officers were off conferring, provided a measure of comfort. Sharing a dream, or a nightmare, with another real person would probably feel like this.

Aside from meeting Craig, this sojourn in Phouc Vinh was blessedly uneventful, terminating in a C-130 flight back to Lai Khe around the 22nd or 23rd. Things were so peaceful there that, for the first time in my tour, I counted up the days I had left in country. Turns out I was about eight months into my 12-month tour, well over the half-way point, and so I allowed myself to think about life after Vietnam. Being caught up on sleep, and not having been shot at much lately, I found I was almost enjoying the army life. I found the climate congenial, the surroundings interesting, and the Vietnamese attractive. Lai Khe, and the army, were feeling a bit like home.

Most of my duties during this interval in the base camp centered around pulling commo watch and general maintenance of the camp; my exalted status as RTO didn't get me out of filling sandbags and other chores, but such tasks didn't take more than three or four hours in a typical day. Commo watch was a 24-hour proposition, but there were usually five or more of us on the roster, so my usual time in the bunker was a couple of two- or three-hour shifts a day. The commo bunker was tight, dug a meter or so into the ground and constructed of sandbags and bars sort of like steel fence posts, which rested on the sandbag walls and were overlaid with waterproof fabric and more sandbags. The bunker was about two meters wide and three meters long, entered through a small entrance cut into the ground and lined with wooden boards scavenged from artillery shell boxes. The interior had a wood floor and wainscoting made of the same material up to ground level, where the sandbags began. We had generator-powered electricity now, and the commo bunker had an overhead electric light, so during the long, boring night shifts I could read, drink coffee, and smoke in comfort. I made friends with some rats that lurked in the interstices of the sandbags, feeding them C-ration fruitcake, which they alone of the inhabitants of Lai Khe seemed to enjoy. As our Lai Khe sojourn continued, some of the guys bought locally manufactured wire cage-type rat traps and set them around the barracks area. The rats, when captured, would be executed using novel and painful methods. Switek was of course the most ingenious of these rat-catchers. Rather than confronting him directly, as I didn't think my advocacy for the rodents would be well received, I made late-night patrols around the hooches before or after my commo shifts, releasing any captives and flattening the cages. I was smart enough to keep quiet when the rat-catchers bitched about the wrecked cages.

We didn't usually get to spend much time in Lai Khe, but it was our base camp and when we did get a few days there it was sort of like being home during a college break. Vietnamese civilians had developed a regulated infrastructure which included Alpha Company's own laundry and tailor shop in a little hooch under the rubber. A Vietnamese family ran this, with an attractive and intelligent young woman usually handling the front counter. Her English was pretty good, and her demeanor was attentive but very professional; I don't think the guys hit on her that often, if at all. I for one didn't like the baggy, oversized jungle fatigues issued by the army, and when I could had mine tailored so the trouser legs were almost tight in the calves and the jacket was cut thinner around the chest and waist. This wasn't primarily for appearance, but to get rid of the excess fabric which impeded movement and took longer to dry. The cost for this kind of custom tailoring was ridiculously low, although often we would go out on an operation before our orders were complete, so it might be weeks before we'd get the finished stuff. The establishment provided embroidered nametags, CIBs, and full-color regimental crests, as well as rank patches and, of course, the Big Red One for our left shoulders. I also got a comfortable, locally manufactured baseball cap there, with a big colorful embroidered 16th Infantry Regiment crest on the front. Lai Khe had gotten so civilized that we didn't need to wear our steel pots when we were off duty. The regulation baseball cap as issued was ugly and uncomfortable, and nobody who'd been in-country any length of time would be caught dead in one. From time to time an itinerant barber would show up and cut hair, and various entrepreneurs would wander around selling luke-warm Cokes, usually carried in a yoke-like arrangement of two tin pans with a piece or two of straw-flecked ice floating in dirty water. All of these folks were regulated in some fashion by the army and the local Vietnamese civil authorities, and they formed part of the background to life in the company area.

The Ville was another matter. Reached by a sandy road through the sprawling army presence, it was within the perimeter of the Lai Khe base, but was separately enclosed by wire and guarded by U. S. Military Police. The series of structures that I came to appreciate as the indigenous architecture were mainly constructed of scavenged lumber and sheets of metal, often and obviously acquired in some manner from soft drink or beer concerns, as they were covered on one side by hundreds of Pepsi or Budweiser lithographs waiting to be cut and rolled into containers for a beverage. Brightly colored and professionally painted signage in almost-but-not-quite-perfect English described the establishments, which included barber and tailor shops, dry goods and souvenirs, and of course bars and massage parlors. I had been down a couple of times early in my tour to buy necessities which the army didn't provide, including a tin foot locker and a thin mattress to put on my steel-sprung army bed frame, but I hadn't returned. For whatever reason, this sojourn in Lai Khe felt different. Maybe with the end of my tour finally, if barely, visible on the horizon, maybe with a growing acceptance of the pervasive fear of death which filled the interstices of my existence, I joined a couple of buddies, freshly showered and in clean fatigues, for a trip to the Ville.

My buds had done this before, and we went straight to one of the café-type establishments, which included an open terrace within a bamboo frame, set with a few small tables and chairs. We ordered beers, and were soon approached by three Vietnamese women, who asked if we wanted them to join us. All of them were small, slim, and dark-haired, wearing simple Vietnamese-type clothes, without much or any makeup. Their hair was clean and they were well groomed and, well, pretty. The lady who chose to sit by me must have been between 20 and 30 years old, with dark hair cut around shoulder length in a Western style, but otherwise not distinguishable from any of the Vietnamese women I had seen on the roads and in the villages. We bought them small glasses of tea, at Vietnamese whiskey prices, and made small talk. Their English averaged fair at best, but they were lively and relaxed. I felt so good to be sitting in clean clothes, on a chair, without a weapon in my hand, drinking a beer and chatting with a woman. While I had some hope that there would be some intimacies involved eventually, I was as content as I had ever been in that moment.

At some point, though, I noticed a line of blue numbers on the left forearm of the lady sitting across the table from me. After a bit I asked her about them. My companion pushed up her sleeve and showed me a similar set. I ran my finger over them: certainly, it was a tattoo. The girls talked together in Vietnamese, and then one tried to explain to me.

"The police do this. Vietnam police, in Saigon. Make a law."

"You mean Diem?" I asked, pronouncing the name "Deem."

More Vietnamese passed between the ladies.

"You mean Diem, I think?" She pronounced it correctly, "Yee-um," and continued, "No, not him. Brother, Ngo Dinh Nhu, he run police, say all working girls get these."

I was bemused. I tried to ask what the reason was, was it registration, for health reasons? This was a difficult question to get across the language barrier, but I persisted.

"Oh no," my lady friend said, when she understood. "This way, no boy will think we are good girls, later, and marry us."

I processed this while the small talk resumed, but it didn't take much processing for me to decide that any government that would tattoo its own citizens to maintain some notion of purity wasn't one I wanted to die to preserve. I had one other opportunity to go to the Ville a few days later, and met up with the same lady. Her grace and beauty continue to amaze me, and I hope she eventually met a young man who had the good sense to ignore her tattoo.

CHAPTER 21

Down Among the Dead Men

Our sojourn in Lai Khe came to an abrupt end on March 31, around mid-afternoon, when Captain Williamson and the other COs were called to battalion HQ. I didn't take the call, but as he left he told Sanchez and me to be prepared to move out on short notice. That didn't sound good to me, but since the Old Man took his jeep and driver I didn't need to follow along, and just hung around the company HQ after I got my gear in shape to travel. Shortly after the Old Man left, the XO sent out the word to the platoons to saddle up and fall in on the road. Captain Williamson came back in a hurry and behind him a bunch of trucks. The guys were already loading up on Cs, and in no time we were heading for the Lai Khe airstrip, me and Sanchez riding in splendor in the back seat of the Old Man's jeep, along with First Sergeant Tolliver, the rest of the troops crammed into the big trucks. Turned out the 1st of the 26th, the same outfit whose perimeter we had been guarding in Phouc Vinh, had run into some nasty shit near a place called Ap Gu. A platoon patrol had run into more VC than they could handle, the platoon leader was dead, and first the rest of that company then another company had been sucked into a firefight in thick jungle. Now we were going in. Oh man, I thought, this feels like the 25th of August, except this time I know enough to be scared. As usual we dismounted and the platoons lined up along the edges of the airstrip. Another company from the 1/16 was already waiting when we got there, but we were first into the choppers when they arrived.

This was not my first hot air assault, so I was able to enjoy the fireworks despite being terrified. The choppers swung out over a large, grassy clearing surrounded by high jungle. In the near distance various fighter-bombers were making runs and large explosions were erupting in their wakes. Cluster bombs and napalm were impacting among the trees. As we lined up to land, the side gunners on the leading choppers opened up with their M-60s. The first wave landed and the guys moved to our right, firing as they went. As usual, I couldn't tell from the chopper whether anything was incoming, but a few seconds later our chopper reared up and touched the ground. Captain Williamson was always the first one out. We followed him as best we could towards the woodline. Since at this stage of an assault he was mostly concerned in getting reports from the platoon leaders, Sanchez was having to keep up with him; I had the luxury of staying a couple steps behind until Devour Six came on and I had to catch up and hand the phone to the Old Man. By then, though, I was pretty confident that there wasn't much of anything incoming. The characteristic stink of exploded ordnance and rich soil filled the air. The available senses were pretty much consumed by the cacophony of the choppers as they touched down and took off, the intermittent roar of the jets, the detonation of bombs, and the rattle of small arms as our troops entered the woodline firing, but I saw no green tracers, and among the clamor I did not hear the characteristic whistle of incoming small arms. So by the time I reached the woodline and could kneel down beside the Old Man, I was breathing a little heavily but I was reasonably confident I was not going to die in the next few minutes.

After the last of the choppers that had carried Alpha Company took off, the Old Man organized the platoons and moved them out across the large, irregular clearing, liberally spotted with clumps of trees, some of them substantial, and surrounded by tall, dense jungle. We had landed in the northeastern quadrant of the clearing, and we set off through the more or less open area towards the southwest, spread out and moving quickly. We were heading towards the perimeter established by the 1/26 the day before. The Old Man pretty much stayed in the center of the clear area, and of course Sanchez, me, Lieutenant Dalton, the artillery FSO and his RTO, the first sergeant, and a couple of other HQ troops followed along. The rifle platoons were moving parallel to us and closer to the woodlines on both sides, and the weapons platoon was pretty much behind us. After a few hundred meters of fast walking I heard a brief whistle and the *whoomp!* of an incoming mortar round, followed shortly after by a few more that landed in the clearing. The rounds were coming from behind us. At this point we picked up the pace right smartly and moved through the remainder of the cleared area. We were all pretty well spread out so these rounds did us no damage, and were answered by a couple of jets, which pounded the area behind us with large bombs, bringing the bombardment to a close. I hoped the jets had found their targets, not just scared them off, but time would tell.

Dark was imminent when we reached our destination: a large clump of trees tucked into a pocket of the clearing near its southwestern end. The 1/26 perimeter was just visible to the southeast, two or three hundred meters across a perfectly open grassy area. The Old Man quickly placed the rifle platoons in a perimeter and we began to dig in. Resupply choppers had dropped some stuff off earlier in the day, and we got a bale of sandbags, as well as some water cans, from the clearing. This was one time when nobody had to be told twice to dig in and make sure the overhead cover was adequate. Fortunately there were plenty of sandbags and lots of trees to donate limbs for roof joists, so when we were finished, around midnight, we all had little bunkers, constructed in the approved 1st Infantry Division fashion, with firing ports to right and left, solid sandbag revetments in the front, and at least one layer of sandbags overhead. Captain Williamson made the rounds of the perimeter several times, encouraging the platoon leaders and checking the progress of the excavations. When we weren't trailing along, Sanchez and I were digging and filling sandbags, as the headquarters group had about eight people total, so we needed a couple of big bunkers, and of course the officers didn't usually dig, though I recall the FSO and the XO pitched in that night. Our little headquarters area was in the northern middle of the company perimeter, right behind the Second Platoon's section of the line. Although we were not in the true jungle, there were trees of various sizes throughout the area. The actual perimeter ended at about the last of the trees, so that to the north and east we were looking across a wide grassy area, with clumps of brush and low hillocks here and there. The open area continued past a line of jungle in the northeastern corner of the clearing, no longer visible in the darkness. Somewhere in that direction was our initial landing zone. Around midnight our bunkers were done, and after one last circuit of the perimeter we were able to set up some commo watches and get some sleep.

I was awakened in the thick darkness by Captain Williamson kicking my boot. "Incoming!"

As I scrambled to my feet and snatched my helmet and radio pack I heard the *pop-pop-pop* of mortar rounds leaving their tubes, not that far away. I was the last one into the HQ foxhole, helmet in one hand and radio pack in the other, sliding in feet first and trying not to bang into anybody. The Old Man was to my right, with Sanchez and then the first sergeant on his right. Our foxhole had good overhead cover, but unlike the fighting positions on the perimeter it had both front and side firing and observation gaps. Sticking my helmet on my head, I shrugged into the radio pack and wrapped the headphones around the helmet's camouflage belt. As I fastened my pistol belt I saw the flashes of exploding rounds in the far darkness to our right front.

"They're hitting the First of the Twenty-sixth," somebody said.

The muffled crump of the rounds impacting on the ground, and the louder crack of tree-bursts, followed on the heels of the flashes. The *pop-pop* of new rounds leaving their tubes overlapped the sounds of explosions.

"Jesus, how many tubes do they have?" I breathed.

Somebody from battalion called for a situation report, and the Old Man held my handset in his left hand while he had the platoon leaders reporting in on Sanchez's handset in his right hand. Maybe 30 seconds had passed since I had been asleep. I was transfixed by the sight of dozens of rounds impacting in the distant treeline, sudden bright red and yellow flashes against a background darker black than the sky. I had time to wonder if we were going to skate when the first rounds landed in our perimeter. There seemed to be at least two calibers of rounds falling, small ones which were probably 60mm, and some much larger ones. The single layer of sandbags overhead suddenly seemed pretty flimsy. I hunkered down as far as I could and still peer over the lip of the firing port. A round landed to my near left and dirt and shrapnel whizzed and pattered overhead. We got some tree-bursts which sent branches as well as shrapnel flying, some of the latter impacting our overhead sandbags with the *thunk!* of an axe biting a tree trunk. I had time to hope everyone in Alpha Company had got the word and was under cover. The rounds were still coming down on our positions when the clearing erupted with green tracers, going from left to right, into the darkness that covered the 1/26's perimeter. Green tracers meant VC, and there were plenty of them out there. The neon-green rounds seemed to arc lazily into the darkness, sometimes rebounding gracefully, sometimes disappearing as they struck. Red tracers started to cross the path of the green ones, coming from right to left, the combination making a Christmas display of fireworks as the intensity of the small-arms fire grew and kept growing. The air was dense with moisture and smoke, so each track of tracer, muzzle flash, or explosion was reflected and magnified; parachute flares began to pop and sizzle, though their brilliant white light was muted by the fog.

"They're in the 1/26 perimeter," came over the battalion net.

From what I could see the fighting across the clearing was now intense and confused, with red and green tracers going every which way. About this time, the rounds stopped falling on our positions and the green tracer started coming right at us.

The light show was now a bit less interesting as my role changed from audience to participant, but I kept my head high enough to watch the gratifying response from our foxholes as plenty of red tracer arced out to our front. The green ones were whizzing overhead, looking to be no more than a few inches above us, but the roar of our answering fire drowned out any more distant sounds. After a bit the frequency of the incoming green rounds peaked and began to yield to the red tracer which sought and found the muzzle flashes in the darkness and extinguished them.

The sky was lightening, and at first light the clearing in front of us was blanketed in a thick ground fog. But as the night drained away the fog lifted and I could see the dark shapes of the enemy in the clearing straight ahead. Almost immediately after the fog lifted artillery rounds started to fall to our immediate front, and the enemy figures were obscured by the gouts of dirt as our barrage rolled after them towards the now-visible woodline to the north. In between the detonations of the artillery, jets swooped in, dropping napalm and cluster bombs, and Huey gunships supplemented the bombing runs with rocket and Gatling gun attacks. The explosions now sent bodies and parts of bodies into the air, as the last of the able-bodied VC faded into the jungle, pursued by streams of red tracer from our positions.

The artillery continued to pound the jungle, but no more green tracers were apparent. The Old Man clambered out of the hole, followed by me, Sanchez and the first sergeant. While the sky was hazy and bright, the sun was still behind the jungle wall to our right, and the ground to our front was still half-covered in fog and smoke. I could see GIs moving around in the 1/26 perimeter. The air was thick with the stink of exploded rounds and gunpowder. To our front, Alpha Company guys were coming out of their foxholes and sitting on the ground behind the overhead cover, with their legs down the entrance hole, and aiming their rifles at the shapes emerging from the fog. Maybe a dozen VC were lying in shell holes or behind undulations in the grassy area they had scraped out during the fight. None of them was firing at this point, and several were waving their hands in the air as they remained prone. First Sergeant Tolliver joined the firing line, and started plinking at the VC with his CAR-15. The Alpha guys opened up on anything moving, or anything that looked like a VC. I had been happy to see the artillery smashing into them, but the ones that were out here now didn't seem like a threat and were trying to surrender. More guys came out of their foxholes and, their elbows resting on the sandbag tops of the foxholes, started taking careful, aimed shots at the moving forms. They reminded me of GIs at a shooting range. My first impulse was to yell at them to cease fire, but I bit that back, realizing that I wasn't going to have much luck with a moral argument after what we'd just been through. The Old Man was talking on the handset and getting reports from the platoon leaders; we had some wounded, including the Second Platoon leader, Lieutenant Denton, who was hit by mortar shrapnel, but nobody had been killed. Denton didn't return after this wound, and was replaced as Second Platoon leader by Jules Sermuskis, a steady and competent officer. The Old Man was talking on the handset and getting reports from the remaining platoon leaders; he was staring at the shooters and seemed accessible, but not inclined to order anybody to stand down.

I thought fast, and spoke up: "Sir, if we could capture some of those wounded VC, maybe we could get some intelligence?"

The Old Man must have been thinking along the same lines as I had. He reached for my handset.

"Devour Six, this is Alpha Six, we got some wounded NVA to our front. We could bring 'm in for interrogation, over."

Lieutenant Colonel Lazzell seemed receptive and put us on hold and checked upstream, while the guys on the line steadily reduced the number of potential survivors to our front. After a bit he came back on with permission to bring some of them in.

"Cease fire!" yelled the Old Man. As the firing slowed and stopped, he collared Sergeant Magee, the acting Second Platoon leader as Denton had headed for the dustoffs, and directed him to send a squad out to police up some wounded, using fire and movement tactics. This was like something out of training, but with real bullets, and some of the guys were not enthusiastic about going out into the field, but after a bit the first fire team moved out in classic infantry fashion, and took up prone firing positions in the middle of the field; the next team then moved to their right and took up similar positions. This leapfrogging continued until the first team reached the woodline. After a bit a couple of VC who were still breathing were located, and some GIs went out and brought them back in improvised poncho litters. Our medics started to try to patch them up while our Vietnamese interpreter began firing questions. They were conscious and responding, but I don't know what eventually happened to them.

Dustoffs had started coming in for our wounded and for the casualties the 1/26 had suffered. Helicopters of various sorts were continuously landing and taking off by now, with some resupply coming in between dustoff flights. Lieutenant Colonel Lazzell showed up as well, and told Captain Williamson that Alpha Company was going to have the privilege of taking the battalion point as we pursued the enemy, determined by now to be elements of our old adversaries, the NVA's 271st Regiment of the 9th Division.

Lazzell put the Old Man in his (Lazzell's) two-seater observation chopper and sent him off to reconnoiter the likely route the VC had taken; we were just a few klicks from the Cambodian border, over which we could not venture, and that was their likely destination. So Captain Williamson took off in the chopper while the rest of us cleaned up as best we could and got our gear in order. Lots of mortar rounds had landed in our perimeter, and in their haste to take cover many of the guys had left their non-essential gear where they had been sleeping, and much of it was now the worse for wear. Greg Murry's web gear had been shredded by a direct hit from a round, and other folks had similar problems. Even the stuff which hadn't been hit was covered with dirt, including my butt pack, gas mask, towel and some other stuff which hadn't been attached to my radio pack. As I did my best to clean up and get my gear sorted, I marveled at the razor-sharp shrapnel fragments sticking in the sandbags of our overhead cover. Without that cover the barrage would have pretty much wiped us out, but instead we were down maybe a dozen guys, none of them with life-threatening wounds. Maybe we should have had a shovel on our CIBs instead of a rifle.

In a few minutes the Old Man was back and we were moving northeast through the clearing-spotted jungle in two columns, the rest of the battalion following behind. Everywhere we went we encountered evidence of a hasty retreat by the VC. Dozens of bodies, which were usually recovered by the VC when they retreated, lay in bunches where violent death had found them. As we passed into thicker jungle, beyond the area which had been our landing zone the day before, we found firing positions, bunkers, and well-concealed shelters, enough for hundreds of soldiers. I didn't see any abandoned weapons, suggesting the retreat had not been a rout, but there was some discarded small- arms ammo and a few mortar rounds strewn about, as well as clothing and other personal items. After a bit of slogging we found some mortar positions, probably the ones from which we had been bombarded: perfectly round holes a meter deep and maybe six or seven meters in diameter, with neatly perpendicular sides. Many empty cases for 82mm rounds, and a few unexpended rounds as well, littered these emplacements. But there was no contact with live VC; the surviving attackers had chosen not to engage us further and had managed to get across the border. In a reprise of August 25, we ran into another battalion that had been vectored into our area by some higher-up who had not informed us, or was unaware of, the likelihood of meeting up. Alert point men from both units exercised restraint, happily, and only greetings were exchanged. Our Old Man and the CO of the lead company of the other battalion turned out to be buddies from West Point and took a few minutes to catch up while giving their RTOs a chance to get acquainted. Aside from that, and gathering up and blowing some of the unexploded ordnance, much to Greg Murry's evident delight, and policing up packs and papers found on the dead, there was nothing for us to do. The VC seemed so thoroughly beaten that the likelihood of an ambush must have been discounted by the brass, for by late afternoon the battalion returned to our old perimeter the way we had come, for once not bothering to take a different azimuth. We spent the night in our old positions.

The next morning was the beginning of another hot and humid day, and we spent the first few hours of daylight getting squared away from the effects of losing the wounded guys and replacing the damaged equipment and consumed ammunition from the preceding couple of days. Around mid-morning I started to notice a bad smell, which at first I thought was my breath; I gave my teeth a second, vigorous brushing, which didn't help. I figured out the smell was from the dozens of decomposing bodies to our front, a sweetish, garlicky stink that settled around us on that hot, windless day. We went out on an uneventful patrol and returned to the perimeter that night, and the smell, of course, was worse. Going in and out of perimeter by necessity took me past many of the bodies, and I was struck by the youth of most of them. These kids looked younger than me, and here were a lot of them who weren't going to get any older. I was appalled by the waste, of them and of us. My parents had always encouraged me to think of medicine as a career, and I had had some interest in that, but seeing these hundreds of dead kids made me wonder if a lifetime in medicine could prevent or postpone as much suffering and death as one day of a war. Preventing a needless war, or even shortening one, seemed a pretty laudable goal at that moment, with the stench of so many dead young men in my nostrils.

We extracted on April 4, in big twin-rotor Chinook helicopters, only the second time I had been in that elderly, noisy, and ungainly type of aircraft, and were deposited at the Quan Loi base camp. This felt like a vacation after the last few days, but it was not to last. The only noteworthy incident occurred shortly after we arrived. The Old Man was making the rounds of our prospective RON when a particularly shiny Huey landed just inside the perimeter, and an oddly dressed civilian jumped out, ducked under the blades, and strode towards us. Captain Williamson was about 6 feet 6 inches tall and most of that was legs, and while he usually took pity on me and Sanchez, on that occasion he was moving as fast as he could without actually running. I didn't have that option, and was trotting just to keep close enough to avoid a court martial for desertion. The dude who got off the chopper had a brightly colored civilian shirt worn over OD jungle pants and shiny combat boots, but when I finally caught up I recognized the eyebrows from the newspaper pictures: it was Westy himself. He gave a few words of encouragement to the Old Man, who was braced at attention, shook his hand, returned a salute, and was back on the chopper and in the air before I could catch my breath. The gist of it was that the Old Man was congratulated for his company's part in the recent fight. I was thankful we hadn't had any more notice of the visit, so we were spared trying to make ourselves pretty for the brass. I never did figure out why Westmoreland was flying around in a flowered shirt over his jungle fatigues, unless it was to signal that he didn't expect a brass band and an honor guard.

CHAPTER 22

Vacation in the Mountains

After one night in Quan Loi we were loaded into C-130s and took a longer-than-usual flight to a town called Song Be in the northeastern corner of III Corps. From there we were choppered, in Chinooks again, further north over a hilly and thickly forested stretch of country near Highway 14. The area we landed in was near another Michelin rubber plantation, now abandoned, which had been under VC control for years. Somebody had decided this was a perfect place for a U. S. Special Forces camp, so the Green Beanies and their native irregulars, called Mike Force for reasons obscure to me, set about building one, which they named Camp Bunard. Our job was to provide security while the construction took place, so we settled in for what turned out to be about three weeks of good weather and little enemy contact. Most of the battalion was present, so there were plenty of other folks to take the rotations of day patrols. Since we were expecting to stay in the same place for a while, we spent a lot of time doing what in the army is called improving our position, which here included digging elaborate sleeping as well as fighting positions, with plenty of sandbags for overhead and lateral cover and, for the guys on the perimeter, actually digging shallow trenches between the fighting positions. I built myself a nice one-man sandbag hooch abutting a larger shelter that three or four of the headquarters guys had constructed. The Old Man and the FSO shared a small tent which was pitched over an excavated rectangle and reveted with sandbag walls. They actually had canvas army cots, with the legs resting in holes in the dirt floor, and a roof of sandbags laid on steel posts overhead. Our company HQ area was

José Garcia and C-130 (1967)

near the top of a gentle hill, with excellent drainage and usually a nice breeze which, despite the heat, made for pleasant days and nights. With plenty of folks to share the commo watch and abundant C-rats, I grew rested and fat. My hooch design called for custom roof joists, and while I was trimming the branches off one such with my sheath knife, despite knowing better, I sliced downward and whacked my left index finger to the bone. Duckwiler, who was to medical procedures as Greg Murry was to explosives, happily sutured the gaping wound and gave me a shot of antibiotic. Getting cut in such a dumb fashion was embarrassing, but getting sutured without a local anesthetic was uncomfortable enough to expiate any shame I felt at the self-inflicted wound. The sound of that little curved needle poking through my skin was actually the worst part.

At some point during our stay in the camp we were sent out to police up some equipment that a Mike Force detachment had left behind when they were attacked by VC. We found a few weapons and a bunch of full packs which, in the absence of clearly identifiable owners, were distributed to needy and deserving infantrymen. I obtained an almost new set of camouflage pattern jungle fatigues, just a little small, and a couple of bags of the rations which were provided to the irregulars. These were similar to the meals–ready–to–eat later generations of soldiers enjoyed, and seemed a nice change from C-rations. One of the ones I got had a sort of smoked mutton main course which was especially tasty. Whether it was the mutton, which my xenophobic American digestive system rejected, as First Sergeant Tolliver suggested, or a pathogen of some sort, I became deathly ill the next day with a high fever, vomiting and diarrhea. I was so weak that I had to crawl across our little company area to vomit in the brush. At least I was so obviously sick that I didn't have to pretend to do anything for a couple of days, and one of the other guys carried my radio. Duckwiler gave me a couple of shots and, after dogging it for two days I was back on my feet.

One of the functions of the Special Forces was to try to win the hearts and minds of the Vietnamese by performing acts of charity, including provision of basic medical services. On this occasion a Special Forces medical team was going to visit a camp of displaced Montagnards, as the tribal peoples of the Central Highlands were called by the French, and then by us. These folks were distinct from the Vietnamese in language, culture, and phenotype, but were assiduously recruited by Special Forces due to their hostility towards the communists. Things were quiet at Camp Bunard, so the Old Man offered to send me along with the small security detachment we were providing for the doc, and I happily accepted. This entailed a short chopper ride over the jungle, then a climb up the side of a small mountain after landing in a natural clearing about halfway to the top of the slope. My job was limited to carrying one of the cases of supplies, and was merely invigorating after becoming used to humping the 60 or 70 pounds of equipment I usually carried. The Montagnard encampment itself was almost invisible, even after we reached it, consisting of small shelters built of bamboo and leaves, hidden amongst the trees and mountain terrain. The doc had been here before and knew and was known by the locals, some of whom approached him for treatment as soon as we arrived. The squad that was providing security spread out into the jungle, but after I put down my bag I was able to wander around. The Montagnards were smaller of stature than most Vietnamese, who were in turn petite by American standards. All were slim, and most were handsome and fit. Older members of the group showed the effects of a hard life, of course, many of them toothless or with missing or obviously damaged limbs. Their garb was simple, colorful, and suited to the climate, in that both men and women tended to be bare chested. Material culture was even simpler than that found in the Vietnamese villages, almost exclusively consisting of handmade wooden implements, baskets and carriers woven of various materials, and a few hand-forged tools. In one of the shelters I noticed an adult individual lying on a straw mat, with his or her back to me, in a fetal position. At first I could not tell whether he or she was alive or dead, and I entered the shelter for a closer look. A young woman, perhaps a relative, was kneeling nearby. She was wearing tribal clothing and ornaments, and was breathtakingly beautiful. I tried to communicate with her regarding the status of the person on the mat, without objective success, but our brief moment of contact left me sure that she understood exactly what I was concerned about, and that she was not impressed by our helicopters, weapons, or medical technology. I was stunned by the knowledge that intelligence and sophistication, and the depth and breadth of human feeling and understanding, had nothing—nothing! to do with the material manifestations of culture. I bowed, left the hut, and found the doc. He knew about the old guy on the mat and shrugged; there was nothing to be done. Shortly after, the last of the wounds sutured, the antibiotics given, and the pills dispensed, I shouldered the much-reduced weight of the bag I had carried up the mountain and we descended to await the return of our chopper. I thought a lot about that brief encounter. It wasn't that I wanted to trade places with the Montagnards. But the fact that they didn't want to trade places with *me* put the complicated and expensive machinery with which we were surrounded in a different perspective. Certainly I could see that Communism, with its notions of enforced conformity to an ideal of progress, wouldn't sit well with the tribal people, but I began to suspect we weren't doing these folks any favors by being here, either.

There were some other spooky elements in the hills around Camp Bunard which we brushed up against a couple of times. One such occasion was a company patrol through some dense forest in a hilly section of the area adjacent to the camp itself. This terrain was not like the jungle at lower elevations, being without the thick, almost impenetrable vegetation that choked the jungle floor. Walking through it was more like walking through a dense thicket of timber in North America, with sight lines measured in meters rather than centimeters. On this trip the company had reached the top of a low hill, though it was hard to judge relative elevation because of the trees. At the crown of the hill we found what looked like a perfect circle perhaps 30 meters in diameter and five or six meters deep at the center, with sides sloping down at a uniform angle of 30 or 40 degrees. The lead platoon had gone ahead and disappeared in the brush to our front when the CP group came to the depression. The day was overcast and windless, and everything around us was dim and still. The Old Man halted the column and consulted his map, which didn't show the terrain feature we were staring at. Whether it had been constructed or was the result of natural weathering and subsidence was unclear, but certainly it was not new; the trees on the rim and in the crater itself were substantial. We knelt down on the rim while the Old Man and the FSO pored over their maps. Without warning, small-arms fire began to our right front, and rapidly reached the level usually heard in the midst of a serious firefight. Turning around, we arranged ourselves on the slope of the crater, peering over the edge while the firing continued. I didn't hear anything like incoming rounds, though. The Old Man called battalion to report possible contact, describing our location as a natural fortress. He then spent some time talking on the company net, and pretty soon the firing died away. No one was hit, and no one appeared certain of why the point platoon had opened fire. Sometimes this could happen, even with veterans.

Near the end of our stay Switek, whose DEROS was approaching, was sent back to Lai Khe to finish the last ten days or so of his tour doing base camp stuff. I really hated Switek, but he had been a fixture in Second Platoon since I arrived, and I figured I should see him off. I was on duty at the time, but I asked the Old Man if I could say goodbye and got permission. Switek and a couple of his buddies were waiting by the edge of the field that the resupply choppers used, with a bunch of other folks going back to Lai Khe, when I came over.

"Hey, Switek," I said.

He looked at me and smiled, I think the first genuine smile I ever saw on his face. "Hey, Clark, fuck you," he said.

"Fuck you too, man," I replied.

We shook hands, the chopper landed, he got on and I never saw him again. But walking back to the CP, I realized that I missed the bastard.

CHAPTER 23

Traveling Around

So after three weeks we flew back to Quan Loi and thence to Lai Khe for a few days. Perhaps because of the relatively peaceful interval, I had spent some time thinking about the year I would still owe on my enlistment after my Vietnam tour was over. The GI rumor mill had it that you could volunteer for another six months in 'Nam, then get an early out from the army. I was actually enjoying the infantry life, thriving on the exercise, friendship, and army stuff, although the moments of stark terror in the midst of combat did not improve with repeated experience. There were other options folks talked about, however, and some of them sounded appealing. I wondered if my RTO experience would make me attractive to any of these outfits, and what the process for getting such a job entailed.

During this Lai Khe interval I wangled a pass to Saigon, where I located USARV headquarters and tried to get some hard intelligence. I was referred to Long Binh, where the relevant office was relocating, and found that most of the options I had heard about were either Special Forces only or units attached to airborne divisions. I was counseled to sign up for jump school after my post-Vietnam leave and try again after I qualified if I really wanted to sleep out in the woods. Other suggestions included a reference to some folks out of country for which I needed a leave and a passport. So I put some of these suggestions into play when I got back to Lai Khe, including applying for leave and signing up for assignment to jump school. I rejoined Alpha Company in time for a C-130 flight to Tay Ninh City, where we stayed an uneventful few days.

The CP was located literally under the muzzles of a section of M-107 and M 110 self-propelled guns. These weapons, mounted on tank-like chassis, fired 60- to 100-kilogram shells through barrels ten meters long at targets over 30 kilometers away. I had often been at or near the receiving end of these shells, and they were effective and accurate as far as I could tell. From time to time these guns would fire a shell or two; a body wallop from a high-pressure air wave would precede the actual sound of the muzzle blast, which then would be followed by a jar coming through the earth. Because of the guns, we had ample supplies of wooden ammunition crates, some of which I used to make a nice raised floor for my sandbag-covered, dug-out sleeping shelter. While the combination of air blast, noise, and earth tremor was daunting at first, within a couple of days this faded down to merely annoying and then barely enough to wake me up for a few seconds. There's nothing like a dry wood floor in your hooch to improve the neighborhood, whatever its drawbacks.

During one of our battalion sweeps out of this base camp, Alpha Company was moving along an azimuth through relatively open country when Bravo Company, several klicks away, took a few sniper rounds. While this encounter didn't quickly develop into a real firefight, where there were snipers there were usually organized units of VC nearby. We were directed to change course and move closer to Bravo, so we could provide support if needed. The only problem was a deep, fast-flowing river than ran across our path. No more than ten meters across, it had no bottom that we could discover, and there were no fords or bridges we could locate. But it turned out that First Sergeant Tolliver had a large coil of nylon rope in his rucksack. After conferring with Captain Williamson, he offered to get us across on what he called a two-rope bridge. I had never heard of that particular device, but the Old Man had Ranger tabs and must have been familiar with the beast. So Tolliver stripped, slid down the steep, muddy bank, and swam across the river holding one end of his coil of rope. Seeing him naked, I was amazed at the scars he had collected, some of which were obviously ornamental, like the ones on his cheeks, and some of which obviously weren't. This was one tough hombre. He clambered up the opposite bank, fastened the rope to a sturdy tree, and returned, dragging the loose end, which

Sergeant Klutts, another Ranger, took from him and fastened to a tree on our side. Running through a few carabineers, the double strand of rope was tightened so that it vibrated like a guitar string, about a meter up the trunk of trees on opposite sides of the stream. Tolliver continued to swim lazily against the current, clearly enjoying the cool, refreshing water. So how is this a bridge, I wondered. Looked more like a couple of tightropes to me. But in a minute, Klutts demonstrated the technique: he took one of the two ropes in both his hands, and put his feet on the other rope, which, despite its tension, was pushed downward by his weight. Moving sideways, he stepped off the bank, and the foot rope went downward so that he was supported by it while holding onto the top rope with both hands, and was able to sidle quickly over the river. While he had to scramble at the end, because of the diminished distance between the ropes where the opposite bank began, he was followed by a few more intrepid types who set up a human chain to help the rest of us scramble the last meter or so. Tolliver continued to maintain station just downstream, to recover anyone who slipped, but as I recall we all made it across. As the ropes stretched, the bottom rope was under water at the midpoint of the crossing, but nobody who made it across, and we all did, was going to complain about wet boots. So in about half an hour we were hustling our dry butts through the scrub to link up with Bravo, which, it turned out, didn't need us anyway. But I at least was pleased as punch to have walked across a river on a two-rope bridge.

And then it was back home again, once more in my least favorite form of transportation, the C-130. While we were back in Lai Khe a new guy, who'd only been in the company a few weeks, was killed on an OP when some other GI fired a Claymore for no apparent reason. He wasn't from Second Platoon and I don't think I ever said a word to him, but I remember his face. He was the first Alpha guy killed since Fred Burris had been run over by the tank back in March.

The following named individual has been reported dead in Vietnam as the result of non-hostile action: Richard A. Hein, Vernal, Utah, age 24. Alpha Co., 1/16 Infantry. Indiv was at listening post when hit by fragments from friendly mine which detonated during practice fire. He was airlifted to the 24th

Evacuation Hospital placed on the very seriously ill list immediately and expired shortly thereafter.

Soon enough we were back on a road-clearing operation, again with no enemy contact. One evening we shared our hillside RON with a platoon of track-mounted 4.2-inch mortars. These heavy mortars fired an 11-kilogram shell with more killing authority than a 105mm howitzer, though with a much shorter range, and were mounted in the bays of M-113 armored personnel carriers, firing through the open roof. The CO of the mortar platoon and the Old Man were schmoozing as we dug in for the night, and their attention turned to a wide field of brown and dry reeds just outside our perimeter at the bottom of the hill. Some of the guys were chopping at the reeds with machetes to try to get decent fields of fire, but there were several acres of the stuff and it was slow going.

The mortar CO had a great idea: "I can drop some willy peter on those reeds and burn 'em right out," he said.

"You think that stuff will burn?" asked the Old Man.

"My willy peter will burn anything," he said proudly, and trotted down to the nearest track. After a couple of minutes he came back to the CP, grinning broadly. "Watch this," he said.

The mortar crew had been busying themselves around their track, and soon we heard the characteristic pop of a round leaving the tube. As we watched, the round shot up into the air, straight up, clearly visible as a black speck against the twilight sky.

"Oh shit," we all said, as the round appeared to hover directly overhead.

"Incoming," a bunch of us yelled, while the Old Man grabbed my radio handset and frantically tried to raise the downslope platoon commander. The guys out in the reeds with machetes looked up and saw us jumping around and yelling; they started to run back towards the perimeter, but too late: the round began its descent. At first it had looked like it would land right back on the track which had fired it, but there was some lateral trajectory after all, and now the round looked like it was going to land right about on the perimeter where the guys were chopping reeds, and this round had a lethal radius of 20 meters. Use of white phosphorus against people is discouraged under most rules of war, due to the particularly nasty effects of a glob of burning phosphorus on human flesh. It isn't smotherable or extinguished by water, burns at 5,000°F, and basically if a piece of it gets on you, it burns its way into your body until it's used up by the process of combustion. But all we could do up at the CP was watch in horror as the black dot continued to accelerate towards impact, going much faster than the guys on the ground could run.

Thump!

The round landed just a couple meters outside the perimeter. We gaped with our mouths open waiting for the explosion, but none came: the round was defective and didn't explode. I couldn't say who was most relieved by this failure, but the mortar platoon CO had to be the most embarrassed. Not only did he put half a dozen GIs in mortal peril, at least for a few seconds, he was also firing blanks. Needless to say nobody suggested he try it again, and after a few apprehensive glances back up the hill, the guys went back out with their machetes and did it the hard way.

After another trip back to Lai Khe we had a few days in the base camp. At some point Sanchez, the Old Man's RTO carrying the company radio, was replaced by a new guy. I was never sure why Sanchez went back to a rifle platoon, but I suspected his drinking got him in trouble. Sanchez was brave, strong, and competent, as witnessed by his six months or so as RTO, and was always sober and ready to go in the field. He was a quiet, polite guy, a good comrade, but when off duty he would often get stinking drunk, and when he was drunk he was combative. On one occasion he and a couple of buddies, including Duckwiler, visited me in the commo bunker while I was on radio watch. I was joking with them, and maybe hassling Sanchez a little, when without warning he launched himself at me, throwing punches as best he could in the confined space. I was utterly surprised, knocked off my folding chair onto the floor, and couldn't do any more than try to protect my head from his boots. The other guys pulled him right off and dragged him out, where he subsided. I wasn't much hurt and didn't make anything of it. I suspected I had crossed some sort of line with my teasing, maybe by trying out some of my Spanish cuss-words which I had learned to parrot but didn't understand in any sort of cultural context, and deserved the bruises. Maybe he had done something similar to somebody where it couldn't be ignored, and the Old Man had to move him somewhere less visible. The new guy, I'll call him Henderson, was a competent, stolid soldier and performed well in his new role, but I missed Sanchez.

Our time off ended with an order to return to Phouc Vinh for another squat in the 1/26 Infantry base camp while we pulled perimeter security and prepared for another operation. One day we ran a company patrol that took us over mostly open country, with small clumps of low trees spotted around grassy lowlands. When we did a more characteristic slog through jungle, we were lucky to travel three or four klicks in 12 hours. Today we moved through hot, spotty sunshine at a brisk pace, and probably covered 20 klicks in a few hours. Nothing happened on route, and we saw no sign of the enemy, but we were unaccustomed to quick, sustained movement. We didn't pass any streams, and the heat was intense, so our canteens were mostly dry and our feet were really sore when we finally connected with a laterite road that led back to Phouc Vinh. The Old Man had taken us to the head of the company column, and waited on the laterite for the stragglers to catch up. I could see he was thinking about something as he watched his bedraggled company dragging their asses out of the scrub and onto the road.

"First Sergeant!" He barked.

First Sergeant Tolliver trotted up to us, standing a few meter ahead of the panting troops. "Sir!"

"Column of fours, First Sergeant!"

Tolliver flashed a big pointy-tooth grin, and moved down the line conferring with the platoon leaders and sergeants. I watched in some awe as the tired, dusty ranks sorted themselves out into a company formation on the laterite, the three rifle platoons in columns of four, each about eight men deep, with their lieutenants and platoon sergeants in the fore, and spaced about five meters apart. None of us had been in a marching column since our last stateside post, or even longer, some of us probably not since our last training outfit. Nonetheless, muscle memory kicked in and the columns and rows formed up.

"Attention!"

While bemusement radiated like sunlight from the hundred or so faces, the backs went straight and the heels came together.

"Port arms! Forward march!"

"Give them a cadence, First Sergeant," came from the Old Man as the Headquarters group stepped out.

"Count cadence, delayed cadence, count—cadence—count!"

And I'm damned if everybody or near enough not to matter picked up the step and bellowed out the count. "We are Alpha—Mighty, Mighty Alpha—your lep' your lep' your lep' ri' lep!"

So we marched singing into Phouc Vinh, and when we weren't singing, we were grinning like bastards. Man, I felt like I could have marched another 20 klicks, but it was only about half a klick before we reached the wire and had to go tactical again, after savoring the amazed stares of the GIs on the perimeter. I understood for the first time why drums and bagpipes counted as weapons of war.

On May 17, as we were getting saddled up prior to leaving Phouc Vinh, I was following the Old Man through the barracks area while he talked on the company net and made the rounds of the platoons. A nearby detonation snapped me out of my daydreaming. Was that an incoming mortar round? Phouc Vinh had been the recipient of a few rounds the day before, though none had landed near our company area. The Old Man hustled towards what we figured was the point of impact; calls of "Medic!" and screams and groans were coming from one of the tin-roofed barrack huts which had been the local billet for some of Second Platoon's guys. As we rounded the corner of an adjacent hut we could see smoke coming out of the affected structure, and several bloodied Second Platoon guys staggering out the door. Was it a mortar round? There was no visible hole in the tin roof, and there had been no more explosions in the 30 seconds or so it had taken us to reach the site. Looking in, the interior of the hut was a shambles, with bodies and smoke everywhere. Medics shoved past us to get to the wounded, and some three-quarter-ton ambulances from the brigade headquarters zoomed in. About all I could do was stand around while the Old Man spoke alternately into the company and battalion nets. While we watched, a couple of guys from brigade came out holding one of the Second Platoon sergeants between them. He had a few scrapes but seemed healthy, but was talking loudly and disjointedly. The guy was one of the younger sergeants who I had thought was a little unstable and sort of a jerk, but otherwise was a pretty good soldier. Turns out he had thrown a grenade at one of the other guys, whether with malice or just negligence I never knew, and it had exploded, killing Mike Braeutigan, a good kid who had joined the company right around Christmas, and wounding ten or so other Second Platoon guys who had been getting their gear together preparatory to moving out. The sergeant who threw the grenade never returned to the company, though most of the wounded guys did eventually. Losing 12 men was a big hit for Second Platoon. The enemy hadn't killed one of us since February, but we seemed to be doing the job for him.

The following named individual has been reported dead in Vietnam as the result of non-hostile action: Michael L. Braeutigan, Sparks, Nevada, age 19. Alpha Co., 1/16 Infantry. Indiv was in billets in unit area when another individual allegedly threw a grenade in the billets.

CHAPTER 24

Looking for Work

I had managed to get passes to Saigon a few times, for various reasons including getting replacement eyeglasses, getting prescription eyeglass inserts for my gasmask, and once doing an errand for a company officer, as well as my trip to scout out reenlistment possibilities. So when my leave was approved in late May I was ready to go. Even though Saigon was only about 50 kilometers from Lai Khe, the roads were too dangerous for Americans to travel except in heavily armed convoys, so routine transport was by air on a catch-as-catch-can basis. Armed with orders permitting travel, a few changes of civilian clothes, and my .45 pistol in a shoulder holster, I hitched a ride to the Lai Khe airstrip and signed a clipboard in the orderly room. Going out I got lucky and left on a Caribou bound for Tan Son Nhut within a few minutes of my arrival. Tan Son Nhut was at the time still expanding, but was already vast and busy with everything from civilian 707s through fighter-bombers all the way to tiny two-seaters which looked like Piper Cubs. After landing, I disembarked and waited for a truck to take me across the field to the hangar-like structure which served as a waiting room for military traffic. From there, I caught a bus which took me and some GIs and other passengers to Saigon proper, where pedicabs and motorized trikes abounded. Boarding one of the latter, I was carried through the busy streets of Saigon to the Mai Loan Hotel, an aging eight-to nine-story example of French colonial architecture, which at that time catered to Western foreigners. I had been there once before for a single night, enlivened around midnight by the clamor of a posse of Vietnamese policemen, noisily and slowly clumping down the stairs and knocking on doors, seeking unmarried couples. The noise and sloth of this approach ensured that no such immorality would be discovered; my room was searched in a perfunctory manner by a host of tiny, uniformed, and giggling Vietnamese, who departed as noisily as they had entered. I realized at that time that I had been expected to have a companion who would have been able to dress and leave ahead of the morals police, and felt somewhat cheated that I had been sleeping alone.

I was able to remedy this defect on my present visit to the Mai Loan. The hotel had a respectably appointed American-style bar on the roof, frequented by off-duty military and civilian types and Vietnamese ladies. So after a day or so spent getting a passport and an exit visa, and some contact information regarding my post-tour plans, I took a shower in my room, changed into a button-down white cotton shirt and jeans, and went upstairs to the bar, where I got a table by myself and had a decent hamburger and a drink. While I was enjoying freedom from heat, dirt, fear, and other sweaty, dirty, scared GIs, I was approached by a Vietnamese woman who asked if I wanted company. The lady was probably in her late twenties or early thirties, rather buxom for a Vietnamese, with a pretty face pitted by old scars. She introduced herself in passable English as Tran Tuyet Nhu, Tran being her family name (in this case a pseudonym), and Tuyet Nhu having the English meaning of peaceful snowfall, or something close. She was smart, confident, seemed happy, and provided at least an honest simulacrum of affection and connection for a couple of days. I even learned a few more words of Vietnamese. Her presence then and later, when I returned from Singapore, was like cool water on the desert.

My stay at the Mai Loan was probably the best part of my leave, although the trip to Malaysia wasn't bad, either. I had been given a number to call in Kuala Lumpur, regarding my post-Vietnam aspirations, but it appeared that I couldn't get a flight into that city because of an embargo of some sort. Having no choice in the matter, I got a ticket for Singapore and figured I'd spend a few days there sightseeing. On June 7, I showed up at the Air Vietnam terminal at Tan Son Nhut, wearing civvies, and was directed in French by a smartly uniformed young Vietnamese woman to an aging but shiny Caravelle jet. After a short uneventful flight I was surprised to find us landing in Kuala Lumpur at a spiffy new airport. We were the only aircraft in evidence, and instead of pulling up towards the terminal, a long, swooping, concrete structure, we stopped in the middle of the tarmac. After a bit a stairway was pushed up to the nose of the plane and a uniformed personage entered the passenger compartment and asked for Peter Clark.

When I stood, he smiled broadly and said, "Ah, Mr. Clark, you come with me, please."

Fortunately all I had was a small carry-on case, so I followed the official down the stairway. No one else left the plane, which started up again as soon as the stairway was pulled back. I was led into a cavernous bay in the terminal building, where I appeared to be the only person aside from a couple of people in the distance doing obscure tasks, and was deposited at a customs counter. Another smiling official had me open my bag. With a sinking heart I remembered that I had a bag of .45 pistol ammunition in there, which I had neglected to leave when I had checked my weapon at Tan Son Nhut. While I was still trying to figure out what I would say when it was uncovered, the official looked at me, smiled very broadly, closed my bag and said something like, "Welcome to Malaysia," and stamped my passport.

I ended up spending two days in Kuala Lumpur, and did in fact meet a couple of Americans in what may have been a job interview of sorts. Both were bland, noncommittal, and appeared interested in our conversation, but nothing came of that meeting, then or later. At some point I opined that if I had been born Vietnamese, I would certainly have been a Viet Cong. In hindsight this probably wasn't a good move from a job applicant's perspective, but as it turned out it didn't matter. My arrival coincided with the start of the Six-Day War, which may have explained the embargo, as Kuala Lumpur was a predominantly Muslim city and Americans were not well-liked, particularly after the rumor was put about that American aircraft had supported the Israeli Air Force when it destroyed the Arab air forces on the ground to begin the war. I may have been in more mortal danger than I would have been in the field in Vietnam, but I was oblivious and checked out quaint little restaurants, an amusement park, and the strangely beautiful National Museum, a giant rendering of a traditional Malay palace, with particular emphasis on shadow puppets and other local arts. I did get a lot of hostile stares and some jostling at the amusement park, but didn't know enough to be scared and just put it down to native exuberance.

My stay in Singapore was less fraught; this was before the age of giant skyscrapers, and the city was still largely low-rise and British colonial, very clean and well-ordered, with most of the historical destinations reflecting the recent British influence. Educational, I suppose, but I was looking forward to getting back to Vietnam.

My leave was involuntarily extended at the end by a real difficulty in getting a flight from Tan Son Nhut to Lai Khe. The drill was report to Tan Son Nhut on the last day of your leave, sign up on the Lai Khe clipboard, and hang out until a flight out materialized and your name was called. Sign-in was around 7:30 a.m., and if you hadn't gotten a flight by around 4 p.m. the NCO in charge would sign you off for the day. At that point you could check in to the transient barracks and spend the night with a bunch of drunken and rowdy GIs, or taxi back to Saigon, change into civvies, and spend the night in air conditioned comfort in a bed with sheets, at least. This was my choice on the 13th and the 14th. I finally hitched a ride in a two-seat spotter plane and landed in Lai Khe late on June 15. When I reached the base area, I found the company area deserted except for a handful of troops—the battalion was in the field on an operation. By then it was too late to catch a resupply chopper, so I spent the night in my bunk.

Next day I was on a resupply chopper to rejoin the unit and recommence humping the battalion radio for the Old Man. My DEROS was July 27, so I was getting close to the 30-day mark; a recurring GI fable held that infantry short-timers were routinely reassigned to duty in the base camp during their last few weeks in country, in part because of their perceived inability to perform due to a reasonable fear of getting wasted when the end of their tour was so close. I was skeptical about this possibility because, based on my observations, unless there was absolutely no useful purpose in keeping a guy in the field, infantrymen tended to get down to their last few days before they were sent off. The companies were always short-staffed, and you never knew when one guy in the right place could make the difference between survival and disaster. Another few weeks in the field wouldn't have been my first choice of how to make the time go by, but my seven-day leave had ended up keeping me away from my post for almost two weeks, I had enjoyed myself thoroughly, and it was time to get back to work. The chopper landed, I was given a sack of something or other to deliver to the first sergeant, and made my way through the battalion RON to the Alpha Company area. In a short time I was back in my place on the roster, just another day at the office.

Later that afternoon, while I was hanging out in the CP area, Rod Floutz came by. He had a congenital condition called hammertoes, where the first joint of the toe bends down at a 90-degree angle to the following joint. This condition, which I also possessed, can make extended walking painful, and is a classic disqualifying disability for infantry soldiers. I had been spotted during a physical screening back in the States, but had insisted that my feet were fine, which they were. I never had any problems. This, however, was back when I wanted to be in the infantry, out of ignorance. Even in my most fearful moments, thereafter, when reassignment to a safer job in some rear area was my secret hope, I figured that, like with the chance to be a typist, the moving finger had writ, and what it writ was, "You've screwed yourself again." Floutz, however, was proving the value of persistence; it seemed to me that he had been less enthusiastic about life in Second Platoon since he had shot the draft dodger back in November. In the meantime he had been awarded the Bronze Star and gotten his sergeant's stripes, and maybe figured it was time to move on. I was happy for him, and wished him well; he was going to a security battalion in Saigon, which was about as good an assignment as an eleven bravo could hope for in the 'Nam.

As I was saddling up that morning, several of my other Second Platoon buddies came by to find out where I'd been and get me up to speed on the happenings of the last ten days. Alpha had seen some action, but most of the fighting had been between Bravo Company and a large VC force, resulting in six dead GIs and a bunch of wounded. Carl Johnson, the guy who was first assigned to José Garcia's gun team back in February, and was then traded for David Ward to accommodate Bob Pointer's desire

Carl Johnson (José Garcia; 1967). Carl died of wounds received on June 17, 1967.

for an all-black gun team, came by and asked to borrow my toothbrush. This was an unusual request, but I automatically said "Sure" and handed it over. As he was walking back to his foxhole it struck me that this was sort of an intimate connection, even for GIs in combat.

What came out of my mouth was, "Wait a minute, what do you want it for?"

Carl stopped, turned around, and replied, "Clean my rifle."

I processed this for a couple of beats, and responded, "Oh, in that case, OK."

A little later Carl returned my toothbrush. That was the last time we talked. After I was saddled up and standing around near the Old Man, waiting for the word to move out, I thought about my hammer toes and decided that, hell, even if I didn't get an end-of-tour reassignment, I wanted to spend my last days in Vietnam with Alpha Company.

CHAPTER 25

June 17, 1967

So on the morning of June 17 we set out through medium-to-high jungle, a light rain falling which often failed to penetrate the canopy, the temperature rising into the mid-90s, all in all not a bad start to a day in the field. The only unusual inconvenience we suffered involved 81mm mortar ammunition. The guys in the rifle platoons were each given a couple of these ten-pound shells packed in foot-long cardboard tubes three inches in diameter. Captain Williamson decided we were going to share the burden, so I ended up with an empty sandbag containing one of the rounds hanging from my radio. All the other CP guys had a round or two, and the Old Man took one himself. We were point for the battalion, with the battalion CP and then Bravo Company behind us. Another infantry battalion, the 2/28, was marching through the jungle a few hundred meters on our left. After several hours of uneventful walking, the column halted. Word came from the point that there was suspected VC activity and the Old Man, with us trailing, moved at a good clip up the column. Near the point, Lieutenant Sermuskis and his RTO were standing next to José Garcia and his gun team. Donnie Gunby pointed out a trail on our right, running parallel to our line of march, that looked well-traveled, and recently at that. Lieutenant Colonel Lazzell came on the radio about then, asking why the hell we were flat on our ass. The Old Man explained what we had found, and Lazzell came up himself. He was pissed that we were stopped, but did have the orbiting fighter-bombers drop a couple of bombs in the jungle to our right front. We were then told to move out smartly, which we did.

Around noon we reached a large clearing and began to move around the right treeline towards the north. The clearing was spotted with random small trees and brush, and was about 500 to 1,000 meters running south to north, maybe half that in width. We had only walked for four or five hours, and here we were in our next RON already. I was grinning. Short-timer's luck, I thought. I could handle a month like this, not a problem. As usual, the headquarters group consisted of the Old Man and his two RTOs. Duckwiler, the company medic, and Lieutenant Dalton, the artillery forward observer, and his RTO were also part of the group. First Sergeant Tolliver was at the end of the company column. So, in the usual course of business, the Company CP group followed the point platoon, in this case the Second, and was followed by the other rifle platoons and the weapons platoon. The activities of the day before, most of which I had missed, had involved cutting down trees and clearing a decoy landing zone near our RON. This march was supposed to create an element of surprise when we appeared at our destination, which was a natural clearing in the midst of heavy jungle. The clearing itself was slightly depressed relative to the surrounding jungle at its southern end, and ankle-high grass sloped gently upwards, towards the north. Spotted with clumps of saplings and brush, the clearing gave pretty good sight lines in all directions up to the treelines, which were likewise spotted with smaller vegetation gradually becoming denser until it became serious jungle. The company moved north along this ragged treeline on the right, where the Second Platoon stopped at about the northernmost edge of clearing. Bravo Company from the 2/28 was supposed to be moving up the left side of the clearing, and after we arrived they were supposed to link up with us on their right. Second Platoon moved into the woodline, taking the northernmost point of the clearing and extending to the right fifty meters or so. First and Third platoons moved through Second Platoon a few meters into the jungle, and Second Platoon came back a few meters as the company reserve. First Platoon was then expected to link up with Bravo 2/28, and Third Platoon turned the corner south to link up with our Bravo Company on Alpha's right, which in turn connected with Charlie Company and covered the eastern side of the clearing.

The battalion recon platoon was set up a few meters further into the jungle on the east, our right. Alpha's weapons platoon moved into the clearing itself and set up their 81mm mortar tubes with mortar platoons from the other companies as they arrived. The rifle companies slid into the jungle and hunkered down. We were all grateful to unload our extra mortar rounds into the custody of the weapons guys. After hanging around the center of the clearing for a few minutes while the mortars started emplacing, and having a quick visit from Lieutenant Colonel Lazzell, the Old Man led the CP group to a spot on the north-east edge of the clearing, around fifty meters from the northern end. We didn't start to dig in because other units were still arriving and our final position in what was going to be a battalion perimeter couldn't be determined until everybody was linked up. The battalion command post was just to our south, in a small clump of trees on the edge of the clearing. Although they were only a few meters past the edge of the clearing, none of the men in rifle platoons was visible from where we were standing. Lazzell and his staff and their RTOs had found a bit of shade and were setting up the long antennas for the radios. Hueys started coming in with ammunition and other supplies, and one or two Light Observation Helicopters had landed as well. It was hot, but not unusually so, and a little hazy. The light rain which had sprinkled us during the morning had stopped and, pretty much, things were as good as they got in the field. There were no signs of any current enemy activity or presence that I could detect, and I considered myself pretty good at that business. I was feeling just lazy and thinking about nothing at all when somebody opened up with an M-16 a hundred meters or so to our right.

In the jungle, you hear the battle more than you see it. And every battle starts the same way: one or a couple of shots. Between the moments the first shots register, and whatever happens next, there is ample time to process and interpret the nature of the battle as it unfolds. The processing goes something like this: That was a shot, that was an M-16 round. Will there be another, or was that some numbnuts who stumbled with his safety off? That was another M-16 round. Damn, that was a third M-16 round. Reject the clumsy numbnuts hypothesis. Maybe a point man who thought he saw a VC? Uh oh, that is a second rifle starting up, and a third/fourth/fifth. More rifles are joining in. Is this just a nervous squad, firing up their sector because numbnuts loosed the first round? That's the crump of an explosion, maybe a grenade? Then a new sound, a baritone report over the M-16's tenor chorus. Was that an AK? That was an AK, one two three more oh shit. And at about that point, two seconds into the battle, the lazy short-timer brain goes and hides and something else takes over.

What we were hearing was a small-to-medium firefight a hundred meters or so to our right as we faced the northern end of the clearing. We couldn't see anything; the rifle platoons were invisible a few meters inside the treeline, and the shooting was coming from somewhere beyond them. I wasn't hearing many incoming rounds, and while we all knew we were engaged, after the first minute or two it didn't seem so bad. My job was to monitor the battalion net, so I knew when Lieutenant Colonel Lazzell jumped into an observation helicopter and took to the air. Almost all the useful emerging intelligence about the battle was auditory, and Lazzell had placed himself where he couldn't hear anything that wasn't coming through his radio headphones in a noisy, open chopper. At that moment, of course, he was connected by radio to his battalion command post, which had set up a little behind us on the right side of the clearing in the modest shade of a cluster of small trees which extended out from the woodline towards the center of the open space. By now all of us in the CP were kneeling out of respect to the odd bullet whickering overhead. I was close to the Old Man on his left, listening to the battalion net while he had the company headset pressed to his right ear. Battalion came on and confirmed that the recon platoon had contact with a small VC force, but had no other details.

Within a few minutes gunships and fighter-bombers started making passes over the jungle to our right. The firing had died down to a sporadic rattle. The rhythm of firing was about the same as the time the platoon from Charlie Company had gotten wiped out when it was lured into an NVA ambush. There wasn't much coming through the battalion net. I had time to feel sorry for the poor bastards out there in the jungle and hopeful that the worst was over when a couple of shots to our front and a couple of bullets whining overhead snapped my head around to the north. This time the firing seemed to start slow, and seemed scattered over the northern end of the clearing, a few AK rounds, a couple of 16s, an M-60 opening up with a few short bursts. Instead of the crescendo of a suddenly engaged platoon, the sounds told of a widespread and deliberate exchange of fire by increasing numbers of troops across a wide front. In retrospect it seemed like a long, long time between the first bullets going over our heads and the tearing, enveloping roar of colliding battalions, but probably only 30 seconds or so elapsed. By then I, along with the rest of the company CP group, was lying flat on my stomach. Captain Williamson had the headset for the company net pressed to his ear and, even though I was a meter away on his left, with Henderson the same distance on his other side, I could barely hear what he was saying. With my earphones I could follow the battalion net, but the ambient noise drowned out the sounds of speech. I did gather that Second Platoon was engaged all along its line, and that First and Third platoons were taking fire as well.

The table of organization calls for an RTO to carry a .45-caliber automatic pistol as a personal sidearm. Captain Howley had mandated that every swinging dick in his company had at least an M-16 and a basic load of ammo, but as the brass got more into such things we had been returned to the TO&E weapons. When that had happened I was delighted not to have to hump the rifle and the minimum load of 200 or so rounds of 5.56 ammo. Now, as the firing increased and green NVA tracers began streaming out of the jungle, my lack of an M-16 made me feel naked and helpless.

One of the First Platoon guys emerged from the jungle, heading toward the center of the clearing; he was bareheaded, had no weapon, and was bloody. Shortly afterwards another trooper came out, without web gear but with helmet, carrying his M-16. Holy shit, I thought, that sucker is running away, the gooks must be on top of them. I pulled out my .45 and chambered a round. Captain Williamson must have heard the slide snapping back, because he turned his head and shouted over the battle noise, "Put that damn thing away before you hurt someone." OK, so maybe I was overreacting, I told myself, and slid the thing back into my holster.

I yelled at the withdrawing trooper, a Second Platoon veteran who should have known better, "If you're not going to use that '16, give it to me!"

Of course he didn't, just gave me a funny look and kept on going, but if he thought he was heading to safety he was going in the wrong direction. By now the center of the clearing was swept with enemy automatic weapons fire, with plentiful green tracer rounds zinging overhead. They seemed close enough that I could have put up a hand and caught one. The weapons platoon must have gotten off a few mortar rounds at the beginning, but they were out in the open, where the middle of the clearing was being scoured by green tracers. The battalion HQ staff on the ground was dead or wounded, or at least not talking on the radio. Over the battalion net Lazzell was trying to coordinate artillery and airstrikes or gunship runs. For obvious reasons the flyboys didn't want to be competing for airspace with incoming cannon shells, but the time interval between shutting off the artillery and getting the air in, when nothing was coming down on the VC, seemed to stretch forever. The alternating artillery fire and airstrikes continued, but all the shells and bombs were falling to the east, our right, and way into the jungle on that side, while the enemy firing by now was coming almost completely from our front. The explosions of artillery rounds, the whoosh of napalm, and the earth-shaking boom of the 500-pound bombs weren't having any effect on the volume of fire to our front, not that I could notice.

Whether it was because we were exposed to the increasingly heavy fire coming into the clearing, or because he wanted to be closer to the action, Captain Williamson got to his feet and led us diagonally across the clearing to the northernmost point, directly behind Second Platoon. I so much did not want to get up, at that point, and test my perception of the height of the tracers overhead, but needs must. As it happened we scuttered the 50 meters or so without injury: Captain Williamson, who at six feet six inches was by far the most at risk from overhead rounds, Lieutenant Dalton, the FSO, his RTO, me, and Henderson. There may have been another couple of guys as well. We all went to ground a few meters south of the serious treeline, lying on soft grass with just a few small trees and brush around. For ten meters or so north of the clearing, brushy pre-jungle gradually thickened and elevated until it became fairly dense, with higher hardwood trees sheltering middle-level thickets. In this transitional area, spotted with thickets of bamboo and clusters of smaller trees, Second Platoon had been waiting for its eventual assignment to a section of what would have been the RON perimeter. Just inside the beginning of the serious jungle, maybe five or six meters away, I could see José Garcia and his M-60, along with Gunby and Ward, his assistant gunners, lying prone behind several small trees. The ground sloped up very gently towards the north, and there were some irregularities here and there, which may have been earthworks or shell craters, but José and his team were pretty much in the open. José was firing short bursts every few seconds. Several other Second Platoon riflemen were also visible in the undergrowth to José's right, and at least one dead or badly wounded GI was lying in that direction. I thought maybe Greg Murry was one of the guys to José's right. I couldn't see who or what was to Joe's left, but he was fully engaged with the enemy to our front. I couldn't actually see any VC, but their rounds were coming out of the jungle to our front from a bunch of locations, and from the sound they were only a few meters into the brush. Greg was the weapons squad leader. Alan Roese was leader of the leftmost rifle squad of Second Platoon, curved around to meet the other Second Platoon squad. Directly to Greg's front and left, elements of First and Third platoons were somewhere in the jungle, supposed to be linked up to the 2/28 on our left.

Here's what José Garcia later told Greg Murry about those first few seconds:

> I heard the VC before I saw them. "Listen, Junior, I hear gooks out there and no one is supposed to be talking Vietnamese." Donnie Gunby replied, "I don't hear anything, you are wrong." Donnie was from the Georgia backwoods and could see things I could not, but I always felt I could hear better and I had a better sense of direction to sound than he did, so we made a good team. As I kept looking in the direction of the voices, I saw a group of VC moving forward ... so I opened fire. Then everyone opened up, and so did the VC. I think that, by our gun opening up, we forced them to spring their ambush a little early.

Bob Pointer's gun crew was just to Greg's right. Bob had set his M-60 down roughly even with Greg's team. Carl Johnson and John Brantley, the assistant gunner and ammo bearer of Bob's all-black gun team, were waiting behind him with their belts and boxes of 7.62. Alan Roese's rifle squad was dispersed between and to the right of the gun teams. Greg, as weapons squad leader, had positioned the machine guns to cover likely areas of approach, José facing a little to the left and Bob a little to the right. Just after José opened up, first one, then a whole bunch of AK rounds started coming out of the jungle. Carl and John jumped up and ran to Bob's position, where he had started putting fire into the greenery.

Greg Murry picks up the account in his own memoir:

Carl and John had left their ammo cans on the other side of a small trail that ran off to the north from the edge of the open area. There was a freshly dug fighting position in the middle of the trail a little north of them. I told Carl and John to get the ammo and bring it to Bob. He had begun firing at figures moving through the brush in front of him and they were shooting at him. Carl jumped up into a low crouch and crossed the trail to his ruck frame that carried his 400 rounds of ammo in two cans. He grabbed the ruck frame and dived back across the trail. As he flew across the trail, he suddenly dropped the ruck and did a half flip to end up on his back close to Bob and the gun. He got up, grabbed the ammo, and took up his position to the left of the gun and prepared a fresh belt to reload Bob's now empty gun. John crossed the trail right behind him, dropped his ammo to Carl's left, and began firing to his front.

José was blazing away furiously at the enemy soldiers attacking to his front and they were firing back at him. Donny was feeding him belt after belt and David and a fourth man, 'Ghost,' were firing their rifles to the front. The vegetation was being shredded to the sides and above both positions. The tempo of incoming enemy rounds increased and it seemed like there was an almost continual cacophony of sound for a long period of time. The perception of time at that point became another phenomenon; it seemed like it stood still. People were shooting, RPGs were swishing in then exploding, mortar rounds were coming in, many of them exploding in the trees above us and spraying shrapnel everywhere, and it seemed like it had been going on my whole life.

I began to hear people calling for medics and I saw Turner, our platoon medic, crawling up to someone a little distance to my right rear. As he got closer to a body that was lying motionless in front of him, a grenade exploded right next to him and threw him 4 feet into the air. He came down and lay motionless for a while near the person he had been trying to get to.

I turned back to observe José's situation when a tremendous volley of fire came through the bamboo and small tree branches in front of José's position, throwing vegetation everywhere. One of the bullets struck 'Ghost's' handguard of his M-16, blowing half of it off. 'Ghost' turned back to me with a smile on his face and said, with a steady voice, "that was close," before facing back toward the enemy and putting fire on them.

I saw José rise up a little to get a better look and then move forward several feet where the ground rose up slightly. He raised his gun a little higher and began to fire long bursts to his front. David moved forward with his ammo and gave it to Donnie who was feeding the ammo into José's gun. When David raised up to move, he was struck in the face by a bullet that entered his head just above his right eye and exited at the top of his head, leaving a square hole about an inch and a half with the skull bone and skin anchored at one end giving the effect of a trap door that had been left open.

I crawled over to him and saw that he was still alive and conscious. I tried to give him some words of comfort, telling him that he would be OK and that we would get him to medical aid soon. He indicated that he heard me with a shaking of his head. At that moment, I saw several RPGs explode in the bamboo to my right front and the enemy fire rate increased even more. Howard and another rifleman from our platoon had moved into the freshly dug enemy fighting position in the middle of the trail and were under heavy attack from somewhere to their front. They were using their ruck sack frames to stop the enemy grenades from coming into their hole. [Lieutenant Sermuskis] was just to the right of their hole, up on one knee, firing well aimed bursts from his CAR 15 up the trail. Both sides were now firing at one another from about 20 meters distance from each other through the thick vegetation.

José continues:

I was told to pull back twice. The first time only a little … I told Gunby to pull back with Ward. When I moved, I hit Ward with my feet … He tried to say "Medic" and then he vomited a thick stream of blood all over my shoulder and face. He had been hit in the eye. I turned away and fired a long burst forward. When I looked back at Ward, he was face down in that mess. I turned his face away from it and told him to play dead. "If you move they will shoot you again." He never responded …. Then here comes an RPG aimed at me that hit a tree behind me and it rained down shrapnel. It got me on the left arm and temporarily paralyzed my left arm and hand … I balanced the M-60 with my right hand and shoulder and kept firing as they kept coming. There was a new man from LA …. Two days before the fight I told him that if fighting broke out, to drop his ammo to my left and then get behind me. He did and was hit and I last saw him face down.

After another interval which might have lasted a few minutes or a few hours, mostly spent by me trying to be very, very flat, Captain Williamson jumped up again and took off towards the center of the open space to our rear.

"We got to get more machine gun ammo," he shouted.

More than anything I wanted to stay hugging the earth, but training took over after a few shameful seconds, in which I wrestled with the possibility of just staying put, and I lurched to my feet, and, staying as close to ground as I could without slowing down, took off after him. I never did actually catch up, but I homed on the tall, thin figure of the Old Man towing Henderson, with another couple of guys running nearby. Resupply choppers had dropped off some stuff in the center of the clearing before the shooting started, and Captain Williamson grabbed a couple of steel boxes of 7.62 machine-gun ammo from a heap on the ground and turned around. I found a box of 7.62, grabbed it, and ran back to the same spot on the edge of the treeline. I passed my box up to Captain Williamson and recommenced lying very, very flat.

At some point a guy I knew from the weapons platoon, I'll call him Slater, appeared on my left and lay down a few inches from me. Captain Williamson was prone on my right and slightly ahead of me; my head was around his knees. Henderson was to his right and ahead. Dalton and his RTO were to my left and ahead, and José and his team were still a few meters into the jungle. Beyond José was dense foliage and tall trees, classic triple canopy jungle. I was aware of other folks still firing into the jungle, and others lying awfully still. Gunby was feeding ammo into José's gun, but Ward was lying very still. I figured he was dead. Another guy was also lying, dead or badly wounded, to José's right. I couldn't see his face. Bullets were constantly whickering overhead, green tracer which seemed to flash by inches above our prone bodies. The sound of incoming rounds continued to increase, and the higher pitched return fire from our weapons seemed to diminish.

Whump!

A mortar or RPG round exploded in the clearing a couple of meters behind us, shrapnel whistling over our prone bodies. A few seconds later, another round landed a meter to my left. Dirt and debris flew over me. The blast tore the fatigue shirt and most of the skin and muscle off

Slater's back, exposing his ribs, bright white against the blood. He started to get up and I grabbed his arm and pulled him flat.

"Stay put, you'll be OK," I shouted into his ear. "That's a million-dollar wound; you're going home."

"Do you think so?" he asked.

"Sure, you'll be fine, I can see it isn't bad," I lied.

Whump!

This time the round landed less than a meter to my right. At the same time as the dirt and smoke washed over me, I knew I was hit on my right leg. It felt like somebody had jumped off a table and landed on it. My ears were ringing and the sounds of the battle had faded. I was suddenly aware of how the earth smelled as I pressed my face into it. It smelled alive, rich, and sour. It smelled so good. This is what I thought with my face pressed into the damp soil: My leg is hit. Maybe it is gone. If it is, if I want to live, I will have to get a tourniquet around the stump. To do that, I will have to move at least enough to get my belt off and get it around the leg, and maybe I will get shot doing that. What's left of the leg may be pretty mangled, and it may be a shock to see it. I will have to overcome the shock, overcome the fear of the bullets flying inches over my head, and attend to the leg if it is bad. That will require a lot of effort. On the other hand, I can do nothing. I can stay with my face in the dirt, and maybe just bleed out, and it will be like going to sleep. So unless I'm going to attend to that leg, there is no point in turning my head. I thought about my options, taking my time to consider them, though probably less than half a dozen seconds passed. Nope, I concluded, I don't want to die just yet, I'll look at the leg and do what I can to live. Do it. I turned my head to my right, keeping it as low as I could, and looked down the length of my body. The sight of a more or less intact fatigue pants leg, with a few red holes in it but no spurting blood or jutting white bone, was just about the best thing I'd ever seen, and it remained in that position until my oldest daughter was put in my arms following her birth by C-section 13 years later.

My next thought was, if I can live through the next couple hours, I'm going home for a while. Forget about any extended tours. Living through the next couple of hours was no sure thing, though. Captain Williamson had been hit in the left foot and leg by the same round that got me, but he didn't appear to be paying any attention to the injury, just listening and shouting orders into the company net handset. He had Henderson's headphone held against one ear. As my hearing started to come back the roar of rifle and machine-gun fire ebbed and flowed like surf on a beach, but it sounded like there were a lot more AKs than M-16s firing and the incoming rounds were thicker than ever, seeming to whistle by a few inches overhead. I raised my head up a little and could see José hunkered down behind his M-60 and a few other guys to his left and right. As I watched he started firing to his front, short bursts a few seconds apart. It crossed my mind that maybe somebody should take some more ammo up to him, but as soon as I had the thought, any impulse to actually do it faded away. I put my face back down in the dirt, thought I was probably going to die, and was sad about that for a couple of seconds. I could hear Lazzell over the battalion net. He had been talking to the Bravo 2/28 company commander.

"Now, I want you to prepare to refuse the flank," he said.

Bravo Six came back, "Devour Six, refuse my flank, over?"

"That's right, refuse your flank. Now, you know what I mean by that, Bravo Six?"

"Yes sir, I know what you mean."

This was such bullshit, of course. Bravo Six knows what refuse the flank means, he's a goddam West Point infantry captain, I thought. I know what it means, and I'm a fucking SP4. As I listened more closely, I realized that Lazzell was an old man who was out of touch, flying around in his LOH without a clue as to what was happening on the ground, giving random orders because he didn't know what else to do as his command got slaughtered. At some point he started talking about gunships and airstrikes, and I was hopeful that he would get us some help, but the strikes came in on the far right, where the firing had started but long since stopped. That was the place the battle had seemed to be happening, when the colonel went up in the chopper and ceased to hear anything coming from the ground and couldn't see anything under the triple canopy jungle. Damn, I wished somebody would talk to him and tell him what was going on. I pushed the handset at Captain Williamson, and he listened a couple of seconds, maybe said a few words, but quickly thrust the handset back and went back to the company net.

Since you're gonna die anyway, I thought, what harm can it do to talk to the colonel? So I pushed the push-to-talk and said, "Devour Six, this is Alpha Six Kilo. Those strikes are not where the VC are, they are too far to the right, the VC are in our front."

"Alpha Six Kilo, put your actual on."

"My actual can't go on right now. We need artillery in our north front."

"I need a casualty report, put Alpha Six on."

"This is Alpha Six Kilo. Alpha Six is a casualty, I am a casualty, we are getting overrun and need some help."

The colonel may have responded, but the brigade commander came on the net at that point. "Alpha Six Kilo, what is your situation?"

"We are being overrun from the north, we are low on ammunition, and we need air and artillery to our front."

"Where do you want it?"

God, am I supposed to call in artillery? This was not what RTOs with a live actual were supposed to do without permission. I was going to be in so much trouble if I lived. Captain Williamson was focused on the company net, though. What the hell.

"Five zero meters north of the treeline at the north end of the LZ," I said.

A couple of Huey gunships made a run across our front about that time, the tearing-paper sound of their Gatling guns rising over the chop of the rotors and the whine of the turbines. The enemy fire slackened off immediately, but a few seconds after the last gunship pass the firing picked up again, if anything heavier than before.

"This is Alpha Six Kilo, we need artillery now," I yelled into the handset.

It seemed just a few seconds later shells were landing to our front, but too far into the woods.

"Gotta bring it down, closer to the treeline, two zero meters," I said, and after those rounds landed there was a definite lull in the incoming fire.

But after a couple seconds it ratcheted back up to a roar. "Bring it right down on the treeline," I shouted.

At about this point Captain Williamson may have noticed I was talking above my pay-grade. "Give me that!" He grabbed my handset. He seemed annoyed, which meant he was truly pissed. I didn't care at this point if I was going to get court-martialed or whatever, as there had seemed little hope of surviving in any event. The captain was talking on both handsets, so there was nothing I needed to do except rest. Turned out I wasn't the only one calling in artillery at that point: our capable FSO, Lieutenant Dalton, and at least one RTO from Third Platoon, Frank Limiero, were also on the net trying to get us the support we needed. But I like to think my two-cents worth helped produce the result.

The howl of the incoming artillery rounds ended in enormous explosions right to our front, the earth shook, and hot, spent shrapnel bounced off my radio and steel helmet and landed on my arms and legs. I didn't mind the burns. I had never heard a sweeter sound. Again I tried to cover myself with my helmet and the radio, pressed my face into the dirt, and reveled in the crash and thunder of the incoming rounds and the peace that came from having nothing left to do. If I had died then, it would have been OK.

Greg Murry's account continues:

> A new sound came into the bedlam of that battle. To the northeast of us, about 5 miles away, a battalion of 105mm artillery was being directed to fire in close support of our defense. The FO, a lieutenant from the field artillery and his RTO, an artillery sergeant, each with a radio, were … coordinating the fires of the 155 and 175mm guns and the massive 8-inch howitzers. They were with the CO, about 20 meters behind us, in the open. With 4 radios in one place, they would have been a tempting target for the snipers to our west, but the snipers were apparently fixated on the mortar crews just past them to the east who were busily firing those shells we had humped in. The attacking enemy soldiers had almost completely overrun the First Platoon in front of us and were now attempting to do the same to the Second Platoon. We were also under a heavy assault from our left flank, and it was José and Bob's guns and crews that were holding the entire left flank of the battalion. In the distance I heard the rumble of 18 tubes of artillery that were aimed right at us. A second later I heard what sounded like an extremely fast freight train from hell, whistle shrieking, wheels screeching, and headed straight for me.
>
> I shoved my face in the dirt as 18 105mm artillery rounds landed in a line about 50 meters to my front. The explosions were so close together that it was

hard to distinguish each round. Dirt was everywhere, tree branches were falling here and there, and eventually some pieces of hot shrapnel fell onto the backs of some of the guys, not breaking the skin but burning their backs. It rained on and off during the battle and those hot pieces of metal, when they landed on our wet clothing, caused steam to rise from our backs.

The firing from both sides slowed down a lot after the first volley of artillery landed but then it picked up again. The FO who was behind us called in some adjustments and a short time later I heard the rumble of the guns again and then the banshee returned again. This would continue for a long time that afternoon. The enemy force continued to press forward. Some more RPGs slammed into the trees above the heads of some of the guys facing north and several of them were wounded. The automatic weapons fire increased again as the enemy attempted to overrun the Second Platoon.

I heard someone calling to throw smoke and I knew that meant close air support by either helicopter or fixed wing or both. A few minutes later a white cloud drifted through the vegetation on our right and came right down our firing line. It was tear gas. Some of the guys started yelling gas and we automatically grabbed for our masks. I put mine on, but I couldn't get any air to come in. The filters were wet. I took it off quickly and stuck my face in the dirt, hoping that the gas would pass over me and not get into my eyes. At this moment a concentrated barrage of RPGs slammed into the trees above our firing line and grenades began to explode all around us. Robert found his crew's position isolated and pulled back so that he was on line with the rest of the firing line, still facing north. Carl came with him; John was lying face down on the ground and not moving. I told José to bring his gun back a ways so we could reform our line. We were almost at the edge of the open area. If we didn't hold here we were through. I had turned around and was looking at the platoon sergeant and another sergeant lying with their feet in the open area and I saw that we had run out of maneuver room. The bodies of the dead and wounded lay around us and in front of our firing line. The artillery continued to crash into the jungle in front of us and now we could hear the F4 Phantom jets passing over our heads as they struck the suspected enemy troop concentrations to our north with napalm, cluster bombs, and regular bombs. At least they weren't bombing us.

When I turned around I realized that we would have to attempt to move our firing line forward in order to secure our dead and wounded. The enemy fire seemed to slow down so I crawled over to Alan, who was a little behind and to the left of me. I told him to get his squad on line and at my signal we would all move forward to regain our positions and get our people. I passed the word to the right and we began crawling forward. All of a sudden a number of RPGs crashed into the trees around us and the automatic weapons fire swept through our area like a blade. Alan was killed with a bullet to the head and many others were wounded or killed. My gunners kept up their fire and, along with some others, they repulsed the enemy's final assault on our position. The fighting tapered off slowly and finally stopped.

Everyone was just lying there in the prone looking to their front when some medics from the battalion aid station showed up and started treating the wounded. One of our men was trying to crawl back to the perimeter, but he had been badly injured in his right arm. He lay on his side, pushing with his legs and waving his other arm as he tried to move toward us. The medics were there encouraging him to continue, because no one wanted to go forward of our line for fear of getting shot. I turned my attention to my own squad. Robert Pointer's crew was in bad shape. John Brantley was dead. Carl Johnson had been hit in the neck at the beginning of the fight and the bullet had severed his jugular vein and resealed it. Carl had continued to feed ammunition to the gun through the entire battle. He was one of the first to be medevac'd after the shooting stopped but we heard later that he had died soon after reaching the hospital. Robert was slightly wounded and was medevaced that evening.

José's crew was not much better. José had been wounded by shrapnel, but would be OK. 'Ghost' was also wounded but would make it. David Ward had been shot in the head and was medevaced. We heard later that he had lost an eye but survived the terrible wound and was sent back to the States. Donnie was the only uninjured man in the squad beside me. I told him to take Joe's gun and face the left flank. I helped him gather the remaining machine gun ammo and directed one of the riflemen from Alan's squad to stay with him. I was feeling guilty, but the details of my guilt would take a while to surface, because I was just starting to come down from what had to have been the most intense adrenalin rush ever.

For an unknowable period the thunder and crash of incoming artillery competed with the roar of automatic weapons coming from our front. Time slowly returned to earth, as the sight and sound and feel and smell of a close artillery bombardment faded. On the underside of the receding sounds of the barrage, the crackle of small arms diminished, and soon was only random bursts and shots, close but not directed at us. Airstrikes and artillery now seemed to be falling steadily further away from our position. For the first time since the battle started, I heard choppers coming into the LZ.

"Time to get up and get moving," muttered the Old Man.

I wasn't sure I was going to be able to get up, but with the Old Man looming over me I made the effort, and found to my great delight that my right leg supported my weight OK and I could move around. For some other interval I followed Captain Williamson and Henderson as we limped about the battlefield. Seriously hurt folks were being taken to the center of the LZ, where dustoffs were beginning to land. I remember searching for cigarettes and finding a pack in the thigh pocket of my fatigues, and pulling it out to find it mangled with shrapnel holes and soaked with blood. Greg Murry showed up, unhurt but explaining that everyone in his squad was dead or wounded.

At about that point I realized my leg felt slippery and my joints weren't quite right. I got a kind of tunnel vision, everything seemed distant, and the nearby sounds were fading. I needed to lie down. I knelt and supported myself on my hands, but that didn't seem to help.

"Captain, I don't think I can carry your radio right now," I said.

The captain gave me a sharp look, but I guess he figured I wasn't goofing off and told me to hand off the radio and get myself a dustoff. Somebody helped me back to the aid station, where miraculously there was an empty stretcher and I got put on it, along with what seemed like lots of other guys, mostly more bunged up than I was. I lay there kind of listlessly, watching the dustoff choppers circle and land. There were still sporadic bursts of automatic weapons fire and the odd round whistled overhead. The battalion chaplain was moving around the stretchers comforting the guys in them. At some point he knelt by my side and took my hand and, although I wasn't religious, I welcomed the touch and his kindness. He had tears in his eyes, and he gave me some words of comfort. At that point I remember waving off one of the teams picking up stretchers, as I felt guilty to be there at all with only a few holes in my leg. After a while the worst cases were moved out, so I let them carry me to a dustoff chopper. When we got there the stretcher racks were full, and the guys carrying me helped me off my stretcher and into the chopper so I could sit on the floor. Another not-so-badly shot-up GI and I were watching blood drip from the bottom of one of the stretchers. We made eye contact and gave each other a small rueful smile, sharing as we were the blessing of the fickle battle goddess and the inseparable mixture of guilt and joy that comes with survival.

Time didn't register during this interval, but I remember being carried at a run from the chopper to the brigade clearing station, getting hooked up to an IV line, and getting a shot of morphine. I started to fade at that

Sketch of José Garcia (Peter Clark; July, 1967). This is Joe, saving my butt. I'm in the background, along with Captain Williamson. The dead VC is an embellishment by about 5 meters, they never got that close, but otherwise it's as I remembered it.

point. The medic shook me hard, saying, "Stay with me, now." The few seconds of oblivion had felt enormously peaceful and good. I realized that dying wouldn't have been so bad, or maybe that was just the morphine.

At least 15 Alpha guys were killed on June 17, including a bunch from Second Platoon. First Platoon was overrun at the beginning of the fight, losing a lot of men, but buying time for Second Platoon to form the line against which the enemy's repeated attacks were broken, and incidentally saving my ass. Third Platoon was not as heavily engaged, but a lot of fighting occurred at its left flank, where the platoon RTO, Frank Limiero, took over functional command of the platoon as their lieutenant became incapacitated. He rallied the survivors, protected the wounded, and kept up the fight while calling in artillery. For these actions he was properly awarded the Silver Star. Our weapons platoon lost four men killed and the rest were wounded. Sometime during the last artillery barrage Slater, the weapons guy on my left who had been so badly wounded, crawled up to where José was lying wounded behind his machine gun and tried to help him manage the gun. José said Slater wasn't able to help much because of his wounds, and lost track of him as the fighting wound down. I never found out if Slater survived.

The battalion's recon platoon lost at least eight dead, and most of the rest were wounded. They had been the first to engage the enemy to our right and were overrun. Bravo Company, just behind the recon, lost just two dead, one of whom was a mortar guy who was in the clearing working his tubes. Two more mortar guys from battalion headquarters were killed as well. Our comrades to the left, Bravo Company of the 2/28, lost nine dead, and Alpha Company of 2/28 lost a guy as well. I haven't listed them here, but they remain in my heart. By the time this fight took place, the army had stopped providing specific information about the cause of death in combat, so I've only added that when it differs from the generic. First, Alpha's dead:

> The following named individuals have been reported dead in Vietnam as the result of hostile action: Individuals were on combat operation preparing a night defensive perimeter in landing zone when they engaged a hostile force in firefight. John A. Brantley, Chicago, Illinois, age 22. Alpha Co., 1/16 Infantry; Emanuel K. Brickhouse, New York, New York, age 20. Alpha Co., 1/16 Infantry; Guy W. Clinger, Lewistown, Pennsylvania, age 21. Alpha Co. 1/16 Infantry; Jerry R. Cook, Alpharetta, Georgia, age 20. Alpha Co., 1/16 Infantry; Ronald D. Edefield, Grand Ridge, Florida, age 19. Alpha Co., 1/16 Infantry; James M. Elchert, Toledo, Ohio, age 20. Alpha Co., 1/16 Infantry; Robert T. Harris, Earle, Arkansas, age 20. Alpha Co., 1/16 Infantry; Edward E. Heyer, Prichard, Alabama, age 22. Alpha Co., 1/16 Infantry; Carl T. Johnson, Houston, Texas, age 20. Alpha Co., 1/16 Infantry. Individual was on a night [sic] combat operation when a hostile force was engaged; Charles P. Kelly, Fullerton, California, age 20. Alpha Co., 1/16 Infantry. Kelly was awarded the Bronze Star with "V" posthumously; Robert S. Maguire, Atascadero, California, age 20. Alpha Co., 1/16 Infantry; Howard A. Mucha, Willoughby, Ohio, age 22. Alpha Co., 1/16 Infantry; Wayne A. Pettersen, Seattle, Washington, age 23. Alpha Co., 1/16 Infantry; Alan J. Roese, Lancaster, New York, age 21. Alpha Co., 1/16 Infantry; Frank G. Romo, Azusa, California, age 22. Alpha Co., 1/16 Infantry.

Bravo Company lost two guys.

The following named individuals have been reported dead in Vietnam as the result of hostile action: Individuals were on combat operation preparing a night defensive perimeter in landing zone when they engaged a hostile force in firefight. Paul E. Kelly, Jr., Smyrna, Georgia, age 21. Bravo Co., 1/16 Infantry; Edward E. Smith, Newport, Kentucky, age 20. Bravo Co., 1/16 Infantry.

And the battalion headquarters company lost nine, seven from recon and two from the battalion CP platoon.

Sammy L. Holmes, Miami, Florida, age 22. HHC, 1/16 Infantry; Douglas Wallin, Rochester, Minnesota, age 20. HHC, 1/16 Infantry; Gary Ernst, Perryville, Missouri, age 20. Recon Plt., HHC, 1/16 Infantry; Douglas A. Logan, Crane, Missouri, age 22. Recon Plt., HHC, 1/16 Infantry; Leroy Reed, Lake Charles, Louisiana, age 20. Recon Plt., HHC, 1/16 Infantry; Martin L. Plotkin, Lynbrook, New York, age 21. Recon Plt., HHC, 1/16 Infantry; Wallace G. Nye, Minneapolis, Minnesota, age 20. Recon Plt., HHC, 1/16 Infantry; Stephen Noggle, Minneapolis, Minnesota, age 20. Recon Plt., HHC, 1/16 Infantry; Charles W. Hook, Friendsville, Maryland, age 20. Recon Plt., HHC, 1/16 Infantry; William N. Cole, Clairton, Pennsylvania, age 20. Recon Plt., HHC, 1/16 Infantry.

CHAPTER 26

Home Again

After a brief time being triaged at the brigade clearing station I was on a gurney in a corridor of the 93rd Evacuation Hospital in Long Binh with an IV drip in my arm. I had lots of company: another outfit had been hit down in the Delta, and the overflow from that battle had ended up here, along with the dozens of other 1st Infantry Division wounded. I saw a couple of guys I knew who were able to walk around, and got a few bits of news about friends, some of which turned out to be accurate, some not. On a gurney near mine, Sergeant Baker from Second Platoon was lying quiet and immobile, pretty much covered with bandages. Somebody said he had been hit five or six times and that many of his bones were shattered. He wasn't expected to live, although he surprised us all on that score. I heard Ward and Gunby were dead, which wasn't true and that José was alive, and somewhere in the hospital, which was true. Carl Johnson was dead. Captain Williamson had eventually been medevaced.

I felt myself slowing down, beginning to comprehend that the quiet, clean, air-conditioned space around me wasn't just a dream fantasy. My boots and fatigue pants had disappeared before I got to the hospital, and I can't remember if I came with my fatigue jacket or not, but when a surgeon came by around midnight I was in a hospital gown. He had a chart in his hand, which he looked at while he asked me some questions: name, where did it hurt, stuff like that. He put the chart on the gurney, did a quick check of my systems, then ran his hands up and down my right leg, twisted my ankle, and then lifted my leg up over his right shoulder and bent it at the knee.

"Jesus Christ, that hurts!" I hissed.

"Good!" he grinned. "Any questions?"

"Am I gonna lose the leg?" I didn't think so, but wanted some reassurance.

"Nope, leg's gonna be fine," he said, taking up the chart and writing quickly in it.

"Thanks," I muttered.

For whatever reason, the sharp pain in my leg when the doc manipulated it cut through the morphine fog. The need to stay in control evaporated and tears started just pouring down my face. I wasn't sobbing or anything, just leaking buckets. The surgeon disappeared and a couple of folks in scrubs materialized on either side of my gurney and pushed me down a corridor between the waiting GIs and into an operating theater. I was lifted onto a brightly illuminated table, aware that various masked folks were busy doing things, both to my body and to objects arrayed on the trays and stands which surrounded us. Tears were still streaming down my face when somebody said, "Start counting backwards from ten."

"Ten, nine, eight ..."

Then waking up in another place, on a gurney again, and somebody talking to me. A hand on my face for a second, then more blessed oblivion.

When I next woke up I was in a ward with a bunch of other beds, mostly occupied by GIs in casts and bandages. Filtered sunlight was coming in through high windows. I could just see the tops of a sandbag wall outside. I had an IV in my left arm. My right leg was still there, covered in moist bandages from toes to mid-thigh, resting in a form-fitting plaster trough. Plastic tubes were snaking out from under the bandages and running over the side of the bed into a bucket on the floor. At some point a nurse came by to see how I was doing. She said a doctor would be by later and gave me shot of something which made me feel really pretty good for a minute before I went back to sleep. When the doc came by, later on, he explained that I had 20 or so penetrating shrapnel wounds which had been surgically joined one to the other. So my leg was basically sliced open from toes to thigh, debrided, and left open to monitor for infection. Most of the shrapnel was out, he said, but the pieces that were left shouldn't cause a problem. He said I was lucky, that the shrapnel had missed the major blood vessels and nerves. I had a couple of non-displaced fractures that didn't need total casts but would require no weight-bearing for a few weeks. At some point they'd sew me up and send me either to Japan or the States for convalescence. I should be walking with crutches in a few weeks and without them in a couple of months. Too early to say if I'd have permanent disability, but good odds I wouldn't.

"Did you save any of the shrapnel you took out?" I asked, thinking of souvenirs.

"Nothing worth keeping," he assured me. "Just junk."

I quickly learned that my medical orders permitted a shot of Demerol every four hours, so my routine became fixed: sleep for four hours, wake up, get a shot, go back to sleep. I didn't want to think about anything at all. A couple of visits from Alpha guys cheered me up. Rod Floutz came by and gave me a hard time for slacking off, and an officer came by and asked if I had been wounded before. I told him about my first one, back in August.

"Did you get the medal?" he asked

I told him I got the orders but not the medal, and so he gave me a Purple Heart in a box.

"Don't get any more of these," he told me. This was the first time I had seen the actual medal close up, a big heavy enameled purple and gold heart with a cameo bust of George Washington on it. I knew I should know better, but I was proud to have that medal.

The days sort of blurred together, sleeping, waking, getting Demerol. The dressings on my leg got changed, the drain bucket got emptied, I learned to pee into a duck. After a week, I got taken back to the OR for my wounds to be evaluated. I was happy to be put to sleep for the process. When I woke up this time, the news stayed good. The wounds were clean and had been closed with a few dozen wire sutures, so my leg looked like a barbed-wire entanglement from above my knee down to my small toe. The open question was whether I would be sent to Japan for recovery or back to the States.

The next day I got orders: Great Lakes Naval Station Hospital, near my home of record in Wilmette, Illinois. From the 93rd, I was sent to Tan Son Nhut on a stretcher and loaded onto a big air force medevac jet with tiers of stretchers along both sides of the cavernous interior. My flight, with a stop in Japan to offload some passengers and pick up some more, seemed to go pretty quickly, probably because I was lying down and sedated to the gills. I recall most of the flight as dark and peaceful.

We landed near Washington, D. C., on a sunny morning, and I was taken out and stowed in a large ambulance-type vehicle for the trip to Walter Reed Army Medical Center. That was probably the best air journey I ever took. If the airlines offered Drugged and Prone Class, with folks to carry you on and off the aircraft, as an option, I think a lot more people would enjoy flying. Of course, I didn't have to pay for the ticket. After spending the night in a ward at Walter Reed, I was loaded onto another ambulance and taken to an airfield where I was placed on an ancient Pennsylvania National Guard propeller-driven transport aircraft, probably a World War II vintage C-46. I shared the bay with a number of other GIs on stretchers bunked along the sides of the aircraft. The medics in the combat zone had been pretty free with the painkillers, but now that I was stateside the medication regimen started to reflect the parsimony with narcotics that characterized peacetime army medicine. So, whether exacerbated from my diminishing level of artificial endorphins or not, the noisy, bumpy flight was more like a trip on a C-130 in Vietnam than a magic carpet ride. Lying in my stretcher, I had plenty of time to imagine various scenarios of aviation disaster as we rattled and banged across the country. We made about five stops to offload wounded GIs before we got to the Glenview Naval Air Station in Illinois, where I was happy to be removed from the aircraft, and along with a half-dozen other troops, loaded onto a bus-like ambulance, again on a shelf along the side of the vehicle, but this time with big windows right at eye level. So I was driven north on the Edens Expressway, having a look at the America that I had almost forgotten. Big shiny cars, mostly filled with pale, fat people wearing bright-colored summer clothes cruised by my window, with the occupants often staring at us, racked along the sides of the military vehicle. I became conscious of the dirt and napalm ash in my hair, which hadn't been washed since before June 17, and how foreign and strange these people looked. I felt a rush of homesickness for Alpha Company, for my family of the last ten months, and a powerful sadness at my loss of them, which has never wholly abated though 50 years have come and gone.

So there I was in a naval hospital, surrounded by sick and wounded swabbies and gyrenes. The orthopedic ward was full, mainly with survivors of the June 8 attack on the USS *Liberty* by Israeli Air Force and Navy units, so I was stuck on a medical ward, one of the few combat wounded in a 20-bed bay. I didn't have much to do at first, as I wasn't ready for any sort of rehab, so I just lay there eating vast quantities of decent navy chow, that I could order three times a day from a menu, with no restriction of ordering, say, two entrees and three desserts.

My mother, who while loving and kind was plagued by demons of her own, was suffering from severe agoraphobia and wouldn't leave the house she had built on family land in Missouri. But my father, who lived and worked in Chicago, visited me often. Best of all, many of my high-school friends from New Trier, a township 20 miles south of the hospital, and my best Reed College buddy, who was now attending Lake Forest College, came by as well. On their first visit, the guys, at least, long-haired and bearded and clad in full counter-cultural regalia, brought me flowers, chocolate, and an American flag. Steely-eyed and suspicious Shore Patrol guys at first followed them up to the ward, convinced the damn hippies were looking for a place to burn that flag, but became reconciled to my weird friends when nothing untoward happened. I asked for and got some drawing materials and made the first of a bunch of sketches, some of which were riffs on the sixties graphic styles and some of which were grimmer attempts to record events in Vietnam.

Life was not all so good: sometime during my first couple of days on the ward, while I was still getting medicated at night, some goddam unknown swabbie stole my Purple Heart out of my bedside table. I wished him joy of it and eventually got another one. One of my wardmates, who had been a crewman on the *Liberty*, complained that he and his buddies didn't get Purple Hearts for their wounds. I wondered if maybe that was because they were hit by friendly fire.

"Didn't seem too fucking friendly to me," he groused.

Eventually the *Liberty* dead and wounded did get their Hearts.

Also, one of the side effects of frequent doses of opiates is constipation. No one had explained this to me and, after about three weeks without taking a shit I began to be worried and complained to the medics who came by from time to time. I was prescribed laxatives, which didn't seem to do any good, so I kept bitching. Finally the laxatives kicked in, plus my opiates had been suspended and I was reduced to Darvon and Tylenol for pain relief, so I had a righteous dump on the very day an exasperated doc had ordered an enema. When the swabbie medic came with the equipment, I protested in vain that it was now redundant but, as he said, orders are orders, and since the doc who wrote the order for an enema is a commander and you are an E-4, you are going to have to get the enema. Which I did. Goddam Navy.

Medical capacity for duty, for soldiers, was measured by something called the Physical Profile, or PULHES, where each letter stood for a particular area: P was physical fitness, U upper extremities, L legs, H hearing, E eyes, and S psychiatric. Each soldier had a value attached to these six categories, with the number 1 being the most fit and number 4 being the worst. A picket fence, or a PULHES profile of 1 1 1 1 1 1, was optimum, if not required, for infantry assignments. Having a number high enough to affect assignment was known among the grunts as "having a profile" and was not an unwelcome burden for those who wanted out of the infantry.

One of the strange side effects of getting wounded in combat, however, was a strong desire to return to the unit, in my case Alpha Company. I had expressed this several times to various folks at the hospital, and was met with rolling eyes and shaking heads. One of the people who was taking notes muttered, "You all say that," incredulous that folks in my condition would want to run towards the location of their damage rather than away from it. And I did want to return, with all my heart, at that time. But I had acquired a profile: 1 1 3 1 1 1, and needed to get that 3 back to a 1. This made me a motivated patient, and I spent a fair amount of time doing the exercises the PT folks were pushing.

As July quickly became August, which faded into September, my leg improved. The wire sutures were removed by a squeamish medic, who had to dig into the skin where it had overgrown the wire, causing me the most acute pain of the entire injury. I got yelled at for a bad attitude by a chief petty officer, who also rated me for my sloppy civilian clothes. Of course all my uniforms were lost or back in Vietnam, and all I had to wear were some second-hand duds my hippy buddies had come up with. The army liaison to the hospital was a flighty SP4 who couldn't be bothered, and of course the local supply folks didn't have army uniforms, so I was stuck unless I wanted to impersonate a swabbie. The CPO took pity on me after a few minutes, during which I stood at attention as best I could on crutches and kept my mouth shut tight. He made some calls, including reaming out the army liaison, so I soon had a basic kit of army clothes, including ribbons and a CIB. My improving orthopedic condition allowed me to take some leave, both to enjoy the company of my friends locally and to visit my mother and other family in Missouri. The latter I did in uniform, on crutches, and the folks on the aircraft and elsewhere couldn't have been nicer. I never had a bad moment wearing the uniform in the States. Navy PT got me bearing weight pretty quickly, and when the time came to leave the hospital, still on a profile but fit for light duty, my chastened army liaison guy gave me my choice of duty stations.

During my two years in college in Portland I had fallen in love with the Great Northwest, so I chose Fort Lewis, Washington as my destination. After a 30-day leave, during which I spent some time with my Lake Forest friends and some in Missouri with my mother and my cousins Jack and Joan, I headed west in my 1958 VW which had been up on blocks in Jack's barn during my absence.

Assigned to a personnel outfit due to my light-duty status, I experienced the administrative side of the army while working to get my leg in shape. This is what I would have been doing if I had taken up the offer the sergeant had made to me back in Long Binh. And, as things turned out, I think I made the right choice. I worked hard taking the advice of an army doc, which included advice on lifting a steel pot with the chin strap around my ankle, gradually adding sand to the helmet as my leg strengthened. Sometime in December I appeared before a medical review team and the hated 3 was removed from my profile: I had the picket fence again. But after six months, I realized, I wouldn't have Alpha 1/16. Normal attrition would have resulted in all, or almost all, of the people I knew leaving. I had been blessed with three outstanding company commanders, and a lot of brave and competent comrades, but I suspected that I had been lucky in that respect. At some point during this interlude I found out that I had been awarded the Bronze Star with V, which was graciously presented to me by the Personnel Center commander. Despite

Bronze Star Presentation (U.S. Army Photograph; 1967)

my knowledge that many more deserving men, including Greg Murry, had not been so honored, I was then and remain proud of my medal. I didn't try to go back, and finished out my enlistment as a platoon sergeant in a Military Police company at Fort Lewis.

A lot of folks seem to have nightmares about their time in combat. I know my dad, who was a radioman in the 8th Armored Division and served with Patton's Third Army during World War II, had terrible dreams which my mother told me came from his experience liberating a concentration camp. I never had what you would call nightmares with Vietnam images, just disturbing dreams. The most common scenario finds me having just completed my tour and feeling so relieved and happy to have been spared. But then someone asks for volunteers to go back to Vietnam and I always, in my dreams, say yes, I'll go. And if I happen to wake up then, with the dream images still accessible, there are always two strong yet totally antagonistic feelings present: bitter despairing fear, and deep enriching love.

Those of you who have had an Alpha of your own will understand perfectly.

HEADQUARTERS 1ST INFANTRY DIVISION
APO San Francisco 96345

GENERAL ORDERS   13 August 1967
NUMBER   5920

AWARD OF THE BRONZE STAR MEDAL

1. TC 320. The following AWARD is announced.

CLARK, PETER F. RA16837711 SPECIALIST FOUR E4 United States Army
Company A 1st Battalion 16th Infantry

Awarded:	Bronze Star Medal with "V" device
Date of action:	17 June 1967
Theater:	Republic of Vietnam
Reason:	For heroism in connection with military operations against a hostile force: On this date, during Operation Billings, Specialist Clark was serving as a radio-telephone operator on a search and destroy mission near Chi Linh. The battalion was preparing a field defensive perimeter when it suddenly was subjected to an intense mortar and ground attack from elements of the 271st Viet Cong Regiment. Specialist Clark repeatedly exposed himself to intensive hostile fire as he provided continuous communications between the company commander and battalion headquarters. He also volunteered to transport munitions when several of the forward positions had almost expended their ammunition. Ignoring debris and shrapnel from the incoming mortar rounds, he made numerous trips between the ammunition supply point and his forward elements until the Viet Cong were forced to retreat. While delivering the ammunition, he received several shrapnel fragments in his legs, but he refused medical attention until all other casualties were cared for. Specialist Clark's bold initiative and undaunted courage significantly contributed to the defeat of a large Viet Cong force. Specialist Four Clark's outstanding display of aggressiveness, devotion to duty, and personal bravery is in keeping with the finest traditions of the military service and reflects great credit upon himself, the 1st Infantry Division, and the United States Army.
Authority:	By direction of the President, under the provisions of Executive Order 11046, 24 August 1962.

FOR THE COMMANDER:

OFFICIAL: FREDERICK C. KRAUSE
                                                    Colonel, GS
                                                    Chief of Staff

S. F. TOMASEK
Captain, AGC
Assistant Adjutant General

Bronze Star Citation (1967)

Acknowledgements

First, my thanks to the three people who caused this book to be written: Greg Murry, Dr. Lewis Sorley, and Jessica Clark. Greg, my army buddy from Vietnam, tracked me down after decades of separation, and asked me to write something for his then forthcoming book, *Content With My Wages: A Sergeant's Story*. I sent Greg a couple of short pieces, which he included in his book. Anyone interested in Alpha Company should read Greg's account of his tour. I have included his description of the June 17 battle, because it couldn't be improved upon, and there is much more of similar virtue in his book.

Greg sent a version of his manuscript to Dr. Lewis Sorley, the dean of academic military historians exploring the American experience in Vietnam, who happened to comment on one of the pieces I had written for Greg, and asked if he could get in touch with me. Greg checked with me, I agreed, and I got an email from Bob Sorley, which started a process, which essentially ended with him ordering me to write a book-length memoir about my year in-country. The habits of obedience are hard to resist, even if learned half a century ago. Bob was the XO of a tank battalion in Vietnam whose tour overlapped with mine, and retired as a lieutenant colonel before beginning his subsequent career in academia and national security.

Writing a book in my spare time seemed a daunting task nonetheless, but I was fortunate in having a published author and military historian to call upon, Dr. Jessica Homan Clark, a brilliant classicist, archeologist, and author of *Triumph in Defeat*, the seminal work on military disasters in Republican Rome, and incidentally my oldest daughter. I had sent Jessica the pieces that I had written for Greg and she gave me some of that positive reinforcement so desirable for an aspiring writer. Jessica was hugely impressed that Bob Sorley has sent me even one email, and, when

I expressed doubts as to whether I could actually write a book-length manuscript while holding down my day job, referred me to the *koan* that, since anyone could write one page a day, and if continued for year, would have a book, then anyone could write a book.

Several Alpha Company comrades read a version of this manuscript, and I would like to particularly thank José Garcia, my brother-in-arms and lifelong role model for his courage, kindness, and decency, and Dennis Howley, my sometime captain and always exemplar of soldierly virtues, for their comments and suggestions. Sheilah Rae Gross and Elizabeth Stephen also read early versions and provided useful criticism and encouragement.

The LBJ Presidential Library in Austin, Texas, contains over 45 million pages of documents, as well as photos, audio and video tapes, and physical artifacts related to the political career of Lyndon Baines Johnson. Among these relics are a hundred or so cardboard archive boxes which contain, in alphabetical order, the files which supported the letters which the White House sent to the next of kin of the men and women who died while serving in Vietnam. The requested files are delivered in their archive boxes, each containing around 50 or so files, and the reader is trusted to locate and refile the papers. These paper files, mostly onion-skin carbon copies or photocopies of original documents, include along with the condolence letters the defense department forms which provide the identifying data of the dead and a very brief, usually formulaic, summary of the fatal event. John D. Wilson, the library's archivist, was amazingly cordial and helpful to me when I visited, as were his staff. Photocopying of the records is permitted, which certainly facilitated the verbatim descriptions, mostly from DD form 1300 or, after February, 1967, DD form 2496, of the deaths of my comrades which are included in my text. Other documents, including some replies by grieving relatives, are often included in the files; the totality of the experience, for me at least, was devastating. For those of you who cannot travel to Austin, there are several online data bases which were helpful to me and which may provide information about particular deaths. The Coffelt Database of Vietnam Casualties and the Virtual Wall are two such. The assistance provided to me by these resources is gratefully acknowledged. If you are interested in the June 17 battle, David Hearne has written a detailed account, *June 17, 1967: Battle of Xom Bo II.*

My thanks to Michal Tsemach, whose kindness and wisdom were skillfully employed to my general benefit throughout the writing process, and Yelena Timoshenko, whose personal support during the transition from manuscript to book was invaluable.

Memory is a slender reed to support a book, and I have buttressed mine with the letters I wrote to my mother and my Aunt Naomi, which they kept and passed on to me, and with the recollections of my comrades and friends. Nicholas Pritzker, boon companion before and after my time with Alpha, was the recipient of many of those memories when they were fresh, and both he, and later, his wife Susan, encouraged this project. To them, my thanks.

While everything I wrote is based on a memory, I cannot claim that every memory is true, only that I believe it is. This is a memoir, after all. I have used the names of real people when I was reasonably certain, and used the phrase, "I'll call him ..." when I was certain of the person but not the name. In a few instances I have chosen to use that phrase even though the persons' names are well remembered, when the events are disparaging of the actors.

My experience as a new author has been enhanced by the wonderful folks at Casemate Publishers. Thanks in particular to my copy editor, Chris Cocks, himself a soldier and writer; Katie Allen and Isobel Nettleton, for the cover and design; Clare Litt and Ruth Sheppard, for final edits; and everyone in London and Havertown who transformed my manuscript into a book.

Throughout I have tried to channel my 20-something sensibilities and my inner voice as I remember it. I have hopefully gained much in wisdom and maturity since I lived the events described, and have tried to overcome the racism and sexism that permeated my culture in the 1960s, but I have also tried not to import my current sensibilities onto the young man that I once was. Certainly the mistakes and errors in this book, whether intentional or not, are my own. But I have done my best not to edit my younger self, or to attempt to improve upon him. I think, and hope, that if I had written this book when I was 22, it would be pretty much as you see it now.